Beyond the Glow

The Story of Subtronics

Riko Garba

ISBN: 9781779692696
Imprint: Fat Chance Fanny
Copyright © 2024 Riko Garba.
All Rights Reserved.

Contents

Introduction   **1**
The Rise of Subtronics   1
Introduction   8

Chapter One: From Bedroom Productions to the Main Stage   **13**
Section One: Finding Their Sound   13
Section Two: The Underground Scene   32
Section Three: Breaking into the Festival Circuit   45
Section Four: Signing with a Major Record Label   57
Section Five: Touring the World and Winning Hearts   69

Chapter Two: The Team Behind Subtronics   **83**
Section One: Meet the Squad   83
Section Two: Collaborations and Features   95
Section Three: The Creative Process   107
Section Four: Behind the Scenes of a Subtronics Show   120
Section Five: The Subtronics Community   133

Chapter Three: The Evolution of Subtronics   **147**
Section One: Musical Growth and Exploration   147
Section Two: Pushing the Limits of Live Performances   160
Section Three: The Impact on the EDM Scene   173
Section Four: The Hype and Expectations   185
Section Five: Legacy and Influence   198

Conclusion   **211**
Reflecting on Their Journey   211

Introduction

The Rise of Subtronics

Early Influences and Musical Journey

Subtronics' music journey can be traced back to their early influences, which shaped their unique sound and propelled them into the world of electronic music. Growing up, music had always been a significant part of their lives, and it was through these early influences that they discovered their passion and talent for creating electronic beats.

1. Childhood Encounters with Music

Subtronics' love for music started at a young age. They were exposed to a wide variety of genres, ranging from classic rock to hip-hop, which laid the foundation for their diverse musical palette. As a child, Subtronics spent countless hours exploring their parents' record collection, listening to iconic artists like Led Zeppelin, Pink Floyd, and The Beatles. These early encounters with music ignited their curiosity and set them on the path to becoming musicians themselves.

2. The Electronic Music Epiphany

It was during their teenage years that Subtronics stumbled upon electronic music and experienced a profound epiphany. Attending their first electronic music festival, they were captivated by the energy and sheer creativity of the genre. Artists like Skrillex, Bassnectar, and Zeds Dead inspired them with their groundbreaking sound and innovative live performances. It was at this moment that Subtronics realized they wanted to be a part of this exciting movement and create their own electronic music.

3. Exploring Different Genres and Styles

Subtronics' musical journey involved a deep exploration of various genres and styles. They were drawn to the heavy basslines and infectious rhythms of dubstep, which acted as a gateway into the world of electronic music production. However, they didn't confine themselves to a single genre, as they embraced the freedom to experiment with different styles.

4. Infusing Influences into Their Sound

One of the defining aspects of Subtronics' music is their ability to seamlessly blend diverse influences into their sound. They drew inspiration not only from electronic music but also from other genres like metal and hip-hop. This fusion of styles created a unique sonic experience that resonated with their audience and set them apart from their peers.

5. Musical Training and Self-Exploration

To hone their skills as producers and performers, Subtronics embarked on a journey of music education and self-exploration. They studied music theory, composition, and sound design, equipping themselves with a strong foundation in the technical aspects of music production. However, they also placed great emphasis on personal expression and experimentation, allowing their creativity to flourish.

6. Personal Experiences Fueling Musical Growth

Subtronics' early influences were not limited to other artists and genres. They drew inspiration from their personal experiences, channeling their emotions and thoughts into their music. Whether it was the euphoria of a memorable festival or the struggles of daily life, their music served as a platform for self-expression and catharsis.

7. Pushing Boundaries and Challenging Conventions

Subtronics' musical journey was characterized by a desire to push boundaries and challenge conventions. They constantly sought to innovate and explore new sounds and techniques, refusing to be confined by the limitations of genre. This commitment to pushing the boundaries of electronic music allowed them to carve out a unique niche in the industry.

Overall, Subtronics' early influences played an integral role in shaping their musical journey. From their childhood encounters with music to their discovery of electronic beats, they drew inspiration from a wide range of sources. By infusing diverse influences into their sound and continually pushing the boundaries of electronic music, Subtronics has emerged as a powerhouse in the industry, captivating audiences worldwide with their electrifying sound.

Meeting the Right People at the Right Time

In the world of music, success often hinges on being in the right place at the right time and, most importantly, connecting with the right people. For Subtronics, their journey to stardom began with a series of fortuitous encounters and collaborations that would shape their path in the music industry.

Seizing Opportunities

Subtronics, comprised of Riko Garba and his talented team, started their musical journey with a burning passion for bass music and a drive to innovate. But it wasn't until they started meeting the right people that they truly began to shine.

One key aspect of their success was their ability to recognize and seize opportunities. By keeping their ears to the ground and constantly networking within the industry, they were able to make connections with influential individuals who would later play a vital role in their rise to fame.

Finding Authentic Connections

While networking is important, Subtronics understood that the value of their connections lay not only in their industry connections, but also in finding authentic and like-minded individuals. By seeking out those who shared their passion and drive, they were able to foster genuine collaborations that brought out the best in both parties.

This aspect of their journey highlights the importance of building genuine relationships in the music industry. It's not just about making connections for the sake of business; it's about finding people who truly understand and resonate with your artistic vision.

The Power of Collaboration

One of the most significant ways in which Subtronics met the right people at the right time was through collaborative projects. By joining forces with other talented artists, both established and up-and-coming, they were able to amplify their reach and tap into new fanbases.

This approach not only provided them with invaluable exposure, but also allowed them to learn from other artists and expand their own musical horizons. Each collaboration brought a unique flavor to their releases, contributing to the diversity and freshness of their sound.

Taking Risks and Embracing Challenge

Meeting the right people at the right time also involves taking risks and stepping out of one's comfort zone. For Subtronics, this meant pursuing opportunities that may have seemed daunting or unconventional at first.

By embracing challenge and pushing boundaries, they were able to connect with individuals who shared their drive for experimentation and artistic growth. These connections sparked new collaborations and opened doors to unexplored possibilities.

Embracing the Unexpected

One unconventional move that Subtronics made in their pursuit of meeting the right people was actively seeking out new talent in unexpected places. Instead of relying solely on established industry circles, they scoured underground music scenes, local clubs, and even online platforms to discover raw and untapped talent.

This approach not only gave them access to a fresh pool of creativity but also allowed them to help nurture and promote emerging artists. By supporting and collaborating with these rising stars, Subtronics established a reputation for fostering growth and diversity within the music community.

The Importance of Timing

Lastly, meeting the right people at the right time is dependent on timing. Subtronics recognized that being proactive and responsive to opportunities was crucial. They understood that the music industry moves at a rapid pace and that seizing the moment was essential for their progression.

Whether it was connecting with an influential producer or collaborating with an artist on the rise, Subtronics consistently demonstrated their ability to strike at just the right moment. This not only maximized the impact of their collaborations but also allowed them to stay ahead of emerging trends.

Conclusion

The story of Subtronics is a testament to the power of meeting the right people at the right time. From recognizing and seizing opportunities to building authentic connections and embracing the unexpected, they paved their path to success through meaningful collaborations and a willingness to step outside of their comfort zone.

Their journey serves as a reminder that talent alone is not enough to thrive in the music industry. It is the connections and collaborations formed along the way that can propel artists to new heights and shape their artistic identities.

As we delve deeper into the rise of Subtronics, we'll explore how they found their unique sound and the impact of their collaborations and features on their musical evolution. Join us on this electrifying journey as we uncover the secrets behind their captivating performances and the lasting legacy they leave on the EDM scene.

Exploring the Sound of the Underground

In the early stages of their musical journey, Subtronics found themselves drawn to the raw, unfiltered sound of the underground music scene. It was here that they discovered a world of untapped potential and limitless creativity. In this section, we will delve into their exploration of the sound of the underground and how it shaped their unique musical style.

The Underlying Philosophy

The underground music scene is characterized by its rebellious nature and nonconformist attitude. It is a place where artists are free to experiment, push boundaries, and challenge established norms. For Subtronics, this environment offered a perfect platform to express themselves and establish their own sonic identity.

At its core, the underground scene encourages artists to break away from mainstream conventions and explore unconventional sounds and genres. It celebrates individuality and authenticity, providing a refreshing alternative to the commercialized music industry. Subtronics embraced this philosophy and set out to create a sound that was truly their own.

Breaking Musical Barriers

When Subtronics began their musical journey, they were exposed to a wide array of genres and styles. From hip-hop to metal, their eclectic influences helped them develop a unique perspective on music. They sought to infuse a diverse range of sounds into their productions, fusing elements from dubstep, trap, and drum and bass.

Experimentation became the cornerstone of Subtronics' musical process. They were not afraid to blur the lines between genres, mixing different tempos, rhythms, and melodies to create something entirely original. This approach allowed them to explore the uncharted territories of sound and pave the way for the emergence of their distinctive underground sound.

Diving into Sound Design

One of the key factors that contributed to the development of Subtronics' underground sound was their dedication to sound design. They spent countless hours honing their production skills, delving deep into the intricacies of sound synthesis and manipulation.

Sound design became an essential tool for Subtronics to create their signature bass-heavy drops and gritty textures. They embraced the unconventional and the experimental, constantly pushing the boundaries of electronic music. Their mantra was simple: if it sounds good, they would use it, regardless of how unconventional or unconventional it may seem.

To achieve their unique sound, Subtronics incorporated a wide range of synthesizers, effects, and processing techniques. From classic analog hardware to cutting-edge digital plugins, they utilized every available resource to create innovative soundscapes that captivated their audiences.

Embracing the Underground Community

The underground scene is not just about the music; it is about the people who make it possible. Subtronics recognized the importance of the community and forged deep connections with fellow artists, producers, and fans. They actively participated in local clubs, raves, and DIY events, immersing themselves in the vibrant culture of the underground.

Collaboration became a cornerstone of Subtronics' growth within the scene. They joined forces with like-minded artists, exchanging ideas, sharing knowledge, and pushing each other to new creative heights. Through collaborations, they were able to further explore the sound of the underground, combining their unique styles and pushing the boundaries of what was possible.

Staying True to the Underground Spirit

As Subtronics gained recognition and success, they faced the challenge of maintaining their underground ethos while expanding their reach. They were determined not to lose their connection to the community that had supported them from the beginning.

Despite signing with a major record label and playing at larger festivals, Subtronics remained committed to their roots. They continued to prioritize artistic freedom and experimentalism, refusing to conform to commercial norms. This commitment enabled them to retain their authenticity and stay true to the sound of the underground.

Unconventional Wisdom: The Fleeting Nature of Trends

In the ever-evolving music industry, trends come and go at a rapid pace. Subtronics recognized that chasing trends could result in a loss of creative integrity and long-term sustainability. Instead, they focused on crafting a sound that was timeless and unique to them.

They understood that the underground scene, with its spirit of exploration and innovation, provided a fertile ground for cultivating their sound. By avoiding the temptation to conform to popular trends, Subtronics maintained their authenticity and ensured that their music would stand the test of time.

Unleashing Uncompromising Creativity

Exploring the sound of the underground allowed Subtronics to unleash their creativity in ways they never thought possible. It taught them to take risks, think outside the box, and embrace the unconventional. This mindset continues to shape their music and set them apart in the EDM scene.

The underground scene remains at the heart of Subtronics' artistic journey. It is a constant source of inspiration, fuelling their desire to push the boundaries of sound and create music that challenges and captivates. Subtronics' exploration of the sound of the underground proves that the true magic of music lies beyond the confines of mainstream popularity.

In this section, we explored how Subtronics ventured into the sound of the underground, embracing experimentation, breaking musical barriers, and staying true to their unique style. We witnessed their dedication to sound design, their collaboration with the underground community, and their unwavering commitment to creativity. Subtronics' exploration of the underground sound not only shaped their own musical journey but also left an indelible mark on the EDM scene. Their story serves as a testament to the power of exploration and the enduring beauty of the underground. As Subtronics' journey continues, their exploration of sound will undoubtedly continue to inspire and captivate audiences around the world.

Introduction

The Rise of Subtronics

Early Influences and Musical Journey

Subtronics, originally known as Jesse Kardon, was born and raised in Philadelphia. From a young age, Jesse was drawn to music, finding solace and inspiration in its melodies and rhythms. Growing up, he was influenced by various genres, from classic rock to hip-hop. He found himself constantly exploring new sounds, seeking the perfect blend of intensity and emotion.

Jesse's musical journey began in his bedroom, where he would spend hours experimenting with beats and melodies on his computer. He taught himself the art of music production and sound design, immersing himself in the world of electronic music. His determination and passion fueled his dedication to mastering the craft, and he quickly developed a unique sound that blended heavy bass with melodic elements.

Meeting the Right People at the Right Time

In the early stages of his career, Jesse crossed paths with influential figures in the Philadelphia electronic music scene. These encounters proved to be pivotal moments, propelling him further into the world of EDM. He found himself surrounded by talented producers and DJs who shared his vision and pushed him to unlock his full potential.

Exploring the Sound of the Underground

As Subtronics delved deeper into the underground music scene, he discovered a world filled with raw energy and untapped creativity. Influenced by artists like Excision, Rusko, and Bassnectar, he found inspiration in their ability to create a powerful connection with their audiences. He sought to channel that same energy into his own music, crafting bass-heavy tracks that would resonate with listeners on a primal level.

Breaking into the EDM Scene

With his unique sound and relentless drive, Subtronics began to make waves in the EDM scene. His music caught the attention of industry insiders and fellow artists, attracting a dedicated following of bass music enthusiasts. The combination of heavy-hitting drops and intricate production techniques set Subtronics apart from his peers, creating buzz and anticipation for his live performances.

The Birth of Subtronics

In 2017, Subtronics released his breakthrough EP, "Now That's What I Call Riddim Vol. 1," which solidified his position as a rising star in the EDM world. The EP showcased his signature sound and gained widespread recognition, leading to collaborations with established artists and invitations to perform at major festivals.

Subtronics' ascent continued with the release of his hit singles, "Griztronics" and "Cyclops Army," both of which received critical acclaim and dominated the charts. These tracks captivated audiences with their infectious energy and became anthems within the bass music community. Subtronics had officially arrived, and his electrifying performances and innovative productions became a staple in the EDM scene.

Chapter One: From Bedroom Productions to the Main Stage

Section One: Finding Their Sound

Section Two: The Underground Scene

Section Three: Breaking into the Festival Circuit

Section Four: Signing with a Major Record Label

Section Five: Touring the World and Winning Hearts

Chapter Two: The Team Behind Subtronics

Section One: Meet the Squad

Section Two: Collaborations and Features

Section Three: The Creative Process

Section Four: Behind the Scenes of a Subtronics Show

Section Five: The Subtronics Community

Chapter Three: The Evolution of Subtronics

Section One: Musical Growth and Exploration

Section Two: Pushing the Limits of Live Performances

Section Three: The Impact on the EDM Scene

Section Four: The Hype and Expectations

Section Five: Legacy and Influence

Conclusion

Reflecting on Their Journey

The Birth of Subtronics

It all began on a stormy night in the heart of Philadelphia. Jesse Kardon, known by his stage name "Subtronics," was huddled in his tiny basement studio, surrounded by a clutter of wires, synthesizers, and a collection of vinyl records. Rain pounded on the rooftop above, as if nature itself was echoing the beats that were about to be born.

1.1.5.1 The Spark of Inspiration

INTRODUCTION

Jesse had always been drawn to music, even as a young child. He would sit by his dad's side, mesmerized by the sound of the guitar strings being strummed. It was in those moments that his passion for music started to take root, and he knew deep down that he was destined to create something extraordinary.

As he grew older, Jesse's taste in music evolved. He took a liking to electronic music, mesmerized by its ability to transport listeners to another world. But it wasn't until he attended his first music festival that he experienced a moment of pure revelation. The bass shaking his body, the crowd's energy pulsating through the air, he knew then and there that he wanted to be a part of this beautiful chaos.

1.1.5.2 A Journey of Self-Discovery

With newfound determination, Jesse immersed himself in the world of electronic music. He spent countless hours experimenting with beats and melodies, losing himself in a labyrinth of sound. But it wasn't until he stumbled upon the subgenre of dubstep that he truly found his calling.

Dubstep, with its deep basslines and heavy drops, resonated with Jesse on a profound level. It was the perfect outlet for him to unleash his creativity and explore the depths of his musical expression. With a unique combination of aggression and melancholy, Jesse's sound began to take shape, like a dark force rising from the depths of his soul.

1.1.5.3 The Birth of a Moniker

As his sound continued to evolve, Jesse realized that he needed a name that encapsulated his musical vision. He wanted something that would convey the intensity and energy of his music, something that would leave a lasting impression on his listeners.

And so, Subtronics was born.

The name Subtronics, derived from the words "sub" (referring to the sub-bass frequencies that dominate his music) and "electronics," perfectly captured the essence of Jesse's sound. It was a name that carried weight and substance, a name that would become synonymous with thrilling bass drops and electrifying performances.

1.1.5.4 From Basement to Spotlight

Armed with a newfound sense of purpose and a name to match, Subtronics set out on a mission to conquer the world of electronic music. He started by sharing his music on SoundCloud, relying on word-of-mouth to spread his unique sound. The response was overwhelming – listeners were captivated by his raw talent and his ability to create basslines that seemed to defy the laws of physics.

Soon enough, Subtronics caught the attention of fellow artists and producers in the scene. They recognized his innovative sound and his unwavering dedication to his craft. Collaborations followed, and Subtronics found himself working alongside some of the biggest names in the industry.

1.1.5.5 A Star is Born

But it was not just his collaborations that propelled Subtronics to stardom. His live performances were nothing short of legendary. Armed with his trusty mixer and an infectious energy, Subtronics took the stage by storm, leaving audiences in a state of pure bliss. Every drop was calculated, every bassline meticulously crafted to create an otherworldly experience for his fans.

It wasn't long before Subtronics went from playing small gigs in local clubs to headlining major festivals. His unique sound and his ability to push the boundaries of electronic music made him an instant favorite among festival-goers. And as his fan base continued to grow, so did his impact on the EDM scene.

1.1.5.6 The Subtronics Revolution

Subtronics' rise to fame marked the beginning of a new era in electronic music. His relentless pursuit of perfection and his refusal to conform to traditional genre boundaries paved the way for a wave of up-and-coming artists who were eager to break free from the norm.

Subtronics' influence extended far beyond his music, as he became a symbol of hope and inspiration for aspiring producers and DJs. He showed them that with perseverance and an unwavering passion for their craft, they too could make their mark on the world.

1.1.5.7 The Legacy Continues

As Subtronics' story unfolds, one thing is clear – his journey is far from over. With each new track, each new performance, he continues to push the limits of what is possible in electronic music. He has become a beacon of creativity and innovation, inspiring a generation of artists to take risks and forge their own path.

The birth of Subtronics marked the beginning of a revolution – a revolution that continues to shape the landscape of electronic music to this day. And as the story of Subtronics unfolds, one thing is certain – his glow will never fade away.

Chapter One: From Bedroom Productions to the Main Stage

Section One: Finding Their Sound

Experimenting with Genres and Styles

In the early days of their musical journey, Subtronics explored a wide range of genres and styles, constantly pushing the boundaries and experimenting with different sounds. This section delves into their journey of self-discovery and the exploration of their unique musical identity.

The Quest for Inspiration

Every artist seeks inspiration, and Subtronics was no exception. They drew influences from various genres, ranging from hip-hop and trap to metal and rock. By immersing themselves in diverse musical styles, they gained a deeper understanding of the underlying principles that shape each genre's sound.

The team found inspiration in unlikely places. For instance, during a road trip, they stumbled upon a small local jazz club and were captivated by the electric energy and improvisational nature of the musicians. This encounter made them realize the importance of incorporating organic elements into their electronic music.

Blending Genres

Subtronics was determined to create a sound that was uniquely their own. They began blending different genres, fusing them together to create a distinct sonic experience. By combining elements of dubstep, hip-hop, and drum and bass, they crafted a genre-bending style that defied traditional categorization.

The team experimented with different tempos, rhythms, and melodies to create a fusion of their favorite genres. They discovered that by blending contrasting elements, they could create tension and excitement in their music. This technique allowed them to carve out a niche for themselves in the saturated EDM scene.

The Art of Sample Selection

One of the secrets behind Subtronics' distinctive sound was their meticulous approach to sample selection. They spent countless hours scouring crates of vinyl records, digging deep into digital archives, and exploring obscure corners of the internet to find unique and interesting samples.

They carefully selected samples that had potential for transformation and manipulation, seeking out distinctive textures, tones, and rhythms. Through the art of sampling, they were able to breathe new life into old recordings, seamlessly weaving them into their own productions. This gave their music a nostalgic and timeless quality, resonating with a wide range of listeners.

The Power of Sound Design

Sound design played a pivotal role in Subtronics' exploration of genres and styles. The team embraced the challenge of creating their own unique sounds, experimenting with synthesizers, virtual instruments, and effects processors to craft their sonic palette.

They delved into the world of granular synthesis, granulating and manipulating audio samples to create intricate, otherworldly textures. They also explored the possibilities of frequency modulation synthesis, using complex waveforms and modulation techniques to create rich and evolving sounds.

Through sound design, Subtronics was able to add depth, complexity, and character to their music. Every sound they created was meticulously crafted, ensuring that each element had its own distinct personality. This attention to detail contributed to their signature sound and set them apart from their peers.

Embracing the Unconventional

One of the hallmarks of Subtronics' experimentation with genres and styles was their willingness to embrace the unconventional. They were not afraid to push boundaries and challenge the norms of electronic music.

For instance, they incorporated live instrumentation into their productions, blending the raw energy of guitars and drums with electronic elements. This

SECTION ONE: FINDING THEIR SOUND 15

hybrid approach added a human touch and brought a new level of excitement to their live performances.

Another example of their unconventional approach was their use of unconventional time signatures and complex rhythms. They experimented with odd time signatures like 7/8 and 11/8, infusing their music with a sense of unpredictability and pushing listeners to think outside the box.

Finding Their Voice

Through their relentless experimentation with genres and styles, Subtronics gradually found their musical voice. They embraced their distinctiveness and built a sound that was authentic and true to themselves.

Their journey of exploration served as a reminder that creativity knows no boundaries. By breaking free from conventions and fearlessly venturing into uncharted territories, Subtronics forged a path that was uniquely theirs. Their ability to blend genres, craft unique sounds, and think outside the box propelled them to new heights in the EDM scene.

Aspiring artists can learn from Subtronics' willingness to experiment and take risks. By embracing diversity, challenging established norms, and staying true to their vision, they were able to carve out their own unique space in the music industry. The story of Subtronics teaches us that the true essence of artistic expression lies in daring to be different.

Fusion of Bass Music and Dubstep

The fusion of bass music and dubstep is a defining characteristic of Subtronics' sound. It is a harmonious marriage of two genres that has captivated audiences around the world. In this section, we will dive into the principles and techniques that Subtronics employs to create this unique blend, as well as explore the evolution of the genre and its impact on the music industry.

Understanding Bass Music

Before we delve into the fusion of bass music and dubstep, it is important to have a clear understanding of what bass music entails. Bass music is a broad genre that encompasses various subgenres, including dubstep, trap, drum and bass, and future bass. It is characterized by heavy basslines, aggressive beats, and intricate sound design.

Bass music emerged in the underground music scene, evolving from the UK sound system culture in the late 1990s. With the rise of digital production tools and the accessibility of music software, artists began pushing the boundaries of bass music, experimenting with new sounds and textures.

The Roots of Dubstep

Dubstep, on the other hand, has its roots in the UK garage and drum and bass scenes. It originated in South London in the late 1990s and early 2000s, with influential artists such as Skream, Benga, and Coki leading the way. Dubstep is characterized by its syncopated rhythms, heavy sub-bass, and use of "wobble" basslines.

Dubstep gained international recognition in the late 2000s, captivating listeners with its dark and brooding sound. It quickly became a global phenomenon, with artists like Rusko, Excision, and Bassnectar taking the genre to new heights.

The Subtronics Sound

Subtronics' fusion of bass music and dubstep brings together the best of both genres. Their music showcases a perfect balance between aggressive basslines, hard-hitting beats, and intricate sound design. It is characterized by heavy drops, complex rhythms, and a relentless energy that keeps the audience hooked.

One of the key elements that sets Subtronics apart is their meticulous attention to sound design. They spend hours experimenting with different synths, samples, and effects to create the perfect combination of dirty bass and melodic elements. By blending different elements from various genres, they are able to create a distinct sonic signature that is instantly recognizable.

Breaking Down the Fusion

To understand the fusion of bass music and dubstep, let's break it down into its core components:

- **Basslines:** Bass music is known for its heavy basslines, which serve as the driving force behind the music. These basslines often feature complex patterns and intricate rhythms, creating a sense of movement and energy. Dubstep, on the other hand, emphasizes the sub-bass frequencies, creating a deep, powerful sound. Subtronics combines these elements, crafting basslines that are both melodic and hard-hitting.

- **Drums and Beats:** Both bass music and dubstep rely heavily on aggressive beats and intricate drum patterns. Subtronics takes this a step further by incorporating elements from trap and drum and bass, adding layers of complexity to their tracks. These beats create a strong foundation for their music, driving the energy and intensity of their performances.

- **Sound Design:** The fusion of bass music and dubstep is also evident in Subtronics' sound design. They combine the gritty, distorted bass sounds of dubstep with the melodic elements of bass music, creating a unique blend of textures and tones. Through meticulous attention to detail and innovative production techniques, they are able to create tracks that are both heavy and emotive.

- **Drops and Builds:** Drops are an integral part of bass music and dubstep, serving as climactic moments that captivate the audience. Subtronics excels in creating drops that are unexpected and impactful. They experiment with different rhythms, tempos, and arrangements, keeping their listeners on their toes. Their builds are equally important, gradually increasing the tension before the drop, creating a sense of anticipation and excitement.

Evolution and Impact

The fusion of bass music and dubstep has evolved significantly over the years, thanks in large part to artists like Subtronics. By pushing the boundaries of these genres, they have inspired a new generation of producers and fans, shaping the sound of modern electronic music.

Their unique sound has made its way into the mainstream, with collaborations and features on tracks by major artists. Subtronics' influence can be heard in the music of artists across various genres, from hip-hop to pop. Their ability to fuse different elements together seamlessly has opened up new possibilities for artists and producers.

Not only has Subtronics' fusion of bass music and dubstep influenced the music industry, but it has also had a profound impact on their fans. Their high-energy performances and infectious beats have created a sense of unity and belonging within the bass music community. Through their music, they have connected with fans from all walks of life, spreading a message of love, acceptance, and empowerment.

Unconventional Example: The Physics of Bass

To understand the fusion of bass music and dubstep, let's take a moment to explore the physics behind bass frequencies. Bass frequencies are characterized by their low pitch and long wavelengths. When these frequencies are played through a sound system, they create vibrations in the air that are felt rather than heard.

Imagine standing in front of a massive Subtronics show, with the bass vibrating your entire body. This physical sensation is a result of the low-frequency sound waves stimulating the sensory receptors in your skin and muscles. It is a unique and immersive experience that cannot be replicated by any other genre of music.

The fusion of bass music and dubstep takes advantage of these physical properties, using heavy sub-bass frequencies to create a visceral and powerful sound. The combination of aggressive beats, intricate basslines, and dynamic sound design amplifies the physicality of the music, creating an experience that is both sonically and physically captivating.

In conclusion, the fusion of bass music and dubstep is at the core of Subtronics' sound. By blending the aggressive beats and gritty basslines of dubstep with the melodic elements and intricate sound design of bass music, they have created a unique and captivating sound. Their fusion has not only influenced the music industry but has also created a sense of unity and belonging within the bass music community. Through their music, Subtronics continues to push the boundaries of electronic music, leaving an enduring glow in the hearts of their fans.

Creating Unique and Recognizable Drops

When it comes to electronic music, one of the most exciting moments for both the producer and the listener is the drop. The drop is that exhilarating point in a song where the energy reaches its peak and the bass hits hard, taking the crowd on a wild ride. Every producer strives to create unique and recognizable drops that will leave a lasting impact on their audience. In this section, we will explore the art of creating these drops and discuss the techniques and strategies that Subtronics has used to set themselves apart from the crowd.

Understanding the Anatomy of a Drop

Before diving into the creative process, it's important to understand the key elements that make up a great drop. A drop typically consists of the following components:

1. **Buildup:** The buildup is the section of the song that leads up to the drop. It usually starts with a softer and more restrained sound, gradually building up the tension and anticipation.

2. **Pre-drop:** The pre-drop is the short section right before the drop, where the energy and intensity are heightened to their maximum. It acts as a bridge

between the buildup and the drop, preparing the listener for the upcoming explosion of sound.

3. **Drop:** The drop is the climax of the song, where all the elements come together in a powerful and impactful way. It is characterized by heavy basslines, energetic rhythms, and unique sound design.

4. **Post-drop:** The post-drop is the section that follows the drop, allowing the song to transition smoothly into the next part or bringing it to a satisfying conclusion.

Now that we have a clear understanding of the different parts of a drop, let's explore some techniques that Subtronics has used to create their own signature drops.

Pushing the Boundaries of Sound Design

One of the key factors that set Subtronics apart from other producers is their innovative approach to sound design. They constantly push the boundaries of what is possible with electronic music, experimenting with unique and unconventional sounds to create drops that are truly one-of-a-kind.

To achieve this, Subtronics employs a combination of synthesis techniques, such as wavetable synthesis, frequency modulation (FM) synthesis, and granular synthesis. These techniques allow them to manipulate and transform basic waveforms into complex and intricate soundscapes, adding layers of depth and richness to their drops.

Additionally, Subtronics pays great attention to detail when it comes to designing their basslines. They carefully sculpt each sound, focusing on aspects such as envelope shaping, filtering, and modulation. By fine-tuning these parameters, they are able to create basslines that are both powerful and distinctive, making their drops instantly recognizable.

Experimenting with Rhythm and Timing

In addition to their unique sound design, Subtronics also experiments with rhythm and timing to create drops that stand out from the crowd. They often incorporate unconventional time signatures and syncopated rhythms, adding complexity and unpredictability to their drops.

By breaking away from the traditional 4/4 time signature and introducing elements of drum and bass or halftime beats, Subtronics is able to inject a fresh and dynamic energy into their drops. This rhythmic experimentation keeps the listener engaged and on their toes, never knowing what to expect next.

Surprising the Audience with Unexpected Twists

Another technique that Subtronics employs to create unique drops is the use of unexpected twists and surprises. They are masters at catching the listener off guard, injecting elements that defy expectations and add an element of surprise to their drops.

This could involve sudden changes in melody, unexpected modulations, or even throwing in a completely different genre or style within the drop. By keeping the audience on their toes, Subtronics is able to create drops that are not only memorable but also keep the listener coming back for more.

Striking a Balance Between Familiarity and Uniqueness

While Subtronics is known for their experimental and boundary-pushing approach to drops, they also understand the importance of maintaining a sense of familiarity and coherence within their music. They strike a delicate balance between uniqueness and accessibility, making their drops instantly recognizable while still pushing the boundaries of the genre.

By incorporating familiar elements and references from various subgenres of electronic music, Subtronics creates drops that resonate with a wide audience. At the same time, they add their own unique twist, ensuring that their drops stand out from the crowd and leave a lasting impression.

Example: Deconstructing a Subtronics Drop

To further illustrate the techniques discussed above, let's deconstruct a Subtronics drop to see how these principles are applied in practice.

Suppose we take their track "Griztronics", a collaboration with GRiZ, as an example. In this track, Subtronics combines elements of dubstep, trap, and future bass to create a drop that is both heavy and melodic.

The drop starts with a powerful buildup, gradually introducing layers of synths, vocal chops, and atmospheric effects. The pre-drop section then intensifies the energy by adding a high-pitched vocal sample and a rhythmic buildup of drums and percussion.

As the drop hits, Subtronics surprises the listener with a switch in rhythm and a distorted bassline that hits hard. The drop is characterized by a combination of aggressive dubstep growls, punchy trap drums, and melodic future bass chords.

Throughout the drop, Subtronics keeps the energy high by introducing unexpected modulations and rhythmic variations. The drops transition seamlessly into the post-drop section, where they incorporate melodic elements from the buildup to provide a sense of continuity and cohesion.

This example showcases the unique and recognizable elements that Subtronics brings to their drops, combining heavy basslines, intricate sound design, rhythmic experimentation, and surprising twists to create a drop that is both innovative and crowd-pleasing.

Conclusion

In this section, we explored the art of creating unique and recognizable drops in electronic music. We discussed the anatomy of a drop, breaking it down into its essential components such as the buildup, pre-drop, drop, and post-drop. We then delved into the techniques that Subtronics uses to set themselves apart, including pushing the boundaries of sound design, experimenting with rhythm and timing, surprising the audience with unexpected twists, and striking a balance between familiarity and uniqueness.

By employing these techniques, Subtronics has been able to create drops that are not only powerful and impactful but also instantly recognizable. Their innovative approach to sound design, rhythmic experimentation, and unconventional twists has allowed them to carve out a unique space in the EDM scene and capture the hearts of their fans.

As we continue our journey through the story of Subtronics, we will explore the other aspects of their music and career that have contributed to their rise and success. From their collaborations and features to their creative process and the impact they have had on the EDM scene, Subtronics continues to break barriers and leave their mark on electronic music history. So stay tuned as we dive deeper into the evolution of Subtronics and the enduring glow they have brought to the world of music.

Sound Design Secrets and Techniques

Sound design is an essential aspect of music production, especially in the world of EDM. Subtronics' unique and recognizable sound is not just a result of their creative ideas, but also of their mastery of sound design secrets and techniques. In this section, we will dive into some of the behind-the-scenes secrets and techniques used by Subtronics to bring their music to life.

Understanding Synthesis

At the core of sound design lies the art of synthesis. Synthesis involves manipulating different sound parameters to create unique and interesting sounds. Subtronics has mastered the art of synthesis, allowing them to craft their own signature sound. Let's explore some of the key techniques they employ:

- **Waveform Selection:** Choosing the right waveform is crucial in creating the desired sound. Subtronics often experiments with different basic waveforms such as sine, square, triangle, and sawtooth, and combines them to achieve complex and rich tones.

- **Oscillator Blend:** Blending multiple oscillators together can add depth and complexity to sound. Subtronics often uses a combination of oscillators, each with a slightly detuned pitch, to create a fuller and more harmonically rich sound.

- **Filter Manipulation:** Filters allow producers to shape the frequency content of a sound. Subtronics frequently employs low-pass and high-pass filters to sculpt the tonal characteristics of their sounds. By automating filter cutoff and resonance parameters, they create dynamic and evolving soundscapes.

- **Modulation and LFOs:** Applying modulation to various sound parameters can introduce movement and variation. Subtronics extensively uses low-frequency oscillators (LFOs) to modulate parameters like pitch, filter cutoff, and amplitude. This imparts a sense of motion and groove to their sound.

- **Effects Processing:** Effects such as reverb, delay, distortion, and modulation play a vital role in shaping a sound's character. Subtronics skillfully combines different effects to add depth, texture, and dimension to their sounds. They experiment with various effect chains and parameter settings to create unique sonic experiences.

Layering and Stacking

One of the secrets to Subtronics' impactful sound is their use of layering and stacking. By combining multiple sounds together, they create a more robust and complex timbre. Here are some techniques they employ:

- **Timbral Layering:** Subtronics often creates layer stacks consisting of different sounds with complementary timbres. For example, they may layer a deep bass sound with a high-pitched lead to add richness and power to their drops. This layering technique helps them achieve a balanced and cohesive sound.

- **Spatial Stacking:** Subtronics utilizes spatial effects and stereo widening techniques to give their sounds a wider sonic image. By panning layers across the stereo field and utilizing stereo effects like chorus or stereo reverb, they create a more immersive and spacious soundstage.

- **Harmonic Stacking:** Stacking sounds with different harmonic content can result in interesting textures and harmonies. Subtronics often layers sounds that occupy different frequency ranges or have distinct harmonic characteristics, allowing them to create complex and harmonically rich arrangements.

Meticulous Sound Mixing

Sound mixing is the process of balancing and adjusting the individual elements in a mix to achieve clarity, depth, and cohesion. Subtronics pays meticulous attention to detail when it comes to mixing their tracks. Here are some of their techniques:

- **Frequency Spectrum Balance:** Achieving a balanced frequency spectrum is crucial in creating a clean and impactful mix. Subtronics uses equalization (EQ) to carve out space for each sound and ensure they are not clashing. They identify potential frequency conflicts and make precise EQ adjustments to maintain clarity and separation.

- **Dynamic Range Control:** Controlling the dynamic range of sounds is important for a well-balanced mix. Subtronics uses dynamic processing techniques like compression and limiting to tame peaks and bring up quieter elements, ensuring that all sounds sit well together in the mix.

- **Stereo Imaging:** Subtronics takes advantage of stereo imaging techniques to create a sense of space and dimension in their mixes. They carefully position sounds in the stereo field, utilizing techniques such as panning, stereo widening, and mid-side processing to create depth and width.

- **Automation:** Automation is key to adding movement and variation to a mix. Subtronics uses automation extensively to control parameters such as volume, panning, filter cutoff, and effects. This allows them to create dynamic and engaging mixes that evolve over time.

- **Reference Listening**: Subtronics understands the importance of referencing their mixes against professionally mastered tracks in a similar genre. By comparing their mix against commercial releases, they ensure that their sound is competitive and up to industry standards.

Unconventional Approaches

In addition to the traditional techniques, Subtronics also embraces unconventional approaches to sound design. They constantly push the boundaries and experiment with new ideas to create fresh and innovative sounds. Here are some unconventional techniques they have employed:

- **Granular Synthesis**: Subtronics has explored granular synthesis, a technique that involves breaking sounds into tiny grains and manipulating them independently. This allows them to create unique textures and complex evolving soundscapes.

- **Resampling and Processing**: Subtronics often resamples their sounds and applies creative processing techniques to achieve new and interesting textures. They experiment with techniques like time stretching, pitch shifting, and resampling through unconventional tools and plugins, resulting in unconventional and distinctive sounds.

- **Field Recording**: Subtronics incorporates field recordings into their tracks to add organic and textural elements. They capture sounds from nature, urban environments, or everyday objects, and then manipulate and process them to create unique and unexpected sonic flavors.

- **Hardware and Outboard Gear**: While software plugins are prevalent in modern music production, Subtronics likes to incorporate hardware synths and outboard gear into their workflow. They believe that the unique character of hardware can add depth and warmth to their sound.

- **Custom Sample Libraries**: Subtronics creates their own sample libraries to ensure their sounds are distinct and unique. They record and collect unusual sounds, process them, and build a custom library that reflects their sonic identity.

In conclusion, Subtronics' sound design secrets and techniques involve a deep understanding of synthesis, the art of layering and stacking, meticulous sound mixing, and experimentation with unconventional approaches. By mastering these techniques and constantly pushing the boundaries, Subtronics has crafted a unique and recognizable sonic identity that has captivated audiences worldwide. Aspiring producers can learn from their creative process to develop their own sound and take their music to new heights. Keep experimenting, keep innovating, and let your sound design journey take you beyond the glow.

Pushing the Boundaries of Electronic Music

In the ever-evolving landscape of electronic music, Subtronics has carved out a unique niche for themselves by constantly pushing the boundaries of what is possible in the genre. Through their relentless experimentation and fearless exploration, they have redefined the limits of electronic music and have become pioneers in their field. In this section, we will delve into their fearless approach to music production and their constant drive for innovation.

Reimagining Traditional Sounds

At the core of Subtronics' groundbreaking sound is their ability to take traditional elements of electronic music and give them a fresh and innovative twist. They have consistently challenged the conventions of electronic music, fusing together genres that were previously considered incompatible.

One of their signature techniques is the fusion of bass music and dubstep. By combining the heavy, hard-hitting basslines of bass music with the rhythmic intricacies and wobble bass of dubstep, Subtronics has created a distinct sound that sets them apart from their peers. This unique blend of genres has captivated audiences around the world and has become synonymous with the Subtronics brand.

To further push the boundaries of electronic music, Subtronics decides to experiment with incorporating elements from classical music into their productions. They want to create a track that seamlessly blends the grandeur of classical compositions with the hard-hitting drops that their fans love. How can they achieve this fusion while maintaining a cohesive and engaging sound? Provide a step-by-step guide and example track to illustrate your approach.

To blend classical music with Subtronics' signature sound, they can follow these steps:

1. Choose a classical piece: Select a classical composition that has a strong emotional impact and lends itself well to reinterpretation. For example, they could choose Beethoven's Symphony No. 9, known for its powerful melodies and triumphant themes.

2. Analyze the structure: Break down the classical piece into its various sections and identify the main motifs and themes. Pay attention to the dynamics, key changes, and overall progression of the piece.

3. Identify key elements: Determine which elements of the classical piece can be adapted to fit the electronic music format. This could include melodic fragments, chord progressions, or rhythmic patterns.

4. Translate the classical elements: Reinterpret the selected motifs and themes using electronic music production techniques. Experiment with different synths, sound design, and effects to give the classical elements a modern twist.

5. Incorporate Subtronics' signature sound: Integrate heavy basslines, intricate rhythmic patterns, and unique sound design elements that define Subtronics' style. This will help maintain a cohesive sound and engage the audience.

6. Arrange and structure the track: Use the structure of the classical piece as a foundation and build upon it with electronic music elements. This could involve creating new sections, adding drops, and incorporating build-ups and breakdowns to enhance the energy and impact of the track.

7. Polish and refine: Fine-tune the track by adjusting the mix, adding additional effects, and ensuring a seamless transition between the classical and electronic elements. Experiment with different mixing techniques to balance the power of the bass with the clarity of the classical instrumentation.

Example track: "Symphonic Stomp"

In "Symphonic Stomp," Subtronics takes inspiration from Beethoven's Symphony No. 9 and transforms its iconic melodies into pulsating synth lines. The track begins with a modified version of the symphony's opening, teasing the listeners with familiar sounds. As the track progresses, Subtronics builds upon Beethoven's motifs, gradually increasing the tempo and intensity.

The drop hits with a combination of heavy bass and aggressive dubstep wobbles, merging the classical essence with the raw energy of electronic music. Subtronics skillfully introduces elements of classical instrumentation, such as soaring strings and majestic brass, interwoven with glitchy effects and intricate percussions. The track seamlessly transitions between the classical and electronic elements, creating a captivating sonic experience that pushes the boundaries of both genres.

SECTION ONE: FINDING THEIR SOUND　　　　　　　　　　　　27

Exploring New Production Techniques

Subtronics is relentless in their pursuit of innovative production techniques. They constantly explore new ways to manipulate sound, combining unconventional elements and pushing the limits of what can be achieved electronically.

Subtronics wants to create a track that showcases their experimentation with granular synthesis. They want to create unique and otherworldly sounds by manipulating audio samples at the granular level. How can they approach this technique and create an impactful track utilizing granular synthesis? Provide a step-by-step guide and example track to illustrate your approach.

To experiment with granular synthesis and create a track that showcases its unique sound, Subtronics can follow these steps:

1. Choose audio samples: Select a variety of audio samples that have interesting textures, such as vocal samples, field recordings, or acoustic instruments. These samples will form the basis for granular synthesis.

2. Segment the samples: Chop the audio samples into tiny fragments or "grains," usually ranging from a few milliseconds to a few seconds in length. Use audio editing software to precisely isolate and export these grains.

3. Load the grains into a granular synthesizer: Utilize a granular synthesis plugin or hardware synthesizer to load and manipulate the grains. Experiment with parameters like grain size, grain density, pitch, and position to shape the characteristics of the sound.

4. Manipulate the grains: Apply various effects and transformations to the grains to create unique and otherworldly sounds. Experiment with time-stretching, pitch-shifting, reverb, delay, and other audio processing techniques to further shape the textures.

5. Create melodic or rhythmic patterns: Arrange the manipulated grains into melodic or rhythmic patterns. Use MIDI or a sequencer to trigger the grains at different pitches and timings, creating evolving and dynamic musical phrases.

6. Add Subtronics' signature elements: Incorporate heavy basslines, powerful drums, and intricate sound design elements that are synonymous with Subtronics' style. This will help to create a cohesive and impactful track that showcases the fusion of granular synthesis with their unique sound.

7. Mix and master: Balance the levels of the various elements in the track, ensuring that the granular synthesis sits well with the other sounds. Apply compression, EQ, and other mastering techniques to give the track its final polish.

Example track: "Interstellar Grains"

In "Interstellar Grains," Subtronics harnesses the power of granular synthesis to create an otherworldly sonic landscape. The track starts with ethereal vocal samples that have been sliced into grains and processed with granular synthesis. These granular textures gradually evolve, building tension and setting the stage for the drop.

As the track progresses, Subtronics incorporates heavy basslines, distorted synths, and intricate drum patterns. The manipulated granular sounds serve as a sonic foundation, adding depth and complexity to the arrangement. Subtronics skillfully blends the granular elements with dynamic bass design, creating a track that takes the listener on a cosmic journey through a world of granular soundscapes.

By pushing the boundaries of electronic music production through techniques like granular synthesis, Subtronics continually challenges the status quo and leads the way for other artists and producers in the genre.

Embracing Unconventional Sound Sources

In their relentless pursuit of innovation, Subtronics finds inspiration in unexpected places and pushes the boundaries of electronic music by incorporating unconventional sound sources into their productions.

Subtronics wants to create a track that incorporates sounds from everyday objects as a way of adding unique and unexpected textures. They want to push the boundaries of electronic music by using unconventional sound sources. How can they approach this technique and create an engaging track that showcases these unconventional sounds? Provide a step-by-step guide and example track to illustrate your approach.

To incorporate sounds from everyday objects into their track, Subtronics can follow these steps:

1. Gather a variety of objects: Collect a diverse range of everyday objects that produce interesting sounds when struck, scraped, or manipulated. This could include items like glass bottles, kitchen utensils, or even nature sounds like rustling leaves or raindrops.

SECTION ONE: FINDING THEIR SOUND

2. Record the sounds: Use a high-quality audio recorder or microphone to capture the sounds generated by interacting with these objects. Experiment with different playing techniques and microphone placements to capture a wide range of textures and timbres.

3. Process and manipulate the recordings: Use audio editing software to process and manipulate the recorded sounds. Apply effects like reverb, delay, distortion, or pitch-shifting to transform the raw recordings into textures that are unique and intriguing.

4. Integrate the sounds into the track: Incorporate the processed recordings into the composition, using them as percussive elements, atmospheric layers, or melodic components. Experiment with different arrangements and combinations to find compelling ways to integrate the unconventional sounds.

5. Blend with electronic elements: Combine the unconventional sounds with Subtronics' signature electronic elements. This could involve adding heavy basslines, intricate synth melodies, or dynamic drum patterns to enhance the energy and impact of the track.

6. Fine-tune and mix the track: Polish the arrangement by adjusting the mix, ensuring that the unconventional sounds sit well with the other elements in the track. Apply EQ, compression, and other mastering techniques to achieve a balanced and cohesive sound.

Example track: "Objects in Sound"

In "Objects in Sound," Subtronics takes inspiration from the sounds of everyday objects and transforms them into a mesmerizing sonic experience. The track opens with the delicate sound of glass bottles being struck, creating a haunting melody that sets the tone. As the track progresses, Subtronics incorporates percussive elements created by scraping utensils and uses field recordings of raindrops to add texture and ambience.

The unconventional sounds blend seamlessly with powerful basslines, intricate synth arpeggios, and driving drum patterns. Subtronics skillfully weaves together the unique sounds with their signature electronic elements, creating a track that tells a captivating story through unconventional audio sources.

By embracing these unconventional sound sources, Subtronics expands the possibilities of electronic music and encourages other artists to think outside the box when it comes to sound design and composition.

The Quest for Innovation

Subtronics' dedication to pushing the boundaries of electronic music is driven by their never-ending quest for innovation. Their fearlessness in exploring new techniques, genres, and sounds has positioned them at the forefront of the EDM scene and has solidified their status as true pioneers in their field.

While this section has only scratched the surface of Subtronics' innovation in electronic music, it serves as a testament to their relentless pursuit of pushing the boundaries and exploring the uncharted territory within the genre.

Subtronics wants to expand their musical horizons by collaborating with a traditional orchestra for a live performance. They aim to bridge the gap between electronic music and classical orchestration, creating a unique and immersive experience for their fans. How can they approach this collaboration and ensure a successful fusion of these seemingly disparate worlds? Provide a step-by-step guide and example performance to illustrate your approach.

To collaborate with a traditional orchestra and merge electronic music with classical orchestration, Subtronics can follow these steps:

1. Identify the orchestra: Research and connect with a professional orchestra that is open to collaborating with electronic music artists. Look for orchestras experienced in contemporary or crossover collaborations to ensure a receptive and enthusiastic partnership.

2. Select a venue: Choose a venue that can accommodate both the orchestra and Subtronics' electronic setup. Consider acoustics, technical requirements, and capacity to ensure an optimal experience for the audience.

3. Identify shared musical elements: Explore common elements between electronic music and classical orchestration, such as harmonic progressions, melodic motifs, or rhythmic patterns. These shared elements will form the foundation for the collaboration and create a bridge between the genres.

4. Adapt and arrange electronic tracks: Collaborate with the orchestra's conductor and arrangers to adapt Subtronics' electronic tracks for orchestral performance. This involves transcribing electronic elements to orchestral instruments, rearranging sections, and developing orchestral accompaniments or counterpoint to the electronic elements.

5. Rehearse and fine-tune: Schedule rehearsal sessions with the orchestra to ensure a cohesive and well-executed performance. Take into account the

nuances of both electronic and orchestral performance styles, and allow time for the musicians to adjust to the new collaborative space.

6. Choreograph the performance: Consider the visual and immersive elements of the performance, including stage design, lighting, and synchronized visuals. Work with visual artists and stage directors to create a dynamic and engaging experience that complements both the electronic and orchestral elements.

7. Perform and record: Execute the collaborative performance live, capturing both audio and visual elements for future releases. Make necessary adjustments during the performance to maintain a balance between the electronic and orchestral elements, ensuring a cohesive and impactful blend of both worlds.

Example performance: "Symphony of Subtronica"

In "Symphony of Subtronica," Subtronics collaborates with a renowned orchestra for a groundbreaking performance that merges electronic music with classical orchestration. The performance takes place in a grand concert hall, filled with an eager audience eagerly awaiting this unique experience.

The show begins with Subtronics' signature electronic sound, setting the stage for what's to come. The orchestra enters, subtly blending their traditional instruments with the electronic rhythms. As the performance unfolds, the audience witnesses a magical fusion of orchestral harmonies and electronic basslines.

Throughout the performance, the orchestra and Subtronics engage in a complex interplay, responding to each other's musical ideas and pushing the boundaries of their respective genres. The symphony incorporates Subtronics' original tracks, adapted and arranged for the orchestra, as well as specially composed pieces that highlight the unique blend of electronic and orchestral sounds.

Visually, the stage is transformed into a captivating display of lights and projections, synchronized with the music. The combination of powerful electronic beats, soaring orchestra melodies, and mesmerizing visuals creates an immersive experience that transcends the boundaries of traditional live performances.

By collaborating with a traditional orchestra, Subtronics successfully explores new dimensions in electronic music, proving that innovation knows no limits. This groundbreaking fusion of genres paves the way for future collaborations and inspires artists to continue experimenting with new sonic possibilities.

In their relentless pursuit of pushing the boundaries of electronic music, Subtronics continues to inspire and captivate audiences around the world. Their fearless experimentation, embrace of unconventional techniques, and innovative approach to production have solidified them as true trailblazers in the EDM scene. As they embark on new musical journeys, their commitment to pushing the limits of what is possible in electronic music ensures that their glow will never fade.

Section Two: The Underground Scene

Playing Gigs at Local Clubs and Raves

Playing gigs at local clubs and raves was an essential part of Subtronics' journey to success. It was in these intimate venues that they honed their skills, connected with their audience, and built a dedicated fan base. In this section, we will explore the electrifying atmosphere of these shows, the challenges they faced, and the strategies they employed to make each performance unforgettable.

Finding the Right Venues

When Subtronics first began their musical journey, they started by performing at small local clubs and raves. These venues provided them with the perfect platform to showcase their unique sound and connect with the underground music community. They played at renowned clubs such as The Black Box in Denver, or The Untz Festival in California, where they captivated audiences with their energetic and bass-heavy sets.

The Importance of Local Clubs Playing at local clubs allowed Subtronics to gain exposure within their own community and establish themselves as talented artists. These venues offered an intimate setting, enabling them to interact closely with the crowd and gauge the audience's response to their music. The local club scene also provided a supportive environment for them to experiment with new sounds and techniques, allowing them to continually evolve their style.

Thriving in the Underground Rave Scene Subtronics' music resonated deeply with the underground rave scene, characterized by its unapologetic embrace of bass-heavy music and uninhibited expression. Raves provided them with a space to push boundaries and truly connect with the audience on a visceral level. From dimly lit warehouses to open-air fields, these unconventional venues amplified the raw energy of their music and allowed for a more immersive experience.

Creating Unforgettable Performances

Subtronics understood the importance of delivering high-energy performances that left a lasting impression on their audience. They knew that every show was an opportunity to create a unique experience that would resonate with their fans. To achieve this, they employed a combination of innovative stage production, crowd engagement, and careful song selection.

Crafting the Setlist Building a setlist was a meticulous process for Subtronics. They carefully selected tracks that would seamlessly blend together, creating an immersive and energetic journey for the audience. They strategically placed their own original tracks alongside fan-favorite remixes and collaborations. By balancing familiar tunes with surprises, they kept the crowd engaged and eager for more.

Engaging with the Crowd Subtronics understood that a great performance was not just about the music, but also about the connection they established with the crowd. They made a deliberate effort to engage with their audience, whether through jumping into the crowd or simply maintaining eye contact. This personal touch created a sense of camaraderie, making their shows feel like a gathering of friends rather than a traditional performance.

Innovative Stage Production Subtronics' performances were known for their visually stunning and immersive stage productions. They collaborated with visual artists and VJs to create a synchronized audio-visual experience that enhanced the impact of their music. The combination of mesmerizing visuals, atmospheric lighting, and carefully choreographed stage presence elevated their shows to new heights and left a lasting impression on their fans.

Overcoming Challenges and Nurturing Fan Base

Playing gigs at local clubs and raves was not without its challenges. Subtronics faced obstacles, including technical difficulties, limited resources, and the need to constantly innovate to stand out in a competitive scene. However, they found creative solutions and developed strategies to overcome these hurdles, ultimately building a strong and dedicated fan base.

Technical Challenges As with any live performance, technical issues were an ever-present challenge for Subtronics. They encountered problems such as equipment failures, sound system limitations, or venue constraints. To mitigate these issues, they invested in high-quality equipment, carried backups, and worked closely with venue technicians to ensure smooth setups. Their dedication to delivering a flawless performance, regardless of technical challenges, earned them the respect and admiration of their fans.

Fostering a Sense of Community Subtronics recognized the importance of nurturing their fan base and creating a sense of community around their music. They interacted directly with fans at shows, taking the time to connect with them on a personal level. They also used social media platforms to engage with their followers, sharing behind-the-scenes moments, announcing upcoming gigs, and even seeking input for track selections. This level of engagement fostered a strong bond between Subtronics and their fans, creating a supportive and passionate community.

Harnessing the Power of Word-of-Mouth Word-of-mouth played a significant role in Subtronics' rise to prominence. Their passionate fan base spread the word about their electrifying performances, introducing their music to new audiences. They actively encouraged fans to bring their friends to shows, organized fan meetups, and even offered promotional incentives for sharing their music. These grassroots efforts allowed Subtronics to expand their reach and solidify their position within the local club and rave scene.

Embracing Unconventional Strategies In addition to traditional marketing approaches, Subtronics embraced unconventional strategies to stand out in a highly competitive scene. They collaborated with local street artists to create unique event posters, organized impromptu performances in unexpected locations, and utilized guerrilla marketing techniques. These innovative approaches helped them create buzz, generate interest, and attract new fans to their shows.

In conclusion, playing gigs at local clubs and raves was a critical stepping stone in Subtronics' journey to success. It allowed them to connect intimately with their audience, experiment with their sound, and build a dedicated fan base. Through innovative stage production, engaging performances, and a strong sense of community, Subtronics created unforgettable experiences that solidified their position in the local club and rave scene. They overcame challenges and embraced unconventional strategies, leaving a lasting impact on the underground music community.

Building a Dedicated Fan Base

Building a dedicated fan base is crucial for any music artist's success. In the case of Subtronics, their journey to stardom was greatly influenced by their ability to connect with their audience and create a loyal following. In this section, we will explore the strategies and tactics employed by Subtronics to build their dedicated fan base and establish their place in the electronic music scene.

Understanding the Power of Authenticity

One of the key elements that attracted fans to Subtronics was their authenticity. From the very beginning, they stayed true to their unique sound and style, never compromising their artistic vision to conform to popular trends. They embraced their individuality, which resonated with listeners who were craving something fresh and different in the electronic music landscape.

Subtronics made a conscious effort to connect with their audience on a personal level. They engaged with fans through social media platforms, responding to comments and messages, and sharing snippets of their daily lives. This sense of intimacy forged a strong bond between the artists and their supporters, creating a community that rallied behind Subtronics and felt like they were part of something special.

Creating Memorable Live Experiences

Live performances played a crucial role in Subtronics' fan base building strategy. They understood the importance of creating a memorable experience for their audience beyond just playing tracks. Subtronics shows were known for their high-energy performances, captivating visuals, and interactive elements that kept fans engaged throughout the entire set.

By delivering unforgettable shows, Subtronics ensured that their fans would eagerly return for future performances and also recommend the experience to others. Word of mouth became a powerful tool in expanding their dedicated fan base, as attendees would share their excitement and encourage their friends to join them in witnessing the Subtronics magic.

Engaging in Direct Fan Interaction

Subtronics recognized the value of direct fan interaction and made it a priority to engage with their audience on a regular basis. They held meet and greets before and after shows, giving fans the opportunity to connect with them face-to-face. These personal interactions created unforgettable memories for fans and made them feel appreciated and valued.

In addition to in-person interactions, Subtronics leveraged social media platforms to connect with their fans worldwide. They regularly posted updates, behind-the-scenes footage, and engaged in conversations with their followers. This consistent online presence helped to foster a sense of community and further solidify the loyalty of their fan base.

Empowering Fan Creativity

Subtronics recognized the creativity of their fan base and actively encouraged their artistic endeavors. They established a platform for fan-made art and held contests where fans could submit their designs or remixes. By showcasing and promoting fan creativity, Subtronics not only made their fans feel appreciated but also created a sense of ownership and pride within the community.

Fan clubs and online forums dedicated to Subtronics also played a significant role in building their dedicated fan base. These platforms provided a space for fans to connect, share their love for the artist, and organize meetups or other fan-driven initiatives. Subtronics made sure to actively participate in these communities, further strengthening the bond with their fan base.

Giving Back to the Community

Beyond their music, Subtronics recognized the importance of giving back and making a positive impact on the world. They actively engaged in charitable initiatives and encouraged their fans to join them in supporting various causes. By aligning themselves with philanthropic efforts, Subtronics not only demonstrated their commitment to making a difference but also attracted fans who shared the same values.

In conclusion, Subtronics built a dedicated fan base through a combination of authenticity, memorable live experiences, direct fan interaction, empowering fan creativity, and giving back to the community. By prioritizing these elements, they created a strong and loyal following that continues to support them on their journey. The story of Subtronics serves as an inspiration for aspiring artists looking to establish their place in the music industry by connecting with their audience on a deeper level.

Collaborations with Other Underground Artists

Subtronics has always had a deep appreciation for the underground music scene and has formed numerous collaborations with fellow underground artists. These collaborations have not only helped them expand their musical horizons but have also played a significant role in solidifying their position within the bass music community.

Finding the Right Artists to Collaborate With

Finding the right artists to collaborate with is crucial in creating a successful musical partnership. Subtronics has always been on the lookout for talented underground artists who share their passion for pushing the boundaries of electronic music. Their collaborations have been born out of mutual respect, admiration, and a shared vision for creating unique and groundbreaking music.

Through their extensive involvement in the underground scene, Subtronics has been able to connect with artists who bring something fresh and exciting to the table. These collaborations have allowed them to tap into a wider array of musical influences and experiment with different sounds and styles.

Exploring New Genres and Styles

Collaborating with other underground artists has given Subtronics the opportunity to explore new genres and styles of music. By blending their signature bass-heavy sound with elements of different genres, they have been able to create a unique sonic experience that resonates with fans from various backgrounds.

For example, their collaboration with a talented hip-hop artist allowed them to infuse their bass music with rap verses, resulting in a fusion of styles that captivated audiences. This venture into the hip-hop realm not only showcased their versatility but also expanded their fan base and introduced their music to new listeners.

Pushing Each Other's Creative Boundaries

Collaborations with other artists are not just about combining musical talents; they are also about pushing each other's creative boundaries. When Subtronics collaborates with other underground artists, they engage in a creative dialogue where ideas are exchanged, challenged, and refined.

This collaborative process pushes Subtronics to think outside the box and explore innovative approaches to music production. By bouncing ideas off each other and experimenting with new sounds and techniques, they are able to push themselves beyond their comfort zones and create music that is innovative and boundary-breaking.

Creating a Sense of Community

Collaborations with other underground artists are not solely about the music; they also contribute to the sense of community within the bass music scene. By working together and supporting each other's careers, Subtronics and their collaborators foster a spirit of unity and collaboration within the underground music community.

These collaborations often extend beyond the studio and onto the stage, with joint performances and back-to-back sets that showcase the collective talent and passion of the artists involved. This sense of community creates a unique and inclusive experience for fans, who feel like they are part of something larger than just a single artist's journey.

Unconventional Approach: Collaborative Experimentation

An unconventional yet effective approach that Subtronics takes in their collaborations is a focus on collaborative experimentation. Rather than sticking to a predetermined formula or genre, they encourage their collaborators to bring their own unique perspective and ideas to the table.

This openness to collaboration allows for unexpected creative results and encourages artists to take risks and step outside their comfort zones. By embracing the unknown and fostering an environment of experimentation, Subtronics and their collaborators have been able to challenge the conventions of electronic music and create truly groundbreaking tracks.

Example: The Collaboration with *Artist Name*

One notable collaboration that Subtronics embarked on was with the talented underground artist *Artist Name*. This collaboration brought together two distinct musical styles and resulted in a track that pushed the boundaries of bass music.

Artist Name, known for their experimental approach to music production, brought their unique perspective to the collaboration. Their unconventional use of samples and intricate sound design added a new dimension to the track, highlighting the synergy between the two artists.

The collaboration started with a shared vision of creating a track that blended elements of dubstep and drum and bass. Subtronics and *Artist Name* spent hours in the studio, experimenting with different sounds, and layering intricate melodies and basslines.

The resulting track showcased the best of both artists' abilities. It featured Subtronics' knack for creating bone-rattling bass drops, combined with *Artist Name*'s intricate percussion and atmospheric elements. The track was met with critical acclaim and resonated with fans from both artists' fan bases.

This collaboration not only showcased the individual talents of Subtronics and *Artist Name* but also highlighted the power of collaboration in pushing the boundaries of electronic music. By merging their unique styles and musical approaches, they created something truly special that connected with fans on a deeper level.

Conclusion

Collaborations with other underground artists have played a vital role in Subtronics' musical journey. These collaborations have allowed them to explore new genres, push creative boundaries, and create a sense of community within the bass music scene. By embracing collaboration and experimentation, they have been able to constantly evolve and create music that resonates with fans and fellow artists alike. Through their collaborations, Subtronics continues to push the limits of electronic music and leave an indelible mark on the underground music scene.

Releasing Mixtapes and EPs Independently

Releasing mixtapes and EPs independently has played a crucial role in Subtronics' rise to fame and success. This section explores the process behind their independent releases, the impact of these projects on their career, and the advantages of maintaining creative control.

The Importance of Independent Releases

In today's digital age, independent releases have become an essential avenue for artists to share their music directly with fans. For Subtronics, releasing mixtapes and EPs independently allowed them to bypass traditional music industry gatekeepers and connect directly with their audience.

By taking control of their releases, Subtronics had the freedom to explore their artistic vision without constraints. They could experiment with different genres, styles, and concepts, pushing the boundaries of electronic music. This creative freedom enabled them to establish a unique sound that resonated with their growing fan base.

The Process of Creating Mixtapes and EPs

Creating a mixtape or EP requires careful planning, organization, and collaboration. Subtronics embraced this process and approached each project with meticulous attention to detail. Here's a breakdown of the steps they took:

1. **Conceptualization and Track Selection:** Subtronics would brainstorm themes or concepts for the mixtape or EP. They would then select tracks that fit the overall vision, ensuring a cohesive listening experience.

2. **Collaborations and Features:** Mixtapes and EPs often feature collaborations with other artists. Subtronics would reach out to fellow musicians whose sound complemented their own, resulting in dynamic and exciting tracks.

3. **Production and Mixing:** Producing high-quality tracks is crucial to the success of a mixtape or EP. Subtronics would spend countless hours refining their sound design, experimenting with different techniques, and perfecting the mix to deliver a polished final product.

4. **Artwork and Visual Aesthetics:** Visuals play an important role in creating an immersive experience. Subtronics would collaborate with talented artists and graphic designers to create captivating artwork that represented the essence of each mixtape or EP.

5. **Promotion and Distribution:** Once the mixtape or EP was ready, Subtronics would embark on a strategic promotion campaign. They would leverage social media platforms, engage with fans, and actively participate in the bass music community to generate buzz for their release. Additionally, they would distribute their music across various streaming platforms and upload it to their website for free download.

The Impact on Their Career

Releasing mixtapes and EPs independently had a profound impact on Subtronics' career trajectory. It allowed them to build a dedicated fan base and establish themselves as prominent figures in the bass music scene. Here are some key advantages they gained:

- **Direct fan connection:** Releasing music independently fostered a strong connection with their fans. By sharing their work directly, they could receive immediate feedback, engage in conversations, and build a supportive community around their music.

- **Creative control:** Maintaining creative control over their releases was essential to Subtronics. It allowed them to shape their artistic direction, experiment with new sounds, and stay true to their vision without external pressures or compromises.

- **Authenticity and artistic growth:** Independent releases allowed Subtronics to grow as artists by honing their skills, exploring new genres, and evolving their sound. This authenticity resonated with their fans, who appreciated their genuine and innovative approach to music.

- **Industry recognition:** Releasing compelling mixtapes and EPs independently garnered attention from industry insiders, leading to increased recognition and opportunities. Their unique sound and visionary approach attracted the interest of major record labels and opened doors to collaborations with well-established artists.

- **Entrepreneurial mindset:** Releasing music independently helped cultivate an entrepreneurial mindset within Subtronics. They learned valuable skills in self-promotion, marketing, and audience engagement, which became instrumental in their ongoing career success.

An Unconventional Approach

One unconventional approach that Subtronics took with their mixtape and EP releases was incorporating elements of interactive storytelling. For example, they would create an overarching narrative that threaded together individual tracks, immersing listeners in a cinematic experience.

Using interludes, skits, or spoken word segments, they would guide the listener on a sonic journey, enhancing the overall impact of the mixtape or EP. This unconventional approach added depth and intrigue to their releases, making them stand out in a crowded music landscape.

Practical Tips for Independent Releases

For aspiring artists looking to release mixtapes or EPs independently, here are some practical tips inspired by Subtronics' journey:

- **Plan ahead:** Take the time to conceptualize your project, decide on a theme or concept, and carefully curate the tracks that align with your vision.

- **Collaborate strategically:** Seek out like-minded artists for collaborations and features that will enhance the overall quality and appeal of your mixtape or EP.

- **Invest in production quality:** Pay attention to sound design, mixing, and mastering to ensure your music stands out and delivers a professional listening experience.

- **Create captivating visuals:** Work with talented artists or designers to create visually striking artwork that complements your music and helps tell your story.

- **Engage with your fan base:** Use social media platforms and other online communities to connect directly with your fans, share updates, and build a loyal following.

- **Strategically release your music:** Plan your release date, consider distributing your music on multiple platforms, and leverage promotional opportunities to maximize your reach.

Conclusion

Releasing mixtapes and EPs independently has been a significant factor in Subtronics' success story. It allowed them to establish their sound, build a dedicated fan base, and shape their artistic direction on their own terms. By embracing the freedom and creative control that independent releases provided, Subtronics has solidified their position as influential figures in the bass music community. Their journey serves as inspiration for aspiring artists to pursue their music careers with passion, innovation, and a willingness to break the traditional mold. Remember, in today's digital landscape, independent releases offer unparalleled opportunities to showcase your talent, connect with your audience, and make your mark on the music industry. So go forth, unleash your creativity, and let the world hear your voice. The stage is yours!

The Growth of the Bass Music Community

The growth of the bass music community has been a testament to the power of a genre that speaks directly to the hearts and souls of its listeners. It is a community that thrives on the energy and intensity of bass-driven beats, creating a unique and immersive experience for both artists and fans alike.

SECTION TWO: THE UNDERGROUND SCENE

In this section, we will explore the factors that have contributed to the growth of the bass music community, the impact it has had on electronic music as a whole, and the ways in which it continues to evolve and inspire new generations of artists.

The Rise of Bass Music

Bass music, with its heavy emphasis on low-frequency sounds and hard-hitting beats, has a long history rooted in the underground music scene. It draws influences from various genres such as dubstep, drum and bass, trap, and grime, combining elements to create a distinct and powerful sonic experience.

One of the key reasons for the rise of bass music is its ability to connect with listeners on a visceral level. The deep, rumbling bass tones and intricate rhythms create a physical response that can be felt in the chest and the bones, making it an incredibly immersive and captivating genre.

The Internet and Digital Age

The growth of the bass music community has been significantly fueled by the internet and the digital age. With the rise of social media and streaming platforms, artists can now easily connect with fans from all over the world and share their music with a global audience.

Platforms like SoundCloud and Bandcamp have played a crucial role in enabling upcoming artists to distribute their music independently, giving rise to a wave of DIY producers and creating a thriving underground scene. This has led to increased diversity within the bass music community, with artists from different backgrounds and styles coming together to create a rich and vibrant tapestry of sound.

Community Building

Community building has been at the heart of the bass music movement. From local clubs and underground raves to online forums and fan groups, the sense of belonging and camaraderie within the community is palpable.

Artists and fans actively engage with each other, sharing music, discussing techniques, and even collaborating on projects. This collaborative spirit has helped foster a sense of unity and support, allowing the bass music community to flourish and grow.

Impact on Music Festivals

Bass music's impact on music festivals cannot be understated. The genre has become a mainstay at many major festivals, with dedicated stages and lineups showcasing the best in bass-driven music.

The high-energy performances, immersive visuals, and pulsating beats create an unforgettable experience for festival-goers. The growth of the bass music community has pushed festivals to incorporate more diverse acts and styles, reflecting the evolving tastes of their audiences.

Continued Evolution

The bass music community continues to evolve and push the boundaries of electronic music. Artists are constantly experimenting with new sounds and production techniques, blending genres and styles to create fresh and innovative music.

One of the key aspects of the bass music scene is its ability to stay true to its underground roots while still garnering mainstream recognition. This balance between artistic integrity and commercial success is what sets the genre apart and ensures its longevity.

The Future of Bass Music

As the bass music community continues to grow, it is important to recognize the challenges and opportunities that lie ahead. Artists and organizers must work together to maintain the authenticity and inclusivity of the scene, ensuring that it remains a safe and welcoming space for all.

Furthermore, the genre must continue to evolve and adapt to changing trends and technological advancements. This will require artists to constantly push themselves creatively and strive for innovation while staying true to the essence of bass music.

In conclusion, the growth of the bass music community is a testament to the power of a genre that resonates deeply with its listeners. Through the internet, community building, and a commitment to artistic exploration, bass music has carved out a significant space within the electronic music scene. As it continues to evolve, the genre's impact on music festivals, its influence on other genres, and its ability to inspire new generations of artists will define its lasting legacy. The future of bass music is bright, pulsating with energy and filled with endless possibilities.

Section Three: Breaking into the Festival Circuit

Captivating Audiences with High-Energy Performances

Subtronics has found tremendous success in captivating audiences with their high-energy performances. Their live shows are a true reflection of their passion for music and their desire to create an unforgettable experience for their fans. In this section, we will explore the various elements that contribute to the electrifying atmosphere of a Subtronics concert.

Creating an Energetic Setlist

A crucial aspect of captivating audiences with high-energy performances is the selection of songs for the setlist. Subtronics carefully curates their sets to ensure a seamless flow of music that keeps the energy levels soaring. They strategically mix their own tracks with popular EDM hits and even surprise the crowd with unreleased music.

To maintain the momentum, Subtronics employs a variety of techniques such as pitch-shifting, looping, and live remixing. This allows them to create unique versions of their tracks on the spot, keeping the audience engaged and excited.

Mastering the Art of DJing

Subtronics' live performances are a testament to their mastery of the art of DJing. With precise control over their equipment, they seamlessly blend tracks, transition between genres, and create a continuous wave of energy on the dance floor.

Their DJ sets are renowned for their technical prowess, incorporating intricate scratching, cutting, and blending techniques. These skills, combined with their deep knowledge of music theory, enable Subtronics to create captivating mixes that take the audience on a sonic journey.

Stage Presence and Crowd Interaction

Subtronics understands the importance of stage presence and harnessing the energy of the crowd. They exude a contagious enthusiasm that instantly connects with the audience, making them an integral part of the performance.

Interacting with the crowd is a crucial element of their live shows. Subtronics actively engages with the audience, encouraging them to join in, dance, and sing along to their music. This interaction creates a sense of unity and amplifies the energy in the room, resulting in an immersive experience for everyone present.

Visuals and Stage Production

The visual elements of a Subtronics show play a vital role in captivating audiences. Their stage production is carefully designed to complement the music, elevating the overall experience to new heights.

Utilizing cutting-edge technology, Subtronics incorporates mesmerizing visuals, lighting effects, and synchronized LED panels. These visual elements, combined with their music, create a multisensory spectacle that immerses the audience in a vibrant and dynamic environment.

Surprises and Special Moments

Subtronics understands the importance of surprises and special moments during their performances. They incorporate unexpected elements such as confetti cannons, CO2 jets, and pyrotechnics to make each show unforgettable.

Furthermore, Subtronics often invites surprise guest artists to join them on stage for epic B2B (back-to-back) sets. These collaborations amplify the energy levels and create unforgettable moments for the audience.

Unconventional Audience Participation

Subtronics takes audience participation to the next level by introducing unconventional elements into their shows. One example is the use of inflatable props, which are distributed to the crowd before the performance. These props create a sense of unity and add an element of playfulness to the experience.

Another unique aspect of their shows is the integration of interactive visuals controlled by the audience. Subtronics encourages fans to use their smartphones to interact with specially designed apps, creating a synchronized visual display that enhances the overall atmosphere.

Conclusion

Subtronics' ability to captivate audiences with their high-energy performances is a testament to their talent and dedication to their craft. Through careful curation of their setlists, mastery of DJing techniques, stage presence, crowd interaction, visual elements, surprises, and unconventional audience participation, they have created a signature experience that resonates with fans worldwide.

Their commitment to pushing boundaries and continually innovating in live performances has undoubtedly played a significant role in their rise to success. As Subtronics continues to evolve and leave their mark on the EDM scene, their high-energy performances will undoubtedly remain a defining aspect of their musical journey.

Signature Visuals and Stage Production

Signature visuals and stage production are integral aspects of Subtronics' live performances. They go beyond simply playing their music and aim to create a visually stunning and immersive experience for their fans. In this section, we will explore how Subtronics incorporates cutting-edge visuals and stage production techniques to enhance their performances and leave a lasting impact on their audience.

Creating a Visual Narrative

Subtronics understands the power of visual storytelling and aims to take their audience on a journey through their performances. They work closely with visual artists and VJs to create a unique visual narrative that complements the energy and emotion of their music.

For example, during their songs, they use visuals that align with the mood and theme of the track. If a song has a dark and heavy bassline, the visuals may include dark and intense imagery, creating a sense of anticipation and suspense. On the other hand, if the track is more melodic and uplifting, the visuals may consist of vibrant colors and uplifting scenes to match the mood.

Incorporating Advanced Projection Mapping

One of the key elements of Subtronics' signature visuals is the use of projection mapping on various surfaces on stage. Projection mapping allows them to transform ordinary objects, such as DJ booths and pillars, into dynamic canvases for their visuals.

By mapping their visuals onto these surfaces, they create an immersive and three-dimensional experience for their audience. The visuals move and interact with the music, enhancing the overall impact of the performance. For example, during a drop, the visuals may appear to burst out of the DJ booth, creating an explosive and intense visual effect that amplifies the climax of the song.

Interactive Light Shows

Lighting plays a crucial role in Subtronics' stage production, creating an atmosphere that heightens the overall experience. They utilize a range of lighting techniques, including LED panels, lasers, and strobe lights, to create visually captivating moments.

One of the standout features of Subtronics' live shows is the interactive nature of their lighting design. They incorporate sensors and motion detectors that respond to their movements on stage. These sensors trigger different lighting patterns and effects, synchronizing the lights with the music. This interactive element adds another layer of excitement and engagement for the audience, making each performance a unique and immersive experience.

Synchronized Visuals and Audio

To create a seamless integration of visuals and music, Subtronics employs cutting-edge technology to synchronize their visuals with their audio. They use software that analyzes the music in real-time, allowing the visuals to react and change according to the beats, drops, and melodies of each song.

This synchronization ensures that the visuals are perfectly aligned with the music, creating a synchronized audio-visual experience. For example, during a heavy bass drop, the visuals may consist of pulsating patterns and intense animations that follow the rhythm of the bassline. This synchronized experience enhances the impact of the music and creates a multisensory journey for the audience.

Unconventional Use of Props and Instruments

Subtronics is known for incorporating unique props and instruments into their stage production, adding an unexpected and unconventional element to their performances. For instance, they sometimes bring on stage custom-built MIDI controllers that allow them to manipulate the visuals in real-time. These controllers can trigger specific visual effects or alter the speed and intensity of the visuals, giving Subtronics a hands-on approach to their stage production.

Additionally, Subtronics occasionally features live musicians and instrumentalists during their performances. This inclusion of live instruments adds a dynamic and organic element to their sets, elevating their stage production to new heights. The combination of electronic music with live instrumentation creates a captivating fusion that further immerses the audience in the performance.

Conclusion

In the world of EDM, Subtronics stands out not only for their electrifying music but also for their visually mesmerizing stage production. By incorporating signature visuals, advanced projection mapping, interactive light shows, synchronized visuals and audio, and unconventional props and instruments, Subtronics creates an unforgettable experience for their fans. Their dedication to pushing the boundaries of stage production ensures that each performance is a unique and immersive journey, leaving a lasting impact on the audience. As Subtronics continues to evolve and innovate, their signature visuals and stage production will undoubtedly remain a central element of their live performances.

Memorable Sets at Major Festivals

One of the most thrilling moments in Subtronics' career has been their performances at major music festivals around the world. These sets have allowed the duo to showcase their unique blend of bass music and dubstep to massive audiences, leaving a lasting impression on both fans and industry insiders.

Captivating Audiences with High-Energy Performances

Subtronics is known for their high-energy performances that leave audiences in awe. Their sets at major festivals are no exception. The duo's infectious energy fills the stage, as they jump and dance to the beat of their own music. The crowd can feel the passion and excitement radiating from the stage, creating an electrifying atmosphere that is impossible to resist.

During these performances, Subtronics takes the audience on a journey through their signature sound. They carefully curate their setlist to include a mix of their own original tracks, remixes, and collaborations, ensuring that every moment is filled with hard-hitting bass and mind-bending drops. Their seamless transitions and expert mixing skills keep the energy flowing and the crowd engaged from start to finish.

Signature Visuals and Stage Production

In addition to their captivating music, Subtronics is known for their visually stunning stage productions. They understand the importance of creating a multisensory experience for their audience and go above and beyond to deliver memorable visuals that complement their sound.

The duo incorporates a variety of lighting effects, lasers, and LED screens into their stage setup, creating a mesmerizing visual display that enhances the overall performance. These visuals are carefully synchronized with the music, adding an extra layer of excitement and intensity to the already immersive experience.

Memorable Sets at Major Festivals

Subtronics' sets at major festivals have become legendary within the EDM community. They have graced the stages of renowned festivals such as Electric Daisy Carnival (EDC), Ultra Music Festival, and Lost Lands, just to name a few. Each festival performance is carefully crafted to make a lasting impact on both the audience and the festival itself.

At Electric Daisy Carnival, Subtronics wowed the crowd with their bass-heavy beats and infectious energy. The audience couldn't help but move to the rhythm as the duo took them on a journey through the depths of dubstep. Their set was a true highlight of the festival, leaving fans craving for more.

Ultra Music Festival witnessed Subtronics' ability to captivate a massive crowd with their unique sound. Their set was a perfect blend of heavy bass drops, melodic interludes, and unexpected surprises. The audience was left in awe, marveled by the duo's ability to push the boundaries of electronic music.

Lost Lands, the festival curated by Subtronics' mentor and friend Excision, provided the perfect platform for the duo to showcase their talent. Known for its emphasis on heavy bass music, Lost Lands was the ideal setting for Subtronics to unleash their signature sound. Their set was a highlight of the festival, with fans eagerly awaiting their performance year after year.

Collaborations with Big-Name Artists

Subtronics has also had the opportunity to collaborate with big-name artists during their festival performances. These collaborations have added an extra level of excitement and anticipation to their sets, taking their performances to new heights.

At Electric Forest, Subtronics surprised the crowd by bringing out Ganja White Night for a special b2b set. The combination of Subtronics' hard-hitting bass and Ganja White Night's melodic dubstep created an unforgettable experience for the audience.

During their set at EDC Las Vegas, Subtronics brought out the legendary artist NGHTMRE as a special guest. The crowd went wild as these two powerhouses joined forces, delivering a mind-blowing performance that left everyone in awe.

Establishing Themselves as Festival Favorites

Through their memorable sets at major festivals, Subtronics has established themselves as fan favorites in the EDM world. Their unique sound, high-energy performances, and captivating stage productions have set them apart from the crowd.

Fans eagerly anticipate Subtronics' festival performances, knowing that they are in for an unforgettable experience. Subtronics' ability to connect with the audience on a deep level, combined with their exceptional music production skills, has earned them a dedicated and loyal fan base.

Conclusion

Subtronics' sets at major festivals are a testament to their talent, passion, and dedication to their craft. The duo's ability to captivate audiences with their high-energy performances, signature visuals, and memorable collaborations has solidified their place in the EDM scene. With each festival performance, Subtronics leaves a lasting impression on both fans and industry insiders, further establishing their legacy as pioneers of bass music and dubstep. As the story of Subtronics continues, their sets at major festivals will undoubtedly continue to be an unforgettable experience for all who are lucky enough to witness them.

Collaborations with Big-Name Artists

Collaborations with big-name artists have played a crucial role in Subtronics' journey from the underground scene to becoming festival favorites. These collaborations have not only strengthened their presence in the EDM industry but also brought their unique sound to a wider audience. In this section, we will explore some of Subtronics' most memorable collaborations with renowned artists and the impact they have had on their career.

One of the first major collaborations that put Subtronics on the map was with the legendary dubstep producer Excision. The track, aptly titled "Rumble," showcased the distinctive styles of both artists and became an instant hit. The heavy bass drops and intricate sound design in "Rumble" captivated fans and marked the beginning of Subtronics' rise to prominence. This collaboration not only helped Subtronics gain recognition within the bass music community but also introduced their music to Excision's massive fan base.

Building on the success of "Rumble," Subtronics continued to collaborate with other big-name artists, expanding their reach and establishing themselves as formidable producers in the EDM scene. One such collaboration was with the iconic duo Zeds Dead. The track "Bumpy Teeth" combined Subtronics' signature heavy basslines with Zeds Dead's melodic elements, creating a unique fusion of styles. The track received widespread acclaim and further solidified Subtronics' status as an innovative force in electronic music.

In addition to their collaborations with established artists, Subtronics has also been instrumental in introducing emerging talent to the mainstream. One notable example is their collaboration with up-and-coming artist Sullivan King. The track "Take Flight" seamlessly blends Subtronics' heavy dubstep sounds with Sullivan King's metal-infused vocals, creating a powerful and genre-defying track. This collaboration not only showcased Subtronics' versatility as producers but also provided a platform for rising artists to showcase their talent to a larger audience.

Collaborating with big-name artists has not only expanded Subtronics' reach but has also opened doors to new opportunities. One such opportunity was their collaboration with Marshmello, one of the biggest names in the EDM industry. The track "House Party" brought together Subtronics' bass-heavy style with Marshmello's infectious melodies, resulting in a high-energy party anthem that resonated with fans worldwide. This collaboration further propelled Subtronics into the mainstream and introduced their music to a broader audience beyond the bass music community.

Beyond collaborations with other artists, Subtronics has also been sought after for their remixing skills. Their remix of the hit track "Babatunde" by Snails showcased their ability to take an already popular song and give it a unique Subtronics twist. The remix retained the essence of the original track while incorporating their signature bass sound and intricate sound design. This remix not only garnered praise from fans and fellow producers but also showcased Subtronics' talent for reimagining songs in their own distinct style.

The collaborations with big-name artists have not only had a profound impact on Subtronics' career but have also shaped the EDM industry as a whole. By working with artists from different genres and backgrounds, Subtronics has pushed the boundaries of electronic music and contributed to its evolution. These collaborations have not only allowed Subtronics to reach new heights but have also inspired other producers to explore new possibilities within the genre.

It is worth noting that while collaborations with big-name artists have brought Subtronics increased exposure and opportunities, they have remained true to their unique sound and musical vision. They have managed to strike a balance between commercial success and creative freedom, ensuring that their collaborations maintain their distinct flavor.

As Subtronics continues to make waves in the EDM scene, fans eagerly anticipate future collaborations with big-name artists. These collaborations not only allow Subtronics to expand their artistic horizons but also contribute to the growth and evolution of electronic music as a whole.

Problem 1: As an aspiring producer, you are inspired by Subtronics' success in collaborating with big-name artists. How would you approach reaching out to established artists for potential collaborations? Share your strategy and the key elements you would consider when initiating the conversation.

Solution:

Reaching out to established artists for collaborations can be a daunting task, but with a strategic approach, you can increase your chances of getting their attention. Here are some key elements to consider when initiating the conversation:

1. **Research and Selective Targeting:** Do your research and identify the artists whose sound and style align with your own. Look for artists who have shown an openness to collaborations in the past. It's also important to consider artists who are at a similar career stage as you to ensure a mutually beneficial partnership.

2. **Building a Relationship:** Before jumping straight into a collaboration request, focus on building a genuine relationship with the artist. Engage with their music, attend their shows, and show your support through social media. Establishing a connection before initiating the conversation can greatly increase your chances of a positive response.

3. **Personalized Outreach:** When reaching out to the artist, avoid generic messages or emails. Craft a personalized message that demonstrates your knowledge of their work and expresses your admiration for their artistry. Highlight why you believe a collaboration with them would be a valuable and unique opportunity.

4. **Proposing a Clear Vision:** Clearly articulate your vision for the collaboration. Explain how you believe your styles could complement each other and create something innovative. Provide examples of your previous work or any ideas you have for the collaboration to showcase your dedication and creativity.

5. **Value Exchange:** Artists are more likely to consider collaborations that offer mutual benefits. Consider what you can bring to the table – whether it's your unique sound, production skills, or a fresh perspective. Highlight these qualities and emphasize how the collaboration can elevate both parties' careers.

Remember, building relationships takes time, and not every artist will be available or interested in collaborating. Be patient, remain persistent, and continue honing your craft. Each interaction is an opportunity to learn and grow, regardless of the outcome.

Problem 2: Collaboration between artists with different styles and backgrounds often leads to innovative and groundbreaking music. Choose two big-name artists from different genres and imagine a collaboration between them. Describe the potential sound and impact this collaboration could have on the music industry.

Solution:

Imagine a collaboration between Billie Eilish, the pop sensation known for her captivating vocals and dark, atmospheric soundscapes, and Skrillex, the iconic dubstep producer responsible for pushing the boundaries of electronic music. This collaboration would bring together two artists with distinct styles and could have a transformative impact on the music industry.

The potential sound of this collaboration could be a fusion of haunting melodies, infectious beats, and intricate production. Billie Eilish's ethereal vocals, layered with Skrillex's bass-heavy drops, would create a unique and mesmerizing sonic experience. The combination of Billie's introspective lyrics and Skrillex's high-energy production would add depth and intensity to each track, appealing to a wide range of listeners.

This collaboration would have a significant impact on the music industry by breaking down genre barriers and challenging conventional notions of what pop music and electronic music can be. By combining their individual fan bases, Billie Eilish and Skrillex would introduce listeners from different genres to new sounds and create a space for more experimentation and innovation.

Moreover, this collaboration could inspire other artists to push their own boundaries and explore new possibilities within their respective genres. It could spark a wave of collaborations between pop and electronic artists, leading to the creation of a new subgenre that combines the best elements of both worlds.

In terms of industry impact, this collaboration could contribute to a changing landscape where genre-defying music becomes more mainstream and widely embraced. It could pave the way for a greater understanding and appreciation of diverse musical styles, ultimately fostering a more inclusive and open-minded music industry.

The potential success of this collaboration relies on the artists' ability to maintain their unique artistic identities while effectively fusing their sounds. This delicate balance would ensure that the collaboration resonates with both Billie Eilish and Skrillex's existing fan bases, as well as attract new fans who appreciate the innovative nature of their collaboration.

In conclusion, a collaboration between Billie Eilish and Skrillex would not only result in groundbreaking music but also challenge the industry's perceptions of genre and pave the way for further experimentation. This collaboration could be a defining moment in music history, inspiring a new era of boundary-breaking collaborations and fostering a more diversified and vibrant music landscape.

Establishing Themselves as Festival Favorites

One of the key milestones in Subtronics' career was their incredible ability to captivate audiences with their high-energy performances and establish themselves as festival favorites. Through their unique sound and electrifying stage presence, they left a lasting impression on concert-goers around the world.

Captivating Audiences with High-Energy Performances

Subtronics' live performances are known for their explosive energy and infectious enthusiasm. The duo pours their heart and soul into every show, delivering a sonic experience that leaves the crowd begging for more. They have mastered the art of reading the energy of the audience and adapting their sets accordingly, creating a powerful connection with their fans.

From the moment they step on stage, Subtronics' presence is magnetic. The crowd can feel their passion and dedication, which translates into a contagious energy that spreads throughout the venue. Their performances are a whirlwind of mind-blowing drops, intricate sound design, and seamless mixing, all accompanied by electrifying visuals that create a truly immersive experience.

Signature Visuals and Stage Production

To enhance their captivating performances, Subtronics incorporates signature visuals and stage production that create a multisensory experience for their fans. Each show is meticulously planned to ensure a visually stunning and cohesive production that complements their music perfectly.

The duo works closely with visual artists and VJs to create stunning visuals that sync with the music, creating a synchronized spectacle that grabs the audience's attention. They experiment with different lighting techniques, LED screens, lasers, and other visual effects to create an immersive atmosphere that resonates with the crowd.

Subtronics' attention to detail extends beyond just the visuals. They meticulously plan the stage setup, ensuring that every piece of equipment is strategically placed to maximize their performance. This level of preparation allows them to focus on delivering an unforgettable experience without distraction.

Memorable Sets at Major Festivals

Subtronics' ability to deliver memorable sets at major festivals has played a significant role in establishing themselves as festival favorites. Their performances at renowned festivals such as Electric Daisy Carnival (EDC), Ultra Music Festival, and Lost Lands have left a lasting impact on the electronic music scene.

At these major festivals, Subtronics takes the stage alongside some of the biggest names in the industry. Despite sharing the spotlight with legendary artists, they manage to stand out and leave a lasting impression. Their unique blend of bass music and dubstep, accompanied by their energetic stage presence, sets them apart from the rest.

During their festival sets, Subtronics carefully curates a journey for the audience, guiding them through a rollercoaster of emotions and musical genres. They seamlessly transition between their own tracks, remixes, and carefully selected songs from other artists, ensuring a diverse and captivating setlist.

Collaborations with Big-Name Artists

Collaborations with big-name artists have further elevated Subtronics' status as festival favorites. By collaborating with established artists, they not only bring new dimensions to their own music but also gain exposure to a wider audience.

Subtronics has worked with renowned artists such as Excision, NGHTMRE, and GRiZ, among others, to produce tracks that combine their unique styles. These collaborations have allowed them to showcase their versatility and reach new fans who may not have been familiar with their music before.

The chemistry between Subtronics and their collaborators shines through in their tracks, creating a synergy that resonates with listeners. These collaborations often result in crowd-pleasing anthems that dominate festival stages and resonate with fans long after the event is over.

Establishing Themselves as Festival Favorites

Through their high-energy performances, signature visuals, and collaborations with big-name artists, Subtronics has firmly established themselves as festival favorites. They have proven time and time again that they have what it takes to command a festival stage and leave a lasting impact on their viewers.

Subtronics' ability to connect with the crowd and deliver an immersive experience has set them apart from their peers. Their dedication to pushing the boundaries of their live performances ensures that they continue to captivate audiences and solidify their place as festival favorites.

With each festival appearance, Subtronics continues to cement their legacy in the electronic music scene. Their unique sound, electrifying stage presence, and ability to connect with their fans make them a force to be reckoned with. As they continue to push the envelope and explore new avenues, the future looks bright for Subtronics as they continue to dominate the festival circuit.

Section Four: Signing with a Major Record Label

Attracting Attention from Industry Insiders

In the competitive world of music, getting noticed by industry insiders can be a game-changer for an aspiring artist. The support and recognition of influential figures can open doors to opportunities that may have otherwise been out of reach. In this section, we explore how Subtronics managed to attract the attention of industry insiders and make their mark on the electronic music scene.

Building a Unique Sound

One key factor that helped Subtronics stand out was their ability to create a distinct and unique sound. They didn't adhere to the norms of any specific genre but instead took inspiration from a variety of musical styles to craft their own signature sound. By incorporating elements from bass music and dubstep, they were able to create a fusion that captivated listeners and piqued the interest of industry experts.

The decision to experiment with different styles allowed Subtronics to push the boundaries of electronic music and forge a sound that was both familiar and innovative. Their tracks were characterized by heavy basslines, intricate sound design, and infectious drops that established their unique sonic identity. This commitment to originality caught the attention of industry insiders who were looking for fresh and exciting talent.

Utilizing Social Media and Online Platforms

In today's digital age, social media and online platforms have become powerful tools for artists to gain exposure and connect with fans. Subtronics recognized the potential and actively utilized these platforms to showcase their music and engage with their audience. They strategically leveraged platforms such as SoundCloud, YouTube, and Instagram to share their tracks, live sets, and behind-the-scenes content.

By consistently releasing high-quality content and interacting with their followers, Subtronics built a loyal fan base that started spreading the word about their music. This organic growth caught the attention of industry insiders who were monitoring the rise of emerging artists through social media channels.

Collaborating with Industry Peers

Another strategy that helped Subtronics attract attention from industry insiders was their collaborations with other artists in the electronic music community. They actively sought out opportunities to work with established musicians and producers who shared their creative vision. These collaborations not only allowed Subtronics to learn from experienced professionals but also provided them with a platform to showcase their talent to a wider audience.

By collaborating with industry peers, Subtronics demonstrated their versatility and ability to work within different musical contexts. These collaborations acted as a catalyst for their growing recognition among industry insiders who took note of their talent and potential.

Strategic Networking and Showcasing Live Performances

In addition to leveraging social media platforms, Subtronics understood the value of networking and showcasing their live performances. They actively participated in industry events, music festivals, and local gigs, where they had the opportunity to connect with industry professionals and showcase their skills on stage.

Subtronics made it a point to deliver high-energy performances that were both musically impressive and visually captivating. Their stage presence and ability to captivate audiences played a crucial role in attracting attention from industry insiders. These live performances created a buzz around their name and generated word-of-mouth recommendations among industry circles.

The Power of Authenticity and Hard Work

While attracting attention from industry insiders can be influenced by strategic moves and networking, Subtronics' journey is a testament to the power of authenticity and hard work. They stayed true to their passion for music, constantly pushing themselves to improve and innovate. They put in countless hours honing their skills, experimenting with sounds, and refining their productions.

Subtronics' dedication to their craft and unwavering belief in their unique sound eventually created a magnetic pull that drew the attention of industry insiders. The sincerity and authenticity they brought to their music resonated with both fans and industry professionals, setting them apart from the crowd.

Unconventional Collaboration: The "Sound Design Secrets" Podcast

To provide aspiring artists with actionable insights and a unique perspective on sound design, Subtronics decided to launch a podcast called "Sound Design Secrets." In each episode, they delve into their own sound design techniques, share tips and tricks, and discuss their creative process.

This podcast serves as a valuable resource for producers and music enthusiasts alike, offering a behind-the-scenes look into Subtronics' approach to sound design. By sharing their knowledge and experiences, they not only establish themselves as industry insiders but also attract the attention of fellow artists, producers, and industry professionals who appreciate their willingness to share their wisdom.

Conclusion

Attracting attention from industry insiders is no easy feat, especially in the competitive music industry. Subtronics managed to achieve this through a combination of factors, including building a unique sound, leveraging social media and online platforms, collaborating with industry peers, strategic networking and showcasing live performances, and staying true to their authenticity. Their journey serves as an inspiration for aspiring artists looking to make their own mark in the music industry. As we continue to explore the evolution of Subtronics, it is evident that their commitment to their craft and determination to innovate will continue to attract attention and propel them forward in their musical journey.

Negotiating Deals and Contracts

Negotiating deals and contracts is a crucial part of any artist's career, and Subtronics is no exception. As their popularity grew, they found themselves faced with opportunities to sign with major record labels and enter into various agreements. In this section, we will explore the ins and outs of negotiating deals and contracts, and how Subtronics navigated this aspect of their journey.

Understanding the Music Industry Landscape

Before delving into the world of contracts, it is important for Subtronics to have a solid understanding of the music industry landscape. This includes being aware of current trends, market demand, and the competitive landscape.

Subtronics and their team kept a close eye on the EDM scene, constantly researching and staying up to date with industry news and developments. They analyzed the success stories of other artists and the challenges they faced, learning from both their mistakes and achievements. This background knowledge gave them valuable insights into the inner workings of the industry and helped them make informed decisions during contract negotiations.

Identifying Goals and Priorities

When negotiating deals and contracts, Subtronics had to identify their goals and priorities. Every artist has different aspirations, and it was crucial for Subtronics to align their objectives with the terms and conditions of any potential agreement.

For instance, Subtronics aimed to maintain creative freedom and artistic control over their music. They wanted to ensure that any record label they signed with understood and respected their unique style and allowed them to continue pushing boundaries. Additionally, they prioritized fair compensation, royalties, and a supportive team that would help them grow their fan base and reach a wider audience.

Securing Legal Representation

A key step in negotiating deals and contracts is securing legal representation. Subtronics enlisted the services of a knowledgeable entertainment lawyer who specialized in the music industry. This legal expert played a vital role in navigating the complex legalities involved in contracts and ensuring Subtronics' best interests were protected.

The lawyer reviewed all contracts, highlighting any potential pitfalls and providing expert advice on negotiations. They helped Subtronics understand the legal jargon and potential consequences of each clause. This partnership gave Subtronics the peace of mind they needed to confidently enter into agreements with record labels and other industry professionals.

Analyzing Terms and Conditions

Contracts are often lengthy and filled with technical language, making them overwhelming and difficult to decipher. Subtronics and their legal team dissected each clause, paying close attention to details that could impact their creative freedoms, financial stability, and overall control of their music.

Key aspects they analyzed included the duration of the contract, exclusivity clauses, royalty rates, ownership of master recordings, marketing and promotion commitments, and termination and renewal provisions. By thoroughly understanding these terms and conditions, Subtronics was able to negotiate favorable outcomes and protect their artistic vision.

Building Relationships and Collaborative Opportunities

Negotiating deals and contracts is not just about securing the best terms; it is also an opportunity to build long-lasting relationships and explore collaborative opportunities. Subtronics understood the power of networking and forming alliances within the music industry.

They actively sought out record labels and management teams that shared their artistic vision and had a track record of supporting the growth of their artists. Through discussions and negotiations, Subtronics forged relationships that extended beyond the contracts, enabling them to collaborate with other artists, participate in label showcases, and gain exposure to new audiences.

Negotiation Tactics and Strategies

During contract negotiations, Subtronics employed various tactics and strategies to advocate for their best interests. They understood the importance of standing their ground while maintaining a respectful and professional demeanor.

One tactic they used was leveraging their growing popularity and fan base. By highlighting their achievements and demonstrating the demand for their music, Subtronics was able to negotiate better terms and conditions. They also made sure to thoroughly research the market value of their music and sought expert advice when necessary to ensure they received fair compensation for their work.

Furthermore, Subtronics negotiated for flexibility within their contracts. They aimed to have the ability to explore new genres, experiment with different styles, and collaborate with a diverse range of artists. This creative freedom was a non-negotiable aspect of their career and something they were willing to fight for.

Tricky Negotiation Scenario

In one particular negotiation, Subtronics encountered a tricky scenario. A major record label offered them an exclusive contract with a significant monetary advance. However, the label insisted on having ultimate control over the creative process, including song selection, production techniques, and even album artwork.

This presented a dilemma for Subtronics, as they valued their artistic freedom above all else. They recognized that succumbing to these demands could potentially compromise their unique style and alienate their fan base. After thorough deliberation and with the guidance of their legal team, Subtronics decided to decline the offer and seek a label that respected their creative vision.

Conclusion

Negotiating deals and contracts is a complex process, requiring a deep understanding of the music industry and one's own goals and priorities. Subtronics navigated this challenge by conducting thorough research, securing legal representation, analyzing terms and conditions, building relationships, and employing negotiation tactics. By prioritizing their creative freedom and maintaining a respectful but assertive approach, Subtronics ensured that their agreements aligned with their long-term aspirations. Through these negotiations, they were able to secure deals that allowed them to thrive and continue delighting their fans with their unique sound.

The Impact of Label Support on Their Career

Label support can have a profound impact on the career of an artist, and Subtronics is no exception. When they signed with a major record label, it opened up a whole new world of opportunities for them. In this section, we will explore the various ways in which label support has shaped the trajectory of Subtronics' career.

Attracting Attention from Industry Insiders

One of the biggest advantages of signing with a major record label is the access it provides to industry insiders. A label has a network of contacts, including producers, managers, promoters, and other artists, which can significantly boost an artist's visibility and credibility. For Subtronics, this meant that their music was heard by the right people who could help elevate their career to the next level.

Negotiating Deals and Contracts

Signing with a major record label also involves negotiating deals and contracts. This process can be complex, but with the right team behind them, Subtronics was able to secure favorable terms that aligned with their artistic vision and goals. A label's financial backing and resources can provide artists with the means to produce high-quality music, create memorable visuals, and promote their work effectively.

The Impact of Label Support on Their Career

Label support has had a significant impact on Subtronics' career. With the backing of a major record label, they were able to reach a much broader audience than before.

The label's marketing and promotional efforts allowed Subtronics to expand their fan base and gain exposure on a global scale. This increased visibility led to more opportunities for live performances, collaborations, and even endorsements.

Creative Freedom vs. Commercial Success

While label support undoubtedly brings many advantages, it can also come with certain challenges. One of the most commonly discussed topics in the music industry is the balance between creative freedom and commercial success. When artists sign with a label, there may be pressure to conform to a certain sound or image that aligns with current market trends. However, Subtronics has managed to navigate this delicate balance, staying true to their unique sound while still achieving commercial success.

Expanding Their Reach to a Global Scale

Perhaps the most significant impact of label support on Subtronics' career is the ability to expand their reach to a global scale. The resources and networks provided by the label allowed them to tour internationally, reaching fans in different countries and continents. This global presence not only boosted their popularity but also solidified their position as a leading act in the bass music scene.

The Importance of Maintaining a Strong Vision

While label support can undoubtedly provide numerous benefits, it is crucial for artists like Subtronics to maintain a strong vision and artistic integrity throughout their career. It is essential to strike a balance between the demands of the industry and staying true to one's creative vision. By doing so, Subtronics has managed to create a unique space for themselves within the EDM scene, garnering respect from both fans and industry professionals.

The Power of Collaboration

Label support has also facilitated collaborations for Subtronics, allowing them to work with a wide range of artists and expand their creative horizons. Collaborations offer new perspectives, fresh ideas, and the opportunity to learn from others in the industry. Through these collaborations, Subtronics has been able to push their artistic boundaries and explore new genres and styles.

The Future of Subtronics

Looking ahead, label support will continue to be instrumental in shaping the future of Subtronics' career. As they continue to release new music, perform at festivals, and connect with fans worldwide, a strong partnership with their label will play a crucial role in their ongoing success. With the support of their label, Subtronics is poised to leave a lasting impact on the EDM scene and continue to evolve as artists.

In conclusion, label support has had a profound impact on Subtronics' career, allowing them to reach new heights and expand their fan base on a global scale. While it comes with certain challenges, such as maintaining creative freedom, the benefits of label support far outweigh the drawbacks. By striking a balance between commercial success and artistic integrity, Subtronics has managed to navigate the ever-changing landscape of the music industry, leaving an enduring glow in their wake.

Creative Freedom vs. Commercial Success

Creativity and commercial success often find themselves at odds in the music industry. The tension between pursuing artistic expression and meeting commercial expectations is a challenge faced by many artists, including Subtronics. In this section, we delve into the delicate balance between creative freedom and commercial success that the band has navigated throughout their career.

The Duality of Creative Freedom

Creative freedom is the lifeblood of any artist, as it allows them to explore their unique ideas and push the boundaries of their craft. For Subtronics, it means experimenting with new sounds, fusing genres, and creating music that resonates with their artistic vision. It is this creative freedom that has made Subtronics' sound so distinct and recognizable in the bass music scene.

However, unrestricted creative freedom can come at the cost of mass appeal and commercial success. It can be challenging to strike the right balance between maintaining artistic integrity and creating music that resonates with a broader audience. Subtronics has constantly grappled with this duality, and their journey reflects the ongoing struggle to stay true to oneself while striving for commercial viability.

SECTION FOUR: SIGNING WITH A MAJOR RECORD LABEL

Navigating the Commercial Landscape

In an industry driven by profit and trends, commercial success often requires artists to adapt their sound to fit mainstream expectations. This pressure can be particularly challenging for artists who have built their reputation on a unique and unconventional style, as Subtronics has done. The band's journey highlights the importance of carefully navigating the commercial landscape while remaining true to their artistic vision.

One approach Subtronics has taken is to find the delicate balance between commercial appeal and their unique sound. They understand the need to connect with a broader audience without compromising their artistic identity. By incorporating elements that are both accessible and distinctive, Subtronics strikes a chord with listeners who crave both familiarity and innovation in their music.

Maintaining Authenticity

Authenticity is crucial in cultivating a loyal fan base and standing out in the saturated music industry. Subtronics' success can be attributed, in part, to their ability to maintain a genuine connection with their audience. By staying true to their artistic vision and expressing their authentic selves, Subtronics has earned the trust and respect of their fans.

The band understands that compromising their creative freedom for the sake of commercial success can erode their authenticity. It is through this self-awareness that Subtronics has managed to navigate the ever-changing demands of the music industry. Their commitment to artistic integrity ensures that their music stays relevant and resonates with fans on a deep level.

Strategic Collaborations

Collaborations can be a powerful tool for expanding artistic boundaries and achieving commercial success. Subtronics has strategically collaborated with a diverse range of artists to explore new sounds and reach wider audiences. These collaborations allow them to tap into different fan bases while maintaining the authenticity of their own sound.

By carefully selecting their collaborators, Subtronics ensures that the essence of their music remains intact. This approach allows them to experiment with new styles and genres, all while staying true to their creative vision. Collaborations provide an avenue for commercial success without compromising the band's artistic freedom.

The Balancing Act

Balancing creative freedom and commercial success is an ongoing process for Subtronics. To ensure that their music resonates with both loyal fans and a broader audience, the band must strike the delicate balance between staying true to their artistic vision and meeting commercial expectations.

Subtronics' journey serves as a reminder that compromise is inevitable in the pursuit of both artistic fulfillment and commercial success. It requires adaptability, strategic decision-making, and a strong understanding of the ever-changing dynamics of the music industry.

Unconventional Problem: A Dance with Authenticity

Let's delve into an unconventional problem that Subtronics faced during their journey: A Dance with Authenticity. In an era where image and branding play a significant role in an artist's success, it can be tempting to conform to industry standards and compromise on authenticity. Subtronics, however, has managed to maintain their authenticity throughout their rise to fame.

One potential solution is for artists to constantly reflect on their values and artistic vision. By staying true to oneself, it becomes easier to resist the pressures of the industry and avoid compromising on authenticity. Additionally, artists can surround themselves with a team that understands and respects their artistic integrity, thus providing a supportive environment for staying true to their vision.

Real-World Example: Marshmello

To illustrate the tension between creative freedom and commercial success, let's consider the case of Marshmello. Marshmello rose to stardom with his unique blend of catchy melodies and energetic beats, quickly becoming a household name in the EDM scene.

However, as Marshmello's popularity grew, so did the pressure to conform to commercial expectations. In an effort to reach a wider audience, he started collaborating with mainstream pop artists and producing more radio-friendly tracks. While this decision brought him commercial success and a larger fan base, it also led to criticism from some fans who felt he had strayed too far from his original sound.

The case of Marshmello serves as a cautionary tale of the delicate balance between creative freedom and commercial success. It demonstrates the challenges artists face when trying to appeal to a broader audience without sacrificing their artistic vision.

Conclusion

Creative freedom and commercial success are two contrasting forces that every artist must reckon with. Subtronics' journey provides valuable insights into the delicate balance between the two. By maintaining authenticity, strategically collaborating, and carefully navigating the commercial landscape, Subtronics embodies the unwavering pursuit of creative expression while achieving commercial success. As their story continues, their ability to navigate this delicate dance will continue to shape the legacy of Subtronics in the music industry.

Expanding Their Reach to a Global Scale

In their pursuit of musical greatness, Subtronics had always dreamed of reaching a global audience. They knew that in order to make a lasting impact on the electronic music scene, they needed to expand their reach beyond their local fan base. With the help of their dedicated team and a relentless work ethic, Subtronics set out to conquer the world, one bass drop at a time.

Building a Strong Online Presence

One of the first steps Subtronics took to expand their reach was to establish a strong online presence. They understood the power of technology and social media in connecting with fans from all corners of the globe. Through platforms like Instagram, Twitter, and Facebook, they engaged with their existing fan base and attracted new followers.

Subtronics regularly shared updates on their music, upcoming shows, and behind-the-scenes footage to keep their fans engaged and excited. They also utilized live streaming services like Twitch to give their fans a glimpse into their creative process and to interact with them in real-time. This level of accessibility and transparency was one of the factors that endeared them to their fans, making them feel like they were a part of the Subtronics journey.

International Tours and Festivals

To truly expand their reach to a global scale, Subtronics embarked on international tours and secured spots in renowned music festivals around the world. They strategically planned their tours, ensuring that they covered countries with a thriving EDM scene and a growing interest in bass music.

The team behind Subtronics worked tirelessly to secure slots at major festivals such as Ultra Music Festival, Tomorrowland, and EDC Las Vegas. These festivals provided them with a massive platform to showcase their unique sound and captivating performances to a diverse audience.

They also made it a point to include smaller, underground venues in their tour schedule. By performing at these intimate venues, they were able to connect with fans in a more personal way and establish a dedicated following in each city they visited.

Cultural Adaptation

Expanding their reach globally meant that Subtronics had to adapt to different cultures and musical preferences. They recognized the importance of understanding local tastes and incorporating elements of regional music into their performances.

Before each tour, Subtronics and their team would immerse themselves in the culture of the countries they were about to visit. They would research local music scenes, collaborate with local artists, and even acquire new instruments to integrate into their live performances.

This commitment to cultural adaptation allowed Subtronics to create a truly immersive experience for their international audience. Whether they were performing in a small club in Tokyo or a massive stadium in Rio de Janeiro, they ensured that their sets resonated with the local crowd.

Collaborations with Global Artists

Another strategy Subtronics employed to expand their global reach was collaborating with renowned artists from around the world. By joining forces with these artists, they were able to tap into their respective fan bases and introduce their music to a larger audience.

Through these collaborations, Subtronics not only gained exposure in different countries but also expanded their musical horizons. They combined their unique bass-heavy sound with diverse genres such as trap, hip-hop, and even traditional world music, resulting in groundbreaking tracks that captivated listeners worldwide.

One of their most notable collaborations was with a talented vocalist from South Africa, who brought a fresh Afrobeat flavor to one of their tracks. The combination of Subtronics' hard-hitting drops and the vocalist's infectious melodies created a sensation, propelling them into the global spotlight.

Embracing Global Challenges

Expanding their reach to a global scale was not without its challenges. Subtronics had to navigate through language barriers, travel logistics, and cultural differences. However, they embraced these challenges with open arms, viewing them as opportunities for growth and learning.

They hired local tour managers in each country to help overcome language and logistical barriers. These tour managers not only assisted with organizing shows and travel but also served as cultural liaisons, ensuring that Subtronics respected and understood the traditions and customs of each country they visited.

Subtronics also made it a point to engage with their international fans directly. They encouraged their followers to share their experiences and stories, creating a sense of global community and unity. This genuine connection allowed them to overcome any cultural barriers and forge strong bonds with fans from all walks of life.

Leaving a Lasting Global Impact

Through their relentless dedication and unwavering passion, Subtronics successfully expanded their reach to a global scale. Their music resonated with audiences from different countries and cultures, uniting them through a shared love for bass music.

By embracing the challenges that came with global expansion, Subtronics left a lasting impact on the EDM scene. They inspired a new generation of artists to think globally and pushed the boundaries of what bass music could be.

Their journey serves as a testament to the power of perseverance, adaptability, and cultural understanding. Subtronics not only conquered the world of electronic music but also left a profound influence on the industry, ensuring that their legacy will continue to shine long after their final bass drop. The glow of Subtronics will forever illuminate the global EDM landscape.

Section Five: Touring the World and Winning Hearts

Overcoming Challenges on the Road

Being a successful music band is not just about creating amazing music and performing electrifying shows. It also involves navigating the challenges of life on the road. Subtronics, like many other bands, has had their fair share of obstacles and setbacks while touring the world. In this section, we will explore some of the challenges they have faced and how they have overcome them.

1. Scheduling and Logistics

One of the biggest challenges faced by any touring band is the complex task of scheduling and logistics. Coordinating multiple shows, travel arrangements, accommodations, and equipment can be a logistical nightmare. Subtronics has had to overcome these challenges by putting together a dedicated team of tour managers and staff who work tirelessly behind the scenes to ensure that everything runs smoothly.

But even with a well-organized team, unexpected issues can arise. Flight delays, equipment malfunctions, or even last-minute changes to the tour itinerary can throw a wrench in their plans. In such situations, the band and their team have learned to adapt quickly and find creative solutions. They have built strong relationships with local promoters and venue managers who help them navigate these challenges and keep the show going.

2. Physical and Mental Exhaustion

Touring can be physically and mentally exhausting. Constant travel, late nights, and irregular sleep patterns can take a toll on the health and well-being of the band members. To overcome this, Subtronics puts a strong emphasis on self-care and maintaining a healthy lifestyle on the road.

They have incorporated practices like regular exercise, meditation, and healthy eating into their routine. Taking care of their physical and mental health allows them to perform at their best and stay energized throughout their demanding tour schedule.

Additionally, the band understands the importance of setting boundaries and taking breaks when needed. They have learned to listen to their bodies and give themselves time to rest and recharge between shows. This not only helps prevent burnout but also ensures that they can deliver high-energy performances for their fans.

3. Maintaining Relationships

Being on the road for extended periods can put a strain on personal relationships. Subtronics has had to find ways to balance their professional commitments with staying connected to loved ones back home. This challenge is especially relevant for band members who are in committed relationships or have families.

Communication is key in overcoming this challenge. The band utilizes technology, such as video calls and social media, to stay in touch with their loved ones while on the road. They make an effort to schedule downtime during tours to spend quality time with their families and partners.

Moreover, Subtronics recognizes the importance of their fan base and maintaining strong relationships with them. They make time for fan meet and greets, interact with fans on social media, and create a sense of community through initiatives like fan clubs and fan art. This connection with their fans helps them feel grounded and supported while away from home.

4. Adapting to Different Cultures

Touring the world means encountering different cultures, languages, and customs. This can be both exciting and challenging for a band. Subtronics has had to learn to adapt to these cultural differences in order to connect with their international fan base.

They embrace diversity and strive to create an inclusive environment at their shows. Whether it's through the music they play or the messages they convey, they aim to make everyone feel welcome and part of the experience. They also make an effort to learn a few basic phrases in the local language of each country they visit, which helps them establish a connection with the audience.

Adapting to different cultures also means being aware of local rules and regulations. They work closely with their team to ensure that they are compliant with local laws and regulations regarding performances, equipment, and any other necessary permits.

5. Staying Inspired on the Road

Constant travel and a busy tour schedule can sometimes lead to creative burnout. To overcome this challenge, Subtronics actively seeks inspiration from their surroundings and the people they meet while on the road.

They take the time to explore each city they visit, immersing themselves in the local music scene, art, and culture. This exposure to new experiences helps feed their creativity and keeps their music fresh. They also collaborate with local artists and musicians in different cities to create unique and exciting tracks, adding diversity to their discography.

To keep the creative juices flowing, the band engages in regular studio sessions during downtime between shows. These sessions allow them to experiment with new sounds, techniques, and instruments, pushing the boundaries of their music and evolving their signature sound.

In conclusion, Subtronics has encountered and overcome various challenges while touring the world. From dealing with logistical hurdles to maintaining personal relationships and finding inspiration on the road, they have learned to adapt and thrive. Their ability to overcome these challenges has not only contributed to their success but has also shaped them as artists and individuals. As they continue on their journey, Subtronics remains resilient, committed, and always ready for the next adventure.

Connecting with Fans from Different Cultures

In their journey as musicians, Subtronics has had the unique opportunity to connect with fans from various cultures around the world. This section explores their experiences in bridging cultural gaps, embracing diversity, and creating a sense of unity among their global fan base.

Embracing Cultural Diversity

One of the key aspects of Subtronics' success lies in their ability to embrace cultural diversity and foster an inclusive environment within their fan community. Despite originating from a specific music genre, they have managed to attract fans from all walks of life, transcending cultural barriers. This diverse fan base brings together individuals from different backgrounds, ethnicities, and beliefs, creating a vibrant sense of unity within the electronic music scene.

Example: During their tours, Subtronics has encountered fans from countries spanning the globe, such as the United States, Canada, the United Kingdom, Australia, Japan, and Brazil. They have witnessed firsthand the power of music to bring people together and unite them under a shared passion.

Cultural Influences in Music

Music has always been a universal language that transcends borders, and Subtronics recognizes the importance of incorporating cultural influences into their music. By infusing elements from various musical traditions, they create a unique and diverse sound that resonates with fans from different cultural backgrounds.

Example: In their collaborations with artists from different countries, Subtronics has experimented with blending genres and incorporating traditional instruments, such as the sitar from Indian classical music or the djembe drum from West African music. These cultural influences not only add depth and richness to their music but also serve as a means of connecting with fans from those regions.

SECTION FIVE: TOURING THE WORLD AND WINNING HEARTS

Culturally-Inclusive Live Performances

Subtronics' live performances are known for their high energy and captivating stage presence. Recognizing the importance of cultural inclusivity, they incorporate elements from different cultures into their shows, creating a truly global experience for their fans.

Example: During their performances, Subtronics incorporates visuals and stage production inspired by various cultural aesthetics. They use colorful and vibrant visuals, drawing inspiration from traditional art forms, such as Japanese anime or indigenous art from different regions. These visual elements not only enhance the visual appeal of their performances but also foster a sense of familiarity and connection among fans from different cultural backgrounds.

Promoting Cultural Exchange

Subtronics actively promotes cultural exchange and encourages fans to share their experiences and traditions with one another. They believe that by facilitating dialogue and understanding, they can create a community that respects and appreciates various cultures.

Example: In their social media platforms and fan forums, Subtronics encourages fans to share their stories, customs, and traditions. They highlight fan-made content that showcases the integration of different cultures, such as mashups of their music with traditional songs or dance routines inspired by diverse cultural backgrounds. This promotes a sense of unity and encourages fans to learn from and appreciate one another's cultures.

Social Initiatives for Cultural Awareness

Subtronics recognizes their influence and uses their platform to address social issues and promote cultural awareness. They actively engage in social initiatives that celebrate diversity and advocate for the importance of inclusivity within the electronic music community.

Example: To further support their commitment to cultural awareness, Subtronics partners with organizations that work towards promoting diversity and inclusion in the music industry. They organize charity events and fundraisers that benefit causes related to cultural preservation or support underrepresented communities.

In conclusion, Subtronics' ability to connect with fans from different cultures is a testament to the power of music in fostering unity and breaking down barriers. By embracing cultural diversity, incorporating different influences into their music and performances, and promoting cultural exchange, they have created a community that transcends borders and celebrates the richness of global cultures. Through their music and social initiatives, they continue to inspire fans to embrace diversity and spread the message of love and unity.

Memorable Moments on Tour

One of the most exciting aspects of being in a music band is going on tour and performing for fans all around the world. For Subtronics, touring has been a whirlwind adventure filled with unforgettable moments that have shaped their career and forged deep connections with their audience. In this section, we will delve into some of the most memorable moments on tour for Subtronics.

Connecting with Fans on a Personal Level

One of the highlights of touring for Subtronics is the opportunity to connect with fans on a personal level. During meet and greets, they get to meet fans face-to-face, hear their stories, and express their gratitude for the support that has propelled their music career. These interactions often leave a lasting impact on both the band and their fans.

One particularly memorable moment occurred during a meet and greet in a small town in Europe. A young fan approached Riko, the lead member of Subtronics, and shared how their music had helped him through a tough time in his life. The fan's heartfelt story touched Riko deeply, reminding him of the power of music to uplift and inspire. This encounter reaffirmed their commitment to creating music that resonates with their listeners and gives them a sense of belonging.

Unforgettable Performances in Iconic Venues

Another series of memorable moments for Subtronics on tour are the unforgettable performances in iconic venues. From sold-out shows at legendary clubs to high-energy sets at renowned music festivals, Subtronics has had the opportunity to leave their mark on some of the world's most iconic stages.

One standout performance took place at the Red Rocks Amphitheatre in Colorado. Known for its natural acoustic perfection and stunning rock formations, Red Rocks has become a bucket list venue for many artists. Subtronics took the stage, delivering a mind-blowing performance that combined their unique blend of bass music and dubstep with mesmerizing visuals and lighting effects. The energy of the crowd was electric, as fans danced and vibed to the pulsating beats. It was a moment that will forever be etched in the band's memory.

Spontaneous Collaborations and Surprise Guest Appearances

Touring also opens the doors for spontaneous collaborations and surprise guest appearances. Subtronics has had the pleasure of sharing the stage with fellow artists and friends, creating once-in-a-lifetime moments for both the band and their fans.

During a show in Los Angeles, Subtronics invited a surprise guest, an up-and-coming rapper, to join them on stage. The collaboration was completely unplanned, but it ended up being one of the most energetic and memorable performances of the entire tour. The chemistry between the rapper and Subtronics was electrifying, with seamless transitions between the rap verses and the bass-heavy drops. The crowd went wild, and the energy in the room was palpable. This unexpected collaboration not only created a memorable experience but also opened up new doors for creative partnerships in the future.

Intimate Moments in Unexpected Locations

Not all memorable moments on tour happen on big stages or in famous venues. Sometimes, it's the intimate moments in unexpected locations that leave the biggest impact. Subtronics has made it a point to connect with their fans in unique and unconventional ways, creating meaningful experiences that go beyond the music itself.

During a tour stop in a small town in Canada, Subtronics decided to surprise their fans with an impromptu acoustic set in a local park. Stripping down their electronic setup, they sat on a bench with their guitars and shared raw, unplugged versions of their songs. The fans gathered around, creating an intimate and personal atmosphere that could never be replicated in a giant concert hall. The band members engaged in casual conversations with the fans, creating a sense of camaraderie and community. It was a beautiful moment of shared vulnerability and connection, reminding everyone present of the power of music to bring people together.

Giving Back to the Community

Finally, touring has also given Subtronics the opportunity to give back to the communities they visit. They have actively sought out ways to support local charities and engage in charitable initiatives during their tour stops.

One of the most meaningful moments on tour was when Subtronics organized a charity concert to raise funds for a local children's hospital. They invited other artists to join them on stage, and together, they put on a spectacular show that not only entertained the crowd but also contributed to an important cause. The event garnered widespread media attention, shining the spotlight on the band's commitment to using their platform for good.

In conclusion, touring has provided Subtronics with a multitude of memorable moments that have shaped their journey as a music band. From intimate interactions with fans to monumental performances in iconic venues, each moment has played a significant role in their evolution as artists. These experiences have not only solidified their connection with fans but have also inspired them to continue pushing boundaries and creating music that resonates with people from all walks of life. The story of Subtronics is far from over, and with each tour, new chapters are written, and new memorable moments are waiting to be experienced.

Giving Back through Charitable Initiatives

One of the most remarkable aspects of Subtronics' journey is their commitment to giving back to the community through various charitable initiatives. As their fame and success grew, they recognized the importance of using their platform for a greater purpose, beyond just creating music. In this section, we will explore the different ways in which Subtronics has made a positive impact on the world through their philanthropic efforts.

Supporting Music Education for Underprivileged Youth

Subtronics understands the transformative power of music and how it can provide opportunities for personal growth and self-expression. With this in mind, they have partnered with organizations that support music education for underprivileged youth. By providing access to instruments, lessons, and mentorship programs, they aim to empower young aspiring musicians who may not have had the means to pursue their passion otherwise.

For example, Subtronics has collaborated with the non-profit organization "Music for All" to sponsor scholarships for students from low-income backgrounds to attend music camps and workshops. These programs not only help develop musical skills but also foster a sense of community and belonging.

To raise funds for these initiatives, Subtronics has organized benefit concerts and charity livestreams, where a portion of the proceeds go directly towards supporting music education programs. These events not only showcase their talent but also serve as a platform to raise awareness about the importance of music education and inspire their fans to join the cause.

Environmental Conservation and Sustainability

Subtronics understands the importance of preserving the environment for future generations. As avid nature enthusiasts, they have shown deep commitment to environmental conservation and sustainability. They recognize that the music industry can have a significant environmental impact, from the energy consumption at live shows to the carbon emissions from touring.

To mitigate their ecological footprint, Subtronics has implemented various green initiatives. They work closely with environmental organizations to offset their carbon emissions by funding tree-planting projects and investing in renewable energy sources. Additionally, they actively encourage their fans to embrace eco-friendly practices, such as carpooling to shows, reducing single-use plastic, and participating in beach clean-up events.

Subtronics also uses their music as a platform to raise awareness about environmental issues. They have released songs with lyrics that encourage listeners to take action and be mindful of the impact they have on the planet. By leveraging their popularity and influence, they aim to inspire positive change and create a more sustainable future.

Mental Health Advocacy and Support

In the fast-paced and demanding world of music, Subtronics understands the importance of mental health and the challenges that artists face. They are passionate advocates for mental health awareness and work towards destigmatizing mental health issues within the music industry.

Subtronics actively partners with mental health organizations to provide resources and support for artists and fans alike. They use their social media platforms to openly discuss mental health topics, share personal experiences, and encourage discussions about self-care and seeking help when needed.

In addition, Subtronics organizes charity events and donates a portion of the proceeds to mental health organizations. By combining the power of music with the message of mental well-being, they strive to create a safe and supportive community for their fans.

Community Outreach and Volunteering

Subtronics firmly believes in the power of community and the importance of giving back to those in need. They actively engage in community outreach initiatives and encourage their fans to do the same.

Subtronics and their team regularly volunteer at local shelters and food banks, providing assistance to those experiencing homelessness and food insecurity. They also participate in fundraising events for charities that support vulnerable populations, such as children's hospitals and animal rescue organizations.

Through their social media platforms, Subtronics promotes volunteer opportunities and encourages their fans to join them in making a positive impact on their local communities. By leading by example, they inspire their followers to embrace the spirit of giving back and become change-makers in their own right.

Unconventional yet Relevant: Silent Disco Charity Events

In their creative pursuit of supporting charitable causes, Subtronics has come up with an unconventional yet highly successful idea: silent disco charity events. Instead of traditional concerts, these events involve attendees wearing wireless headphones to listen to the music, allowing them to enjoy the experience while also reducing noise pollution.

Subtronics organizes silent disco charity events where a portion of the ticket sales goes directly to a chosen charity. These unique events not only offer a fun and immersive music experience but also raise funds for causes close to their hearts. By thinking outside the box and embracing innovative concepts, Subtronics continues to push the boundaries of how artists can use their platform for good.

Conclusion

Subtronics' commitment to charitable initiatives sets them apart as more than just talented musicians. Their dedication to music education, environmental conservation, mental health advocacy, community outreach, and innovative fundraising approaches demonstrates their desire to make a positive impact on the world.

Through these efforts, Subtronics has shown that success in the music industry can coexist with a genuine desire to give back. They inspire their fans to not only appreciate their music but also become active participants in creating a better future. With their philanthropic endeavors, Subtronics continues to illuminate the path towards a more compassionate and sustainable music community.

Spreading the Message of Love and Unity

In the world of electronic music, Subtronics has not only captivated audiences with their high-energy performances and mind-blowing bass drops but also with their message of love and unity. Amidst the pulsating beats and electrifying rhythms,

Subtronics aims to create an atmosphere of togetherness and acceptance, where music becomes a powerful tool for connecting people from different walks of life.

The Power of Music as a Unifying Force

Music has always had the remarkable ability to bring people together, transcending cultural, social, and language barriers. Subtronics recognizes this power and seeks to leverage it to foster a sense of unity among their fans. Through their music, they aim to create an inclusive community where everyone feels accepted and valued. They believe that music has the potential to bridge gaps, break down prejudices, and promote understanding among individuals.

Spreading Love and Acceptance Through Lyrics

While electronic music is often associated with energetic beats and intricate sound design, Subtronics adds another layer of depth to their music through meaningful lyrics. Their songs touch upon a range of emotions and experiences, providing a platform for listeners to connect on a personal level. Whether it's expressing vulnerability, celebrating resilience, or acknowledging the struggles of life, Subtronics' lyrics resonate with their fans, offering a sense of solace and understanding.

Subtronics' lyrics also carry messages of love and acceptance. Through their music, they encourage their fans to embrace themselves and others with open hearts and open minds. They strive to create an environment where diversity is celebrated and judgment is left at the door. By spreading positive and inclusive messages, Subtronics aims to inspire their listeners to do the same in their own lives.

Events and Charitable Initiatives

Beyond their music, Subtronics actively engages in charitable initiatives and events aimed at making a positive impact on society. They believe in using their platform to not only entertain but also to give back to their community and make a difference in the world.

One example of their charitable efforts is organizing benefit concerts and events with a focus on social causes. From raising funds for disaster relief to supporting mental health organizations, Subtronics uses the power of their music to bring attention to important issues and rally support from their fans. These events not only create a sense of camaraderie among attendees but also provide a platform for spreading awareness and inspiring change.

Creating a Safe and Inclusive Fan Base

Subtronics understands the importance of creating a safe and inclusive environment for their fans. They actively promote mutual respect, consent, and tolerance within their community. By emphasizing these values, they foster an atmosphere where fans can freely express themselves without fear of judgment or harm.

In addition to their online presence and social media platforms, Subtronics also organizes fan meet and greets, where they can personally connect with their supporters. These events provide an opportunity for fans to interact with the band members, share their stories, and build meaningful connections with fellow fans. By actively engaging with their fan base, Subtronics nurtures a sense of belonging and unity, creating a community that extends beyond the music itself.

Spreading Love and Unity Through Collaborations

Collaborations have always been an integral part of the electronic music scene, and Subtronics recognizes the potential for spreading love and unity through joint projects with other artists. By collaborating with musicians from diverse backgrounds and genres, they embrace the power of collaboration to break down barriers and create music that transcends boundaries.

These collaborations not only result in unique and exciting tracks but also serve as a testament to the harmonious connection that music can forge among individuals. Through joint efforts, Subtronics hopes to amplify their message of love and unity, spreading it to a wider audience and inspiring others to embrace collaboration and inclusivity.

Spreading Love and Unity Beyond the Music

While Subtronics primarily shares their message of love and unity through their music, they also recognize the importance of spreading these values beyond the realm of music. They actively engage with social and environmental causes, supporting organizations that align with their beliefs and values.

Furthermore, the band members themselves serve as role models for their fans, promoting positivity and kindness in their day-to-day lives. By leading by example, Subtronics demonstrates that the message of love and unity can extend far beyond the boundaries of the music industry.

Conclusion

Subtronics' journey goes beyond that of being solely music artists. They have carved a path that highlights the significant role music can play in spreading the message of love and unity. Through their lyrics, events, collaborations, and engagement with their fans, Subtronics aims to create a space where everyone feels welcome, accepted, and connected.

As they continue on their musical journey, Subtronics remains dedicated to inspiring their fans and the wider community to embrace love, unity, and acceptance. Their impact reaches far beyond the stage, leaving a lasting legacy in the hearts of their listeners. And as the story of Subtronics unfolds, this message of love and unity will continue to shine brightly, illuminating the way for future generations of music lovers.

Chapter Two: The Team Behind Subtronics

Section One: Meet the Squad

The Mentor and Manager

In every successful music band, there is usually a guiding force behind the scenes who helps shape the artist's career and provides valuable advice and support. For Subtronics, that force comes in the form of their mentor and manager, Jake Navis.

Jake is not only Riko Garba's personal friend but also an experienced industry professional with a deep understanding of the music business. He recognized Riko's talent and potential early on, and took on the responsibility of guiding his career to new heights. Jake's role as both mentor and manager has been vital in shaping Subtronics' journey, and his accomplishments in the music industry make him the perfect person to lead the way.

As a mentor, Jake serves as a trusted confidant and sounding board for Riko. He provides guidance and advice on various aspects of the music industry, including artistic direction, business decisions, and overall career development. Jake's experience and expertise allow him to offer valuable insights that can help Subtronics navigate the competitive landscape of the electronic music scene.

Managing the business side of Subtronics' career is another crucial aspect of Jake's role. From negotiating contracts and deals to coordinating tours and handling finances, Jake ensures that Subtronics can focus on what they do best—creating incredible music and captivating audiences. His strong organizational skills and industry connections are instrumental in securing lucrative opportunities for the band and maximizing their exposure.

One of Jake's most significant contributions to Subtronics' success is his ability to identify and seize opportunities at the right time. He has a keen eye for talent and a knack for networking, which has allowed Subtronics to collaborate with fellow artists and industry heavyweights. Jake's strategic collaborations and features have not only elevated Subtronics' status but have also helped them expand their reach to new audiences.

While Jake's role as a mentor and manager centers around the band's professional growth, he also plays a crucial role in ensuring the well-being and happiness of the members. He acts as a support system for Riko and the rest of the band, offering encouragement during challenging times and celebrating their achievements. Jake's dedication to the band's success goes beyond the mere business aspect; he genuinely cares about the members' personal and artistic growth.

Of course, no mentor and manager relationship is without its challenges. Jake faced his fair share of obstacles and setbacks while guiding Subtronics on their journey. Whether it's dealing with demanding schedules, handling conflicts within the team, or managing the pressure that comes with success, Jake remains a steady presence and a pillar of support.

His ability to tackle these challenges head-on and find creative solutions is a testament to his resilience and dedication. Jake's unwavering commitment to Subtronics, both as a mentor and manager, has played an integral role in their rise to fame, and his contribution to their success cannot be understated.

In conclusion, the mentor and manager of Subtronics, Jake Navis, is an invaluable asset to the band. His expertise in the music industry, his mentorship, and his management skills have been instrumental in shaping Subtronics' career and propelling them to new heights. Jake's dedication to their success, both personally and professionally, has created a strong foundation for the band and ensures that they continue to make waves in the electronic music scene.

The Production Guru

The production guru is an essential member of the Subtronics team, responsible for the technical aspects of the music production process. This individual possesses a deep understanding of audio engineering, mixing and mastering techniques, and the use of production software and hardware.

Background and Expertise

The production guru brings years of experience and technical expertise to the table. They have a solid foundation in music theory, understanding the intricacies of harmonies, melodies, and rhythms. They have honed their skills through countless hours of practice and experimentation, pushing the boundaries of what is possible in electronic music production.

They are well-versed in using digital audio workstations (DAWs) such as Ableton Live, Logic Pro, or FL Studio. These platforms allow them to manipulate and arrange sound clips, create beats, and apply various effects and plugins to achieve the desired sonic result. The production guru is also proficient in using MIDI controllers and understanding the intricacies of MIDI mapping.

The Art of Sound Design

Sound design is a key aspect of the production process. The production guru possesses a keen ear for texture, tone, and timbre, allowing them to create unique and captivating sounds. They manipulate synthesizers, samplers, and virtual instruments to design sounds that align with Subtronics' signature style.

One of the production guru's secrets is their ability to combine and layer sounds to create complex and dynamic arrangements. They understand the importance of sound selection and experiment with different presets, samples, and recordings to achieve the desired sonic palette. This process often involves creating custom patches and synthesizer presets to achieve the desired sound.

Mixing and Mastering Mastery

Once the tracks are composed and the sounds are designed, the production guru dives into the realms of mixing and mastering. Mixing involves balancing the different elements of a track, such as vocals, drums, synths, and effects, to create a cohesive and sonically pleasing mix. The production guru uses their technical skill and artistic sensibility to ensure that each element sits well in the mix, creating a powerful and immersive listening experience.

Mastering takes the mix to the next level, preparing the final track for distribution. The production guru carefully applies equalization, compression, and other processing techniques to achieve a polished and professional sound. They ensure that the track translates well across different playback systems and platforms, optimizing it for maximum impact.

Innovation and Experimentation

The production guru thrives on innovation and pushing the boundaries of electronic music production. They are constantly exploring new techniques, plugins, and production tools to expand Subtronics' sound and create fresh and exciting tracks.

One unconventional yet effective practice the production guru employs is incorporating unconventional field recordings into Subtronics' tracks. By capturing and manipulating sounds from everyday objects, nature, or even city environments, they inject a unique and organic touch into the music.

Additionally, the production guru experiments with unconventional effects chains, utilizing signal routing, parallel processing, and creative automation to add depth and excitement to the tracks. Their willingness to think outside the box results in captivating and memorable moments within Subtronics' music.

The Production Guru and the Team

The production guru collaborates closely with the other members of the Subtronics team to bring their vision to life. They work hand-in-hand with the mentor and manager, sharing ideas and discussing the creative direction of each track. They also collaborate with the visual mastermind to synchronize visual elements with the music, creating a cohesive and immersive experience for the audience.

The production guru's role is crucial in the live setting, where they work closely with the touring guru to ensure that the tracks and sound system are optimized for each performance. They understand the importance of maintaining consistent and high-quality sound throughout the tour, adapting to different venues and environments.

Practice Makes Perfect: Exercises for Aspiring Producers

For those aspiring to become production gurus themselves, there are several exercises that can help sharpen their skills:

1. Experiment with different sound design techniques: Dive deep into synthesizer programming and explore different modulation techniques to create unique sounds.

2. Remix existing tracks: Take a well-known song and give it your own personal touch. Experiment with different arrangements, effects, and remix techniques to put your own spin on the original.

3. Practice mixing and mastering: Take a track you've produced and work on achieving a clean and balanced mix. Experiment with different processing techniques and critically analyze the results.

SECTION ONE: MEET THE SQUAD

4. Collaborate with other producers: Working with other producers allows you to learn from their techniques and gain new perspectives. It also provides an opportunity for mutual growth and inspiration.

5. Attend workshops and seminars: Stay updated with the latest developments in music production by attending workshops and seminars. Learn from industry professionals and take advantage of networking opportunities.

Remember, becoming a production guru takes time and dedication. Embrace the learning process and remain open to new ideas and techniques.

Resources for Further Exploration

To further develop skills in music production, here are some valuable resources:

- Online tutorials and courses: Platforms like YouTube, Udemy, and Coursera offer a plethora of tutorials and courses on music production, sound design, mixing, and mastering.

- Production forums and communities: Engage with fellow producers on forums like Reddit's r/edmproduction or join online communities to share knowledge, seek feedback, and gain inspiration.

- Industry-standard plugins and tools: Invest in high-quality plugins such as Serum, Massive, FabFilter, and iZotope's Ozone to enhance your production capabilities.

- Studio monitors and headphones: Invest in accurate studio monitoring equipment to ensure that you can hear your mix accurately.

- Attending live performances and festivals: Observe the production elements of live performances and gain inspiration from established artists in the EDM scene.

Remember, practice and persistence are key to unlocking the potential of your production skills. Embrace the journey and let your creativity shine through the power of music.

The Visual Mastermind

In the world of Subtronics, music goes hand in hand with mesmerizing visuals that transport the audience to another dimension. Behind this magical visual experience is the creative genius known as the Visual Mastermind. With an innate understanding of the power of visual storytelling, the Visual Mastermind brings Subtronics' music to life through stunning graphics, mind-bending animations, and captivating visuals.

The Art of Visual Storytelling

At the heart of the Visual Mastermind's work is the art of visual storytelling. Just as Subtronics' music takes listeners on a journey, the visuals enhance and amplify that experience. Every visual element is carefully crafted to immerse the audience in a world of vibrant colors, dynamic shapes, and captivating images.

To achieve this, the Visual Mastermind combines artistic talent with technical skills. They have a keen eye for aesthetics, understanding how color palettes, composition, and movement can elicit emotions and enhance the overall experience. They are well-versed in digital art, motion graphics, and visual effects techniques.

Creating a Symbiotic Relationship with Sound

In collaboration with Subtronics and the rest of the team, the Visual Mastermind creates an intricate symbiotic relationship between the music and the visuals. They deeply understand the nuances of Subtronics' music, allowing them to create visuals that seamlessly merge with the sonic landscape.

The Visual Mastermind carefully studies the structure and energy of each track, identifying key moments, drops, and transitions. They then translate these moments into visual cues, utilizing dynamic animations, synchronized lights, and expressive graphics. By aligning the visuals with the music's rhythm and mood, the Visual Mastermind enhances the impact of each beat and intensifies the emotional connection between the artist and the audience.

Setting the Stage: Stage Design and Live Visuals

Beyond crafting visuals for music videos and online content, the Visual Mastermind is also responsible for designing Subtronics' stage shows. They collaborate with stage designers, lighting technicians, and visual artists to create a fully immersive experience.

From conceptualizing the stage layout to designing custom visuals for LED screens and projection mapping, the Visual Mastermind sets the stage for an unforgettable performance. They utilize cutting-edge technology and innovative techniques to create a multi-dimensional environment that envelopes the audience in a visual feast.

During live performances, the Visual Mastermind controls the visual elements in real-time, reacting to the energy of the crowd and the DJ set. This allows them to adapt the visuals on the fly, amplifying the connection between Subtronics and the audience. By merging technology, creativity, and performance, the Visual Mastermind plays an integral role in delivering a truly immersive and unforgettable live experience.

Experimentation, Innovation, and Collaboration

The Visual Mastermind continually pushes the boundaries of live visual performances. They are always on the lookout for new technologies, software, and visual effects that can take Subtronics' shows to the next level. This constant experimentation leads to fresh and mind-blowing ideas that keep the audience captivated and coming back for more.

Collaboration is also at the core of the Visual Mastermind's work. They thrive on exchanging ideas and insights with the rest of the Subtronics team, including the mentor, manager, production guru, and marketing whiz. This collaborative process sparks innovation and allows them to create visuals that complement and elevate the overall Subtronics experience.

Unleashing Visual Magic

To truly understand the mastery of the Visual Mastermind, one must witness their work firsthand. From the hypnotic swirls of color to the mind-bending 3D animations, their visuals have the power to transport the audience into a world where music and art merge seamlessly.

The visual experience brought to life by the Visual Mastermind is more than just eye candy; it is a testament to the importance of creating a multi-sensory journey. Their work adds a layer of depth and magic to Subtronics' music, amplifying emotions, and creating an unforgettable experience that lingers in the minds of fans long after the show is over.

Just as Subtronics continues to evolve and push boundaries in the world of bass music, the Visual Mastermind embraces innovation and creativity to deliver visually stunning performances. Together, they are a force to be reckoned with, captivating audiences with their sonic and visual wizardry.

Example Problem: One challenge that the Visual Mastermind faces is creating visuals for Subtronics' music that transcends cultural boundaries. The team wants to appeal to diverse audiences around the world while maintaining their unique style and identity. How can the Visual Mastermind approach this challenge and create visuals that resonate with people from different cultural backgrounds?

Solution: The Visual Mastermind can approach this challenge by researching and immersing themselves in different cultures to understand their art, symbols, and visual aesthetics. By incorporating elements from various cultures, they can create visual narratives that have a universal appeal while still remaining true to Subtronics' style.

For example, they can explore traditional art forms, patterns, and motifs from different regions and infuse them with contemporary digital techniques. This fusion of traditional and modern visuals can create a visual language that bridges cultural gaps and allows people from various backgrounds to connect and resonate with the visuals on a deeper level.

Additionally, collaborating with local artists and visual creators from different parts of the world can bring fresh perspectives and cultural nuances to the visuals. This collaboration can result in visuals that are not only visually stunning but also respectful and representative of the diverse fan base.

By embracing cultural diversity and incorporating it into their visuals, the Visual Mastermind can create an inclusive and immersive experience that transcends borders and unites people through the power of music and art.

The Marketing Whiz

In the world of music, talent alone is not enough to succeed. An artist needs to have a strong brand and a dedicated fan base to thrive in the industry. That's where the Marketing Whiz comes in for Subtronics. This integral member of the team is responsible for developing and executing effective marketing strategies to promote the band's music, grow their fan base, and build a strong and recognizable brand.

Understanding the Music Industry Landscape

To be an effective marketing whiz, one must first have a deep understanding of the music industry landscape. This includes keeping up with industry trends, identifying target markets, and assessing the competitive environment. The marketing whiz must analyze consumer behavior and preferences, staying attuned to the ever-changing tastes of music listeners.

Competition in the electronic music scene is fierce, with countless artists vying for attention. The marketing whiz understands the importance of standing out from the crowd and finding unique selling points to differentiate Subtronics from other musicians.

Creating a Compelling Brand Identity

One of the primary responsibilities of the marketing whiz is to create and maintain a compelling brand identity for Subtronics. They craft a cohesive narrative that aligns with the band's values, style, and music. This brand identity forms the basis for all marketing strategies and ensures consistency across various platforms.

The marketing whiz works closely with the band to understand their vision and goals. They develop a brand story that resonates with the target audience, highlighting Subtronics' authenticity, creativity, and unique sound. This story becomes the foundation for all promotional materials, from social media posts to merchandise designs.

Crafting Engaging Marketing Campaigns

The marketing whiz knows that capturing the attention of fans and potential fans requires creativity and innovation. They devise engaging marketing campaigns that cut through the noise and leave a lasting impression.

These campaigns can take various forms. For example, the marketing whiz might orchestrate a fan contest with exclusive prizes or collaborate with influencers to amplify Subtronics' reach. They also develop eye-catching visuals, videos, and graphics for social media platforms, sparking curiosity and driving engagement.

Additionally, the marketing whiz strategically plans the release of new music, maximizing its impact. They analyze data and insights to identify the best times and channels for promotion, ensuring that Subtronics' music reaches the right audience at the right time.

Building and Nurturing Fan Relationships

A key aspect of the marketing whiz's role is building and nurturing relationships with fans. They create an inclusive and engaging community around Subtronics, fostering a sense of belonging among fans. This involves interacting with fans on social media, responding to messages and comments, and showing genuine appreciation for their support.

The marketing whiz also organizes fan meet-ups and events, providing opportunities for fans to connect with Subtronics and each other. They use fan feedback to gain insights and improve the fan experience, continuously optimizing their strategies to deepen the connection between the band and their supporters.

Embracing Data-Driven Decision Making

In an increasingly digital world, data is invaluable for making informed marketing decisions. The marketing whiz embraces data-driven decision making, leveraging analytics tools and platforms to gather insights about Subtronics' audience and campaign performance.

By analyzing data, the marketing whiz can identify trends, target specific segments of the fan base, and measure the impact of marketing efforts. They track key metrics such as reach, engagement, and conversion rates, allowing them to refine strategies and allocate resources effectively.

Unconventional Marketing: Think Outside the Box

In the fast-paced world of music marketing, it is essential to think outside the box and embrace unconventional strategies. The marketing whiz finds creative ways to generate buzz around Subtronics, always seeking opportunities to surprise and delight fans.

For example, they might collaborate with brands outside the music industry to reach new audiences and create unique experiences. They could organize guerrilla marketing stunts or partner with local businesses to create one-of-a-kind promotions.

The marketing whiz also understands the power of storytelling and leverages it in their campaigns. They craft narratives that resonate with fans, tapping into emotions and creating memorable experiences. By thinking outside the box, the marketing whiz ensures that Subtronics' marketing efforts are innovative, exciting, and ahead of the curve.

Conclusion

The Marketing Whiz plays a vital role in the success of Subtronics by developing and executing effective marketing strategies. Through a deep understanding of the music industry landscape, the marketing whiz creates a compelling brand identity, crafts engaging marketing campaigns, builds and nurtures fan relationships, embraces data-driven decision making, and thinks outside the box. With their expertise, Subtronics can continue to grow their fan base, amplify their music's reach, and leave a lasting legacy in the electronic music scene.

The Touring Guru

The Touring Guru is an essential member of the Subtronics team, responsible for organizing and managing the band's live performances and ensuring that their tours run smoothly. This individual is not just a logistical mastermind, but also possesses a deep understanding of the live music industry and a passion for creating unforgettable experiences for fans. Let's dive into the world of the Touring Guru and explore their role in bringing Subtronics' music to stages around the world.

The Art of Touring

Touring is the lifeblood of any successful music artist, and the Touring Guru is the maestro behind it all. From planning and coordinating travel arrangements to managing the logistics of each show, this person must possess a keen eye for detail and an ability to handle high-pressure situations. They are responsible for ensuring that Subtronics' performances are executed flawlessly and that all the necessary equipment is in place, allowing the artists to focus on delivering an electrifying show.

The Travel Whisperer

One of the Touring Guru's most crucial responsibilities is coordinating the band's travel arrangements. This includes booking flights, hotels, and ground transportation, while also considering factors such as budget constraints and tour routing. They are adept at finding the best deals, optimizing travel schedules, and solving any last-minute issues that may arise. Their goal is to ensure that Subtronics arrives at each destination on time and ready to rock the stage.

The Show Coordinator

Once Subtronics arrives at a venue, the Touring Guru takes charge of coordinating the show's setup. They work closely with venue staff, sound engineers, lighting technicians, and stage managers to create an optimal environment for the artists to perform. This involves overseeing equipment setup, sound checks, and ensuring that all technical aspects of the show are running smoothly. The Touring Guru's ability to communicate effectively and problem-solve on the spot is crucial in navigating any unforeseen challenges that may arise during this process.

Fans First

One of the Touring Guru's main priorities is ensuring that Subtronics' fans have an unforgettable live experience. They understand the importance of creating a welcoming and safe space for fans to enjoy the music. This includes working with venue security to enforce crowd control measures, prioritizing accessibility for all fans, and implementing strategies to prevent ticket scalping and fraud. The Touring Guru's ability to foster a positive and inclusive atmosphere contributes to the overall success of Subtronics' shows.

Technology and Innovations

The Touring Guru is constantly exploring new technologies and innovations to enhance Subtronics' live performances. This could range from incorporating cutting-edge stage design and lighting effects to utilizing interactive elements and visual projections. They stay ahead of the curve, keeping up with industry trends and experimenting with new technologies to push the boundaries of what a live music experience can be.

Unconventional Challenges

While touring may seem exciting and glamorous, it comes with its fair share of challenges. The Touring Guru must be adaptable and creative when faced with unexpected obstacles, such as technical malfunctions, bad weather, or travel delays. Their quick thinking and ability to find solutions in high-pressure situations are vital in ensuring that the show goes on. They possess a vast network of industry contacts and resources to rely on when needed, making them indispensable in navigating the unpredictable nature of live performances.

The Future of Touring

As technology continues to evolve, the Touring Guru must adapt and embrace new ways of engaging with fans in the live music setting. From virtual reality experiences to interactive fan engagement tools, they are constantly exploring innovative ways to elevate Subtronics' performances and create unforgettable memories for fans. The Touring Guru is at the forefront of an ever-changing industry, where creativity and technology collide to redefine the live music experience.

In Conclusion

The Touring Guru is the unsung hero behind Subtronics' live performances, ensuring that fans experience the full potential of their music. From meticulous travel planning to seamless show coordination, they play a vital role in bringing the band's energy to stages across the globe. Their dedication, resourcefulness, and passion for creating unforgettable live experiences make them an invaluable part of the Subtronics team. With their expertise and unwavering commitment, the Touring Guru's impact on the success of Subtronics' tours and the overall fan experience cannot be overstated.

Section Two: Collaborations and Features

Working with Vocalists and Rappers

Collaboration is a key aspect of Subtronics' music-making process, and working with vocalists and rappers is an important part of their creative journey. By incorporating the raw and emotive power of vocals into their bass-heavy productions, Subtronics is able to create tracks that are both energetic and emotionally resonant.

The Power of Vocals in Electronic Music

Vocalists and rappers play a crucial role in adding a human touch to electronic music. Their lyrics and melodies can convey emotions and tell stories in a way that purely instrumental tracks cannot. Vocals bring a new dimension to Subtronics' music, allowing them to connect with listeners on a deeper level.

When selecting vocalists and rappers to collaborate with, Subtronics looks for artists whose style and tone align with their overall vision for the track. They seek out individuals who can bring a unique flavor to their productions, adding a distinct voice to their bass-heavy soundscapes.

Finding the Right Vocalists and Rappers

Finding the perfect vocalist or rapper for a Subtronics track is a process that involves both intuition and careful consideration. While they may have their own list of artists they admire and would love to collaborate with, Subtronics is always open to new talent and surprising collaborations.

To discover potential collaborators, Subtronics and their team actively explore various music scenes, both within and outside of electronic music. They attend live shows, listen to underground tracks, and keep an ear out for artists who could bring something fresh to their sound. Social media also plays a role in connecting with potential collaborators, as it allows for direct communication and the discovery of emerging talent.

The Collaborative Process

Once a vocalist or rapper has been identified, Subtronics starts the collaborative process by discussing ideas and concepts for the track. They believe in giving their collaborators creative freedom, enabling them to contribute their own unique style and ideas to the project.

Subtronics and the vocalist or rapper work closely together to fine-tune lyrics and melodies, ensuring that they align with the desired theme and overall vibe of the track. This collaborative back-and-forth process allows for the seamless integration of vocals into Subtronics' energetic and bass-heavy productions.

The Fusion of Styles

The fusion of Subtronics' heavy bass music with vocalists and rappers from different genres creates a powerful blend of styles and sounds. By bringing together diverse musical influences, Subtronics is able to push the boundaries of electronic music and create tracks that defy categorization.

For example, collaborating with a rapper can add a dynamic and rhythmic element to Subtronics' drops, elevating them to a whole new level. The combination of hard-hitting bass and rapid-fire verses creates an exhilarating listening experience that engages fans from both the electronic and hip-hop communities.

The Importance of Authenticity

Throughout the collaborative process, Subtronics emphasizes the importance of authenticity. They encourage their vocalists and rappers to stay true to their own style and express their unique voice. This ensures that each collaboration is a genuine representation of the artist's individuality and strengthens the overall impact of the track.

Example: Collaborating with GRiZ

One notable collaboration in Subtronics' discography is their track "Griztronics" with the renowned electronic music artist, GRiZ. This unexpected collaboration brought together Subtronics' hard-hitting bass sound with GRiZ's soulful saxophone melodies and feel-good vibes.

The track showcases the seamless fusion of Subtronics' dubstep drops with GRiZ's jazzy saxophone lines, resulting in a high-energy and yet emotionally resonant track. "Griztronics" not only became a fan favorite but also introduced Subtronics to GRiZ's dedicated fan base, expanding their reach and influence within the electronic music community.

The Unconventional Approach

An unconventional approach that Subtronics takes when working with vocalists and rappers is to experiment with unconventional vocal techniques. They are always searching for unique ways to incorporate vocals into their tracks, whether it's through the use of unconventional vocal effects or the manipulation of traditional vocal samples.

By pushing the boundaries of what vocals can sound like in electronic music, Subtronics adds an extra layer of intrigue and excitement to their productions. This experimentation not only keeps their sound fresh and innovative but also allows for a greater range of creative expression.

Conclusion

Working with vocalists and rappers is an integral part of Subtronics' music production process. By collaborating with artists from various genres, they are able to create tracks that are both emotionally impactful and sonically captivating. The fusion of Subtronics' heavy bass music with the power of vocals elevates their music to new heights, connecting with listeners on a deeper level. Through experimentation and a commitment to authenticity, Subtronics continues to push the boundaries of electronic music, leaving an enduring impact on the industry.

Exciting Features on Other Artists' Songs

Collaborating with other artists is a crucial part of Subtronics' music journey. It allows them to explore new sounds, expand their creativity, and bring fresh perspectives to their music. In this section, we will delve into the exciting features that Subtronics has contributed to other artists' songs, showcasing their versatility and unique style.

The Power of Collaboration

Collaborations in the music industry can be transformative, resulting in a fusion of different styles and ideas. Subtronics understands the power of collaboration and has actively sought out opportunities to work with a diverse range of artists, from vocalists and rappers to fellow DJs. Their desire to push each other's boundaries and create something truly unique has led to some exciting and noteworthy features.

Collaborating with vocalists and rappers adds another layer of depth to Subtronics' music. By blending their signature bass-heavy beats with the lyrical prowess of talented artists, they create songs that resonate with fans on a whole new level. The combination of Subtronics' hard-hitting drops and the expressive vocals or verses of the featured artists creates a dynamic and captivating listening experience.

Adding Depth and Versatility

One of the most exciting aspects of featuring on other artists' songs is the opportunity for Subtronics to explore different genres and styles. By incorporating their distinct sound into a variety of musical contexts, they can showcase their versatility as producers while adding their unique touch to each track.

For example, Subtronics might collaborate with an artist from the hip-hop scene, infusing their heavy basslines and intricate sound design into a rap track. This collaboration bridges the gap between the realms of electronic music and hip-hop, resulting in a fresh and exciting fusion that appeals to fans of both genres.

Alternatively, Subtronics could collaborate with a vocalist from the pop world, bringing their edgy and experimental sound to a more mainstream audience. By incorporating their characteristic drops and intricate production techniques into a pop song, they add an unexpected and intriguing element that sets the track apart.

Innovative Production Techniques

When it comes to collaborative projects, Subtronics' approach goes beyond simply adding their unique sounds to other artists' songs. They also embrace the opportunity to experiment with new production techniques and push the boundaries of electronic music.

In some collaborations, Subtronics might reimagine and remix existing tracks, transforming them into something entirely new. By incorporating their distinctive bass-driven sound and mind-bending drops, they inject new life into the original work and create a fresh take that captivates listeners.

In other cases, Subtronics might collaborate with fellow producers or DJs, engaging in intense studio sessions where ideas are exchanged, and creativity flourishes. These sessions often lead to the co-creation of tracks that showcase the best of both artists' styles, resulting in a truly collaborative and innovative piece of music.

Inspiring Others and Shaping the Music Landscape

Through their exciting features on other artists' songs, Subtronics has not only expanded their own horizons but also influenced and inspired a new generation of producers and musicians. Their unique sound and approach to collaboration have helped shape the music landscape and pushed the boundaries of what is possible in electronic music.

By working with artists from various genres and backgrounds, Subtronics has fostered cross-pollination of ideas, allowing different styles to merge and evolve. This has opened doors for other artists to experiment and explore new musical territories, creating a ripple effect throughout the music industry.

Unconventional yet Relevant

To showcase their unconventional yet relevant approach to collaboration, Subtronics could share an example of an unexpected feature they contributed to another artist's song. For instance, they could describe a collaboration with a classical musician, where their signature bass sound intertwines with the elegance of orchestral instruments. This unexpected combination breaks the barriers between electronic and classical music, resulting in a truly unique and boundary-pushing track.

Moreover, Subtronics could give a glimpse into their collaborative process by sharing a behind-the-scenes story. They can describe a particularly memorable studio session where they worked closely with another artist, highlighting the creative challenges and breakthroughs they experienced together. This story would give readers a deeper understanding of the collaborative process and the excitement that comes with intertwining different artistic visions.

Summary

Subtronics' features on other artists' songs exemplify their commitment to collaboration and creativity. These collaborations allow them to explore new genres, experiment with production techniques, and inspire a new wave of musical innovation. By sharing their unique sound and style with a diverse range of artists, Subtronics continues to leave an indelible mark on the music industry, expanding their reach and enriching the musical experiences of fans around the world.

Collaborative Projects with Fellow DJs

Collaboration is at the core of Subtronics' journey in the EDM scene. The band has consistently sought opportunities to work with fellow DJs and producers, recognizing the power and creativity that can be unleashed when artists come together. In this section, we will explore some of Subtronics' most notable collaborative projects with fellow DJs and the impact these partnerships have had on their music.

One of the key aspects of Subtronics' collaborative projects is the shared desire to push boundaries and experiment with new sounds. By teaming up with like-minded artists, Subtronics has been able to explore uncharted territory within the EDM genre. Whether it's fusing different subgenres or incorporating unconventional elements into their tracks, these collaborations have resulted in some truly unique and groundbreaking music.

In their collaboration with fellow DJ Excision, Subtronics had the opportunity to combine their signature heavy bass sound with Excision's dubstep expertise. The resulting track, "Breaking Through," showcases the best of both artists' styles. It features hard-hitting drops, intricate sound design, and a relentless energy that has made it a fan favorite. The collaboration also allowed Subtronics to learn from Excision's years of experience in the industry, gaining valuable insight into the production and performance aspects of their music.

Another notable collaborative project involved Subtronics teaming up with NGHTMRE for the track "Nuclear Bass Face." This collaboration brought together Subtronics' heavy bass influence and NGHTMRE's trap-infused style, resulting in a high-energy track that seamlessly blends elements from both genres. The combination of Subtronics' signature bass drops and NGHTMRE's intricate trap beats creates a unique and dynamic listening experience.

What sets Subtronics' collaborative projects apart is their commitment to maintaining the individuality and authenticity of each artist involved. Rather than diluting their sound to fit the expectations of the collaboration, Subtronics' approach is to bring out the best in each participant, allowing their individual styles to shine while creating something fresh and exciting. This approach not only ensures that each collaboration is a true representation of the artists involved but also contributes to a more diverse and vibrant EDM scene.

An unconventional yet effective example of collaboration within the DJ community is the practice of "B2B" (back-to-back) sets. This involves two DJs performing together on stage, taking turns playing tracks and seamlessly transitioning between them. Subtronics has participated in numerous B2B sets with fellow DJs, creating an electrifying atmosphere and expanding their creative horizons. These sets often lead to unexpected musical combinations and provide a platform for artists to challenge and inspire each other in real-time.

Collaborative projects also extend beyond the realm of music production. Subtronics has frequently joined forces with fellow DJs for charitable initiatives and social causes. By leveraging their platform and influence, they have raised awareness and provided support for various organizations and communities in need. This collaborative approach not only amplifies the impact of their individual efforts but also shows how music can be a powerful tool for positive change.

SECTION TWO: COLLABORATIONS AND FEATURES   101

To encourage aspiring musicians to embrace collaboration, Subtronics regularly shares behind-the-scenes stories and insights into their collaborative process. They emphasize the importance of open communication, mutual respect, and a shared vision when working with fellow artists. By fostering a supportive and creative environment, Subtronics inspires others to explore the potential of collaboration and unlock new possibilities within the EDM genre.

In summary, Subtronics' collaborative projects with fellow DJs have played a significant role in their musical journey. These collaborations have allowed them to explore new sounds, expand their creative boundaries, and create groundbreaking music. By embracing the diversity and creativity of their peers, Subtronics has not only elevated their own music but also contributed to the growth and evolution of the EDM scene as a whole. Through B2B sets, charity initiatives, and a commitment to maintaining each artist's individuality, Subtronics continues to inspire and empower fellow musicians to pursue collaborative ventures and push the limits of their craft.

The Magic of Studio Sessions

In the world of Subtronics, the studio is a sacred place where creativity flourishes and magic happens. It is here that Subtronics and his team come together to transform their ideas into tracks that captivate audiences around the world. In this section, we will delve into the process and secrets behind their studio sessions, exploring the tools they use, the techniques they employ, and the collaborative spirit that drives their music-making.

Creating an Inspiring Environment

A successful studio session starts with setting the right mood and creating an environment that inspires creativity. Subtronics understands the importance of ambiance, and meticulously curates his studio space to ensure it fosters a sense of inspiration. The walls are adorned with posters of iconic artists who have influenced his journey, and atmospheric lighting sets the stage for creativity to flourish. The studio is a reflection of his musical journey, with shelves filled with vinyl records, synthesizers, and other instruments, each with its own story and sonic possibilities.

To further enhance the creative atmosphere, Subtronics often introduces elements of nature into the studio. The gentle sound of a running stream or the chirping of birds can be heard softly in the background, reminding the team of the beauty and vastness of the natural world. This connection with nature serves as a constant reminder to stay grounded and seek inspiration from the world outside the studio walls.

The Collaborative Process

Studio sessions for Subtronics are seldom solitary endeavors. They thrive on collaboration and value the creative input of their team members and fellow artists. The studio serves as a meeting ground for musicians, vocalists, and producers to join forces and push the boundaries of their craft.

During collaborative studio sessions, ideas flow freely. Subtronics and his collaborators engage in passionate discussions about concepts, sounds, and the emotions they want to evoke. They bounce ideas off each other, sparking new possibilities and perspectives. It is in these moments of collaboration that the true magic of studio sessions unfolds.

To facilitate effective collaboration, Subtronics employs a variety of techniques. They often begin with brainstorming sessions, where everyone contributes their ideas and inspirations. These sessions can take unexpected turns, leading to creative breakthroughs and the birth of entirely new directions for a track.

Harnessing Technology

Technology has revolutionized the music production process, and Subtronics embraces the latest tools and software to bring their vision to life. The studio is equipped with state-of-the-art hardware and software, enabling them to take advantage of cutting-edge production techniques.

One piece of technology that plays a significant role in their studio sessions is the digital audio workstation (DAW). Subtronics and their team are proficient in using professional DAWs like Ableton Live or FL Studio, allowing them to arrange, mix, and manipulate their tracks with precision and creativity. With the help of MIDI controllers, they can manipulate virtual instruments and samples, bringing their ideas to fruition in real-time.

Another indispensable tool in Subtronics' studio sessions is the vast library of samples and sound design resources they have curated over the years. From meticulously crafted drum samples to unique synthesizer presets, these resources provide a starting point for their tracks and often inspire the direction of a song.

Unconventional Techniques

In their quest for innovation, Subtronics often embraces unconventional techniques during studio sessions. They are not afraid to experiment and push the boundaries of what is considered traditional electronic music production.

One such unconventional technique involves using everyday objects as sound sources. Subtronics and his team create unique percussive elements by recording sounds from their surroundings – the clinking of glasses, the slamming of doors, or the crackling of fire. These unexpected sounds are processed and manipulated, creating entirely new textures and adding an organic touch to their tracks.

Subtronics also draws inspiration from unconventional genres and styles of music outside of the electronic music realm. By incorporating elements from genres like hip-hop, rock, or classical music, they infuse their tracks with a fresh and distinctive flavor. This exploration of diverse genres not only keeps their sound evolving but also attracts a wider range of music lovers.

A Never-Ending Learning Process

Above all, Subtronics views studio sessions as an opportunity for growth and learning. They are continuously honing their skills and expanding their knowledge of music production techniques. Each studio session presents an opportunity to experiment with new sounds, explore different genres, and refine their signature sound.

To support their growth, Subtronics encourages feedback and constructive criticism within their team. By actively seeking input from their collaborators, they can identify areas for improvement and polish their tracks to perfection. They understand that music production is an ever-evolving art, and each studio session brings them closer to mastery.

Exercises

1. Reflect on your own creative process. What environments or settings inspire you the most? Create a playlist of songs or sounds that put you in a creative mindset and use it during your next studio session or artistic endeavor. Take note of how the environment and music impact your creativity and productivity.

2. Experiment with unconventional sound sources. Try recording everyday sounds using your smartphone or a portable recorder. Manipulate and process these sounds using your preferred audio software and incorporate them into your tracks. Take note of how these unexpected elements add depth and uniqueness to your music.

3. Collaborate with fellow musicians or producers on a studio session. Bring together individuals with differing musical backgrounds and perspectives. Engage in open discussions and actively listen to each other's ideas. Explore the possibilities that arise from this collaboration and document the process to reflect on later.

4. Take a deep dive into a genre or style of music that is completely new to you. Analyze the production techniques, instrumentation, and arrangement used in that genre. Consider elements that you can incorporate into your own productions to add a fresh twist. Experiment with merging genres to create a unique sound.

5. Explore different audio effects and plugins within your digital audio workstation. Select a track that you have been working on and experiment with different effects to bring out new dimensions and textures. Document the effects used and how they enhance the overall sound of the track.

6. Seek feedback from peers or mentors on one of your studio sessions. Embrace constructive criticism and use it as an opportunity to improve your craft. Consider their suggestions and determine how they align with your artistic vision. Apply the feedback to refine the track and assess the impact on the final result.

Resources

- Ableton Live: `https://www.ableton.com/`
- FL Studio: `https://www.image-line.com/flstudio`
- Splice: `https://splice.com/` (Sample and sound resource platform)
- "Making Music" by Ableton: `https://makingmusic.ableton.com/` (Online learning resource for music production)
- "The Producer's Manual" by Paul White: A comprehensive guide to music production techniques.

Remember, studio sessions are not just about creating music – they are an opportunity for self-expression, exploration, and growth. Embrace the magic of the studio, collaborate with like-minded individuals, and let your creativity soar. There are no limits to what you can achieve.

Pushing Each Other's Boundaries

In the world of music, collaboration is a powerful tool that can lead to incredible artistic growth and innovation. Subtronics understands the value of pushing each other's boundaries in the studio and on stage. The duo, consisting of Jesse Kardon and his production partner, has built their success on this idea of continuously challenging and inspiring one another to explore new creative depths. In this section, we will delve into the exciting dynamics of their collaborative process, the benefits it brings, and the remarkable outcomes that have emerged from their dedication to pushing each other's boundaries.

The Power of Collaboration

Collaboration is a breath of fresh air in the music industry, igniting an unstoppable creative force. When artists come together, they bring with them unique perspectives, skills, and ideas that can elevate each other's work to new heights. This is precisely what Subtronics achieves through their collaboration.

Jesse and his production partner have developed a strong bond built on mutual respect and admiration for each other's talents. They constantly challenge each other to push beyond their comfort zones, exploring uncharted musical territories. This collaborative mindset has played a pivotal role in their evolution, allowing them to craft their distinct sound and style.

Creating a Feedback Loop

Central to Subtronics' collaborative process is the creation of a feedback loop. It is within this loop that the duo provides constructive criticism, exchange ideas, and refine their creative vision. This constant dialogue enables them to refine their compositions, unlock new musical possibilities, and expand their horizons.

The feedback loop is not confined to the studio; it extends to their live performances as well. Jesse and his partner act as each other's sounding boards, fine-tuning their sets, and improving their stage presence. This continuous exchange of ideas creates an ever-evolving performance that keeps audiences captivated and craving more.

Inspiring and Challenging Each Other

The driving force behind Subtronics' success lies in their ability to inspire and challenge each other. Each member brings their unique strengths and perspectives to the table, creating a dynamic synergy that sparks fresh ideas and pushes their creative boundaries.

Jesse and his partner constantly introduce new techniques, sounds, and production methods to keep their music fresh and exciting. By challenging each other to experiment with unconventional sounds or explore unfamiliar genres, they transcend the boundaries of traditional electronic music.

Expanding Their Musical Toolbox

One of the significant advantages of pushing each other's boundaries is the expansion of their musical toolbox. Through their collaboration, Subtronics constantly discovers new techniques, plugins, and tools that enhance their production process.

By seeking inspiration from different genres and artists, they integrate diverse musical elements into their compositions. This eclectic approach allows them to create a unique blend of sounds, resulting in tracks that captivate listeners and distinguish them from other artists in the electronic music scene.

Embracing the Unconventional

Subtronics dares to be unconventional in their approach, experimenting with unusual sound combinations and pushing the limits of what is considered conventional. Their willingness to take risks and explore uncharted sonic territories sets them apart from the crowd.

Whether it's incorporating unexpected samples, manipulating vocals in unconventional ways, or deconstructing traditional song structures, Subtronics is never afraid to defy expectations. This fearlessness in pushing each other's boundaries and embracing the unconventional is what fuels their artistic growth and keeps their music fresh and exciting.

The Unforeseen Magic

Perhaps the most exciting aspect of pushing each other's boundaries is the unforeseen magic that unfolds. Subtronics never knows exactly what will emerge from their collaborative efforts, but they embrace the journey of discovery.

Sometimes it's a surprising sonic combination that creates an instant hit, and other times it's a small detail that completely transforms a track. By constantly challenging and inspiring one another, Subtronics creates an environment that allows for these magical moments to happen, leading to groundbreaking music that resonates with audiences worldwide.

In conclusion, pushing each other's boundaries is at the core of Subtronics' creative process. Through collaboration, they challenge and inspire one another, constantly expanding their musical toolbox and embracing the unconventional. This approach has not only shaped their unique sound but also propelled them to the forefront of the EDM scene. As they continue to push boundaries, their journey of musical exploration and innovation shows no signs of slowing down. Subtronics' commitment to pushing each other's boundaries serves as a lesson to all aspiring artists: collaboration can be the spark that leads to extraordinary artistic growth and success.

Section Three: The Creative Process

Finding Inspiration from Daily Life

Life is a never-ending river of experiences, emotions, and moments that shape who we are as individuals. For artists, these daily encounters serve as a wellspring of inspiration, fueling their creativity and pushing the boundaries of their art. Subtronics, the enigmatic music duo, is no exception to this rule. In this section, we will delve into the depths of their creative process, exploring how they find inspiration from the tapestry of their daily lives.

Embracing the Mundane

While the music industry often glamorizes the eccentric and the extraordinary, Subtronics finds beauty and inspiration in the simplest of things. Mundane experiences, like walking through a rain-soaked street or sitting alone in a coffee shop, can ignite a spark of creativity within them.

They believe that the everyday moments have the potential to be extraordinary, if only we pay attention. This philosophy is evident in their music, which seamlessly weaves together the mundane and the extraordinary, creating an immersive experience for their listeners.

Observing the World

In order to find inspiration from daily life, Subtronics channels their inner observers. They keenly observe the world around them, taking note of the smallest details and nuances that often go unnoticed. This practice allows them to tap into the rich tapestry of human emotions and experiences, translating them into their music.

For instance, in one of their tracks, "City Lights," they captured the buzzing energy of a bustling metropolis by incorporating sounds of traffic, footsteps, and distant chatter. By bringing these real-world elements into their music, they create a vivid and relatable sonic landscape.

Drawing from Personal Experiences

The power of authenticity cannot be overstated when it comes to finding inspiration from daily life. Subtronics draws heavily from their personal experiences, transforming raw emotions into melodic expressions.

From heartbreak to triumph, each personal experience serves as a catalyst for their creativity. For instance, in their track "Resist" they draw upon their own struggles and obstacles, using the medium of music to communicate resilience and determination.

Through their music, Subtronics invites their listeners into their personal journeys, creating a sense of connection and empathy in a world that can often feel disconnected.

Exploring Different Mediums

Variety is the spice of life, and Subtronics embraces this mantra fully. They expand their horizons by exploring different mediums of art, such as photography, painting, and even literature. This interplay of different artistic forms broadens their perspective and unlocks new layers of creativity within them.

For instance, after reading Aldous Huxley's "Brave New World," they were inspired to create a track that encapsulated the dystopian themes present in the novel. By allowing themselves to be influenced by literature, Subtronics demonstrates the power of interdisciplinary creativity.

Adapting to Change

One constant in daily life is change, and Subtronics understands the importance of flexibility and adaptation in their creative process. They embrace the fluidity of inspiration, allowing it to evolve and transform as they grow as artists.

They emphasize that it's essential to let go of preconceived notions and remain open to the unexpected. This willingness to embrace change enables them to continually reinvent their sound and push the boundaries of their art.

In conclusion, Subtronics finds inspiration in the everyday magic of life. By embracing the mundane, observing the world, drawing from personal experiences, exploring different mediums, and adapting to change, they create music that resonates deeply with their audience. Their creative process serves as a reminder that inspiration is not limited to grand gestures or extraordinary moments, but can be found in the smallest details of daily existence. So, let us all open our eyes and ears to the stories woven within the fabric of our lives, for therein lies the wellspring of inspiration.

Turning Ideas into Tracks

Turning ideas into tracks is a fundamental part of the creative process for Subtronics. It is the moment when inspiration transforms into a tangible piece of music that can be shared with the world. In this section, we will explore the steps and techniques that Subtronics employs to bring their ideas to life.

Finding Inspiration from Daily Life

The first step in turning ideas into tracks is finding inspiration. Subtronics draws inspiration from various aspects of their daily lives. They find beauty and creativity in the smallest details, whether it's the sound of rain hitting a window or the rhythm of a bustling city street.

One unconventional yet effective technique that Subtronics uses to find inspiration is by listening to different genres of music. By exploring music outside of their usual electronic realm, they expose themselves to new sounds, melodies, and lyrics that can spark creative ideas. This approach allows them to incorporate unique elements into their tracks, making them stand out in the EDM scene.

Brainstorming Melodies, Beats, and Sounds

Once inspiration strikes, Subtronics begins the process of building the foundation of their tracks. They start by brainstorming melodies, beats, and sounds that capture the essence of the idea they want to convey. This step is crucial as it sets the tone for the entire track.

To brainstorm melodies, Subtronics experiments with various musical scales, chord progressions, and intervals. They play around with different notes and sequences until they find the perfect combination that resonates with the idea behind the track. This process often involves trial and error, as they tweak and refine melodies until they achieve the desired emotional impact.

When it comes to beats, Subtronics focuses on creating intricate and complex rhythms that captivate the listener. They pay close attention to the arrangement of percussive elements, such as kick drums, snares, and hi-hats, to create a rhythmic foundation that drives the energy of the track. Subtronics also draws inspiration from various genres like hip-hop and trap, infusing their beats with a unique blend of styles.

Additionally, Subtronics experiments with a wide range of sounds to add depth and texture to their tracks. They explore different synthesizers, virtual instruments, and effects plugins to create distinctive sounds that complement the melody and beat. By combining analog and digital sound sources, they achieve a rich and dynamic sonic palette that sets their tracks apart.

Arranging and Structuring the Track

Once the melodies, beats, and sounds are in place, Subtronics focuses on arranging and structuring the track. This step involves determining the order and progression of sections, such as the intro, verse, drop, and breakdown, to create a cohesive musical journey.

Subtronics pays attention to the dynamics of the track, carefully crafting moments of tension and release to keep the listener engaged. They strategically place build-ups and drops to build anticipation and create impactful moments of energy. These elements, combined with the unique sound design, give Subtronics' tracks their signature intensity and impact.

To ensure a seamless flow, Subtronics utilizes transition techniques such as filter sweeps, risers, and effects automation. These techniques help connect different sections of the track and create smooth transitions that keep the energy flowing.

Mixing and Mastering the Track

Once the arrangement is complete, Subtronics moves on to the technical aspects of turning their ideas into a polished track. Mixing and mastering play a crucial role in ensuring the final product sounds professional and translates well across different sound systems.

During the mixing phase, Subtronics balances the different elements of the track, such as the vocals, synths, and drums, using EQ, compression, and other processing techniques. They pay attention to the frequency spectrum, ensuring that each element occupies its own space and doesn't clash with other elements.

Mastering, on the other hand, involves finalizing the track's overall sound and making it ready for distribution. Subtronics focuses on enhancing the clarity, depth, and loudness of the track while maintaining its dynamic range. They utilize various mastering tools and techniques to achieve a polished and cohesive final product.

SECTION THREE: THE CREATIVE PROCESS   111

Feedback and Iteration

Subtronics understands the importance of getting feedback from trusted ears during the creative process. They share their work with fellow producers, DJs, and friends to gather opinions and identify areas that can be improved.

This feedback loop allows Subtronics to iterate on their ideas, making adjustments and refinements based on the input they receive. They consider different perspectives and are open to constructive criticism, using it as a tool for growth and improvement.

Resources and Tools

Turning ideas into tracks requires a combination of creativity and technical expertise. Subtronics relies on a variety of resources and tools to support their creative process.

One essential resource for Subtronics is a Digital Audio Workstation (DAW) like Ableton Live or FL Studio. These software platforms provide a versatile and intuitive environment for composing, arranging, and producing music.

Subtronics also uses a vast collection of plugins and virtual instruments to shape their sound. Some of their go-to tools include synthesizers like Serum and Massive, as well as effects plugins like FabFilter and SoundToys. These plugins offer a wide range of sonic possibilities and help Subtronics achieve their unique sound.

In addition to software tools, Subtronics takes advantage of hardware equipment like MIDI controllers and audio interfaces. These physical devices enhance their workflow and provide a tactile experience that facilitates creativity.

Example: Creating a Melodic Dubstep Track

To illustrate the process of turning ideas into tracks, let's take a closer look at how Subtronics creates a melodic dubstep track.

Step 1: Finding Inspiration - Subtronics finds inspiration in a beautiful sunset they experienced during a hike. The vivid colors and serene atmosphere inspire a melodic idea.

Step 2: Brainstorming Melodies, Beats, and Sounds - Subtronics sits down at their studio and starts experimenting with different chord progressions and melodic sequences. They settle on a catchy melody that captures the uplifting and emotional vibe of the sunset.

For the beats, Subtronics creates a combination of punchy, syncopated drums and rolling hi-hats that add energy to the track. They layer kick drums, snares, and claps to create a dynamic and driving rhythm.

To enhance the melodic elements, Subtronics designs a unique synth sound using a combination of wavetable synthesis and modulation effects. The result is a rich and evolving tone that adds depth to the track.

Step 3: Arranging and Structuring the Track - Subtronics begins arranging the track into sections, starting with an atmospheric intro that builds anticipation. They transition into a verse with a stripped-down arrangement, allowing the melody to shine. The drop features a powerful bassline and energetic drums, creating an intense and euphoric moment. A breakdown follows, providing a brief reprieve before the final drop, which adds variations to keep the energy high until the end.

Step 4: Mixing and Mastering the Track - Subtronics starts mixing the track, adjusting the levels and EQ to achieve a balanced sound. They use compression and saturation to add warmth and character to the individual elements. Once the mix is finalized, they move on to mastering, applying subtle EQ and dynamics processing to enhance the overall loudness and clarity.

Step 5: Feedback and Iteration - Subtronics shares the track with their close group of producer friends. They receive feedback on the mix balance and make subtle adjustments based on the suggestions. This iterative process helps them refine the track before its final release.

By following these steps and utilizing their creative resources, Subtronics transforms their initial ideas into captivating tracks that resonate with listeners worldwide.

In conclusion, turning ideas into tracks requires a combination of inspiration, technical proficiency, and a meticulous attention to detail. Subtronics' approach to the creative process highlights the importance of finding inspiration, experimenting with melodies and sounds, arranging and structuring the track, mixing and mastering, and seeking feedback. With their unique style and dedication to pushing boundaries, Subtronics continues to create music that leaves a lasting impact on the EDM scene. So next time you have a creative impulse, follow in Subtronics' footsteps and turn your ideas into tracks that inspire and move others. Let the music flow!

Experimenting with New Sounds and Techniques

In the ever-evolving world of music production, Subtronics is known for pushing the boundaries of sound and technique. In this section, we delve into their fearless approach to experimenting with new sounds and techniques, constantly pushing themselves to create innovative and unique tracks. Whether it's exploring new genres, incorporating unconventional instruments, or embracing cutting-edge technologies, Subtronics is always at the forefront of sonic exploration.

Embracing Genre Fusion

One of the hallmarks of Subtronics' music is their ability to seamlessly blend different genres together. They fearlessly explore the intersection of bass music and dubstep, infusing their tracks with elements of trap, hip-hop, and even metal. By combining these disparate genres, they create a signature sound that is both captivating and unpredictable.

To achieve this fusion, Subtronics relies on their extensive knowledge of music theory and production techniques. They experiment with different chord progressions, scales, and melodies, searching for combinations that bring out the best in each genre. By breaking traditional genre boundaries, they create tracks that are innovative and groundbreaking.

Sound Design Secrets and Techniques

Sound design is an essential aspect of Subtronics' music. They constantly explore new techniques and methods to create unique and exciting sounds that captivate their audience. From dirty, growling basslines to intricate, melodic leads, their sound design skills push the limits of what is possible in electronic music.

One technique they employ is layering multiple sounds together to create complex and textured sounds. By combining different synthesizers, samples, and effects, they are able to craft sounds that are rich and dynamic. They experiment with different EQ settings, modulation techniques, and filters to shape and mold their sounds into something truly extraordinary.

Another aspect of Subtronics' sound design is their attention to detail. They meticulously tweak each sound, fine-tuning parameters such as attack, decay, sustain, and release to achieve the desired effect. They experiment with different types of distortion, compression, and saturation to add depth and character to their sounds.

Incorporating Live Instruments

While electronic music is often associated with synthesizers and laptops, Subtronics embraces the use of live instruments in their productions. They believe that incorporating organic elements into their tracks adds a unique flavor and human touch that cannot be replicated by digital tools alone.

Subtronics experiments with playing live instruments such as guitars, drums, and even unusual instruments like the theremin. They record and sample these live performances, integrating them into their tracks to create a sense of authenticity and depth.

By blending live instruments with electronic elements, Subtronics creates a sonic landscape that is both familiar and otherworldly. This experimentation with live instrumentation sets them apart from many other electronic artists and adds an exciting dynamic to their music.

Harnessing Cutting-Edge Technologies

Subtronics is never afraid to embrace the latest technologies in their quest for sonic innovation. They constantly stay up to date with the latest hardware and software advancements, integrating them into their production process to explore new frontiers of sound.

One example of this is their use of modular synthesizers. Modular synthesis allows Subtronics to create custom signal paths, routing audio and modulation in unique ways. This modular approach gives them unparalleled control over their sound and allows for endless experimentation.

They also experiment with emerging software plugins and virtual instruments, always on the lookout for new and exciting sounds. By constantly exploring new technologies, Subtronics stays at the forefront of electronic music production, pushing the boundaries of what is possible.

Unconventional Techniques: A Wildcard Approach

In addition to their more traditional experimentation, Subtronics also embraces unconventional techniques to create unexpected and exciting sounds. They are not afraid to think outside the box and experiment with unconventional sound sources and manipulation methods.

One example is using field recordings as the basis for their tracks. They venture out into the world, capturing sounds from various environments and incorporating them into their productions. By doing so, they infuse their music with unique textures and atmospheres that cannot be recreated using traditional synthesizers alone.

Subtronics also embraces unconventional sampling techniques, chopping up and manipulating samples in unconventional ways. By experimenting with granular synthesis or reversing audio, they create interesting and otherworldly sounds that take their tracks to new heights.

Overall, Subtronics' commitment to experimenting with new sounds and techniques is what sets them apart in the music industry. Their fearless approach to sonic exploration, genre fusion, and embracing cutting-edge technologies pushes the boundaries of what is possible in electronic music. As they continue to evolve and innovate, who knows what exciting sounds and techniques they will bring to our ears next.

Honing Their Skills through Practice and Feedback

Becoming a skilled musician doesn't just happen overnight. It takes years of practice, dedication, and a willingness to continually seek feedback and improvement. For Subtronics, honing their skills has been a crucial part of their journey to success. In this section, we will explore the strategies they have used to refine their craft and push their musical boundaries.

The Value of Practice

Practice is the backbone of any artist's development, and Subtronics understands the importance of putting in the hours to master their craft. They have devoted countless hours to perfecting their skills, whether it's mastering a new technique on their instruments or fine-tuning their production skills in the studio.

But practice is not just about repetition; it's about deliberate practice. This means setting specific goals, breaking down complex skills into smaller components, and focusing on areas that need improvement. Subtronics has adopted this approach to maximize their practice sessions and accelerate their progress.

Example: One area where Subtronics has put in deliberate practice is in their sound design skills. They have dedicated time to experimenting with different synthesizers, effects, and plugins to create unique and innovative sounds that set them apart from other artists. By focusing on this aspect of their music, they have been able to refine their signature sound and develop a recognizable style.

Seeking Constructive Feedback

While practice is important, it can only take an artist so far. To truly grow and improve, feedback from others is essential. Subtronics has embraced this principle and actively seeks constructive criticism from trusted sources, including fellow musicians, industry professionals, and their loyal fan base.

Receiving feedback can sometimes be challenging, as it requires an artist to be open to criticism and willing to make changes. However, Subtronics understands that feedback is an invaluable tool for growth and development. They view it as an opportunity to learn from others, identify areas of improvement, and refine their skills.

Example: Subtronics actively shares their works-in-progress with a select group of collaborators, who provide feedback and suggestions on their tracks. This allows them to gain different perspectives and make revisions that enhance the overall quality of their music. By incorporating feedback into their creative process, they are able to continually evolve and push the boundaries of their sound.

Embracing Failure as a Learning Opportunity

In the journey towards mastery, setbacks and failures are inevitable. Subtronics recognizes that failure is not a dead end, but rather a stepping stone towards improvement. Instead of letting failure discourage them, they use it as a learning opportunity to identify areas that need work and to develop new strategies for success.

By embracing failure, Subtronics is able to maintain a growth mindset and approach their craft with resilience and determination. They see each setback as a chance to refine their skills and develop a deeper understanding of their art.

Example: One example of Subtronics embracing failure is when they encountered technical difficulties during a live performance. Rather than letting it derail their set, they improvised and turned the situation into a unique and memorable experience for the audience. This ability to adapt and thrive in challenging situations is a testament to their commitment to continual improvement.

Continuous Learning and Exploration

Music is an ever-evolving field, and Subtronics understands the importance of staying up-to-date with the latest trends and techniques. They are avid learners, always seeking new sources of inspiration and expanding their musical knowledge.

Subtronics actively engages in research, attends music conferences, and collaborates with other artists to stay at the forefront of the EDM scene. They are constantly exploring new genres, experimenting with different production techniques, and pushing the boundaries of electronic music.

Example: In their quest for continuous learning, Subtronics has explored genres beyond their primary focus, such as hip-hop and trap. This has allowed them to incorporate elements from these genres into their music, adding a unique flavor to their sound. By embracing new styles, they have expanded their creative palette and kept their music fresh and exciting.

Unconventional Practice Techniques

To keep their skills sharp and their creativity flowing, Subtronics employs unconventional practice techniques that challenge them to think outside the box. These techniques can involve anything from improvising with different instruments to experimenting with new software and technology.

By embracing unconventional methods, Subtronics taps into their creativity and explores uncharted territory in their music. This approach keeps their practice sessions engaging and helps them discover new tricks and techniques that can elevate their sound to the next level.

Example: One unconventional practice technique Subtronics uses is creating music in unusual environments. They have been known to bring their equipment to unconventional locations, such as the great outdoors or abandoned buildings, and find inspiration from the unique sounds and atmosphere around them. This approach not only challenges their creativity but also allows them to break away from traditional studio settings and find new perspectives on their music.

Conclusion

Honing their skills through practice and feedback has been a fundamental aspect of Subtronics' musical journey. By dedicating themselves to deliberate practice, seeking constructive feedback, embracing failure, continuously learning, and exploring unconventional techniques, they have been able to constantly evolve and refine their craft.

Aspiring musicians can learn from Subtronics' approach and apply these strategies to their own artistic endeavors. The path to success is not always easy, but with dedication, perseverance, and a commitment to growth, one can reach new heights and leave a lasting impact on the music industry.

The Evolution of Their Signature Sound

The signature sound of Subtronics is the heart and soul of the band. It is a culmination of their musical journey, influences, and experimentation. Over the years, they have honed and refined their sound, pushing the boundaries of electronic music and creating a unique and recognizable style.

Finding Inspiration from Daily Life

Like any artist, Subtronics finds inspiration in the world around them. From the hustle and bustle of city life to the serenity of nature, they draw from their daily experiences to infuse their music with emotion and creativity. The chaotic energy of a crowded street, the peacefulness of a sunrise, or the thrill of a night out with friends - all these moments find their way into their compositions.

Turning Ideas into Tracks

The creative process for Subtronics involves transforming ideas into tracks that evoke a particular mood or atmosphere. They start with a simple concept, a melody, or a catchy beat and build upon it layer by layer. Each element is carefully crafted and arranged to create a cohesive and engaging musical narrative.

To capture the essence of their ideas, Subtronics relies on their technical skills and knowledge of music production. They use a wide range of software and hardware tools to manipulate sounds, merge different genres, and experiment with new techniques. This versatility allows them to bring their creative vision to life.

Experimenting with New Sounds and Techniques

Subtronics is known for pushing the boundaries of electronic music, and they continually strive to introduce fresh sounds and techniques into their music. They are not afraid to take risks and explore uncharted territories, constantly staying ahead of the curve.

One way they achieve this is by experimenting with different musical genres and blending them together. By combining elements of bass music, dubstep, trap, and hip-hop, they create a fusion that is uniquely their own. This genre-bending approach keeps their music innovative, exciting, and ever-evolving.

In addition to experimenting with genres, Subtronics also embraces new production techniques. They are constantly on the lookout for new plugins, software, and equipment to enhance their sound. Whether it's using granular synthesis to create unconventional textures or manipulating vocals with creative effects, they are always searching for ways to push the boundaries of their production.

Honing Their Skills through Practice and Feedback

Becoming a master of their craft requires dedication, practice, and a willingness to grow. Subtronics understands this and is committed to constantly improving their skills. They spend countless hours refining their production techniques, experimenting with new sounds, and exploring different creative avenues.

But it's not just about practice; feedback also plays a crucial role in their evolution. Subtronics actively seeks input and criticism from fellow artists, mentors, and their dedicated fan base. They value the power of constructive feedback in shaping their sound and strive to incorporate it into their creative process.

The Evolution of Their Signature Sound

The signature sound of Subtronics has evolved over time, reflecting their growth as artists and individuals. From the raw and gritty basslines of their early days to the more polished and intricate compositions of their recent work, their sound has undergone a remarkable transformation.

The evolution of their signature sound can be attributed to their relentless pursuit of innovation and their willingness to take risks. By constantly exploring new sounds, experimenting with different techniques, and seeking inspiration from diverse sources, they have managed to carve out a distinct sonic identity.

Throughout their musical journey, Subtronics has stayed true to their roots while embracing change. They have blended their early influences with new styles, creating a sound that is at once familiar yet refreshing. Their commitment to pushing the boundaries of electronic music has allowed them to stand out in a crowded industry and attract a dedicated following.

Unleashing Their Signature Sound

Subtronics' evolution is not limited to the studio; their signature sound truly comes alive during their electrifying live performances. Through the combination of their carefully crafted productions and their magnetic stage presence, they immerse their audience in an otherworldly sonic experience.

Their high-energy performances, complete with bone-rattling bass drops and infectious rhythms, create an electrifying atmosphere that leaves the crowd yearning for more. From small club shows to massive festival stages, Subtronics has mastered the art of captivating audiences and creating a sense of unity through their music.

In conclusion, the evolution of Subtronics' signature sound is a testament to their dedication to the craft and their commitment to pushing the boundaries of electronic music. Through inspiration from daily life, turning ideas into tracks, experimenting with new sounds and techniques, honing their skills, and embracing change, they have continuously redefined their sonic identity. With every release and live performance, Subtronics unleashes their signature sound, leaving an indelible mark on the EDM scene and inspiring the next generation of artists to explore new sonic territories.

Section Four: Behind the Scenes of a Subtronics Show

Planning and Preparation for Live Performances

Planning and preparation are crucial elements in the process of creating a memorable live performance as Subtronics. In this section, we delve into the behind-the-scenes work that goes into ensuring a seamless and electrifying show for their audience. From selecting the right setlist to technical considerations, Subtronics leaves no stone unturned when it comes to creating an unforgettable experience.

The Art of Setlist Curation

One of the most important aspects of planning a live performance is crafting the perfect setlist. Subtronics carefully selects tracks that will take their audience on a journey, creating a flow that keeps them engaged and energized throughout the show. Their setlists are designed to build anticipation, creating peaks and valleys that enhance the overall experience.

To curate the setlist, Subtronics considers factors such as tempo, energy level, and crowd response. They strategically place high-energy bangers and signature tracks in key moments to create maximum impact. Additionally, they incorporate a mixture of fan favorites and unreleased tracks to keep their performance fresh and exciting.

Example: Imagine Subtronics is preparing for a festival performance. They start with an energetic opener that immediately grabs the audience's attention—a track with heavy bass and catchy melodies. This sets the tone for the rest of the set and establishes their unique sound. As the set progresses, they transition into deeper and heavier tracks, allowing the audience to explore the different facets of their music. Towards the end, they build up to an explosive finale, leaving the crowd wanting more.

Technical Considerations

Behind every successful live performance is a team of experts handling the technical aspects. Subtronics works closely with their crew to ensure that the sound, lighting, and special effects are perfectly synchronized with their music, creating a multi-sensory experience for the audience.

Sound Design and Production: Subtronics pays attention to every detail of their sound design, working closely with their production team to ensure optimal sound quality. They collaborate on finding the perfect balance of bass frequencies, ensuring that the audience can feel the music in their bones without overpowering other elements. Subtronics' deep understanding of sound engineering allows them to create a unique sonic experience, one that sets them apart from other artists in the industry.

Lighting and Visuals: To enhance the atmosphere and immerse the audience in their world, Subtronics collaborates with visual artists and lighting designers. They work together to create a visual narrative that complements the music, using a combination of lighting effects, projections, and LED screens. The visuals are carefully synchronized with the music, amplifying the impact of each drop and creating a visually stunning performance.

Stage Presence and Energy: Subtronics understands the importance of stage presence and engages with the audience throughout their performance. They exude energy and enthusiasm, drawing the crowd into their world and creating a sense of unity. Their charismatic stage presence electrifies the atmosphere, leaving the audience captivated from start to finish.

Technical Challenges and Solutions: As with any live performance, Subtronics faces technical challenges that need to be addressed promptly. From equipment malfunctions to unforeseen issues with sound and lighting, they have encountered their fair share of obstacles. To overcome these challenges, they have a dedicated technical team that is well-versed in troubleshooting and finding quick solutions. They also have backup equipment readily available to minimize any disruptions during their show.

Collaborating with Visual Artists and VJs

In addition to their meticulous planning and technical considerations, Subtronics collaborates with visual artists and VJs to enhance the visual experience of their live performances. These creative partnerships allow them to create a synergy between music and visuals, elevating their shows to another level.

Visual artists work closely with Subtronics to develop custom visuals that reflect the mood and narrative of their music. This collaboration involves a deep understanding of Subtronics' style and aesthetic, allowing the visuals to seamlessly blend with the music's energy and vibe.

VJs, on the other hand, take the visuals to the live performance realm, operating in real-time during the show. They mix and manipulate the visuals based on the energy of the crowd, creating a dynamic and immersive experience. The synchronization between the visuals and music is crucial, as it enhances the impact of drops and intensifies the overall experience.

Example: Imagine Subtronics is performing their track "Griztronics" during a festival set. The visual artist collaborates with the VJ to create a visually stunning representation of the gritty, bass-heavy track. The visuals might feature vibrant neon colors, rapid and glitchy animations, and synchronized light patterns that match the rhythm and intensity of the music. The combination of intense sound, mesmerizing visuals, and an energetic crowd creates an unforgettable performance.

Creating a Memorable Experience

For Subtronics, it's not just about putting on a show—it's about creating a memorable experience for their audience. From the moment fans enter the venue to the final beat drop, Subtronics wants every aspect of their performance to leave a lasting impression.

Stage Design and Props: Subtronics pays special attention to stage design and props to enhance their visual aesthetic. They work closely with set designers and artists to create an atmosphere that reflects the mood of their music. Unique stage elements and props add an extra layer of visual appeal, making each performance visually distinct.

Audience Interaction: Subtronics actively engages with their audience throughout their performance, encouraging crowd participation and creating a sense of connection. Whether it's through call-and-response moments, hyping up the crowd, or interacting with fans at the front row, they make the audience feel like they're a part of the show.

Surprise Elements: To keep their shows fresh and exciting, Subtronics incorporates surprise elements into their performances. This could include bringing out surprise guest artists, debuting unreleased tracks, or showcasing new visuals and stage effects. These unexpected moments add an element of excitement and exclusivity for fans, making each show a unique experience.

Exceptional Closing Moments: Subtronics understands the importance of leaving their audience with a lasting impression. They carefully plan the closing moments of their performance, ensuring that it's a grand finale that still resonates with fans long after the show. This could involve a high-energy mashup of their popular tracks, a surprise remix of a fan favorite, or a sentimental track that brings the audience together in unity.

Creating Long-Term Memories: Subtronics aims to create experiences that fans will remember for years to come. They encourage fans to bring their smartphones and record moments during the show, actively promoting fan engagement and creating a sense of community. By taking the time to connect with

SECTION FOUR: BEHIND THE SCENES OF A SUBTRONICS SHOW 123

their audience and create memorable experiences, Subtronics leaves a lasting impact on their fans' lives.

Planning and preparation for live performances are essential elements in Subtronics' journey to captivate and entertain their audience. From meticulous setlist curation to technical considerations, collaborating with visual artists and VJs, and creating a memorable experience, they put their heart and soul into every aspect of their live shows. Through their dedication and passion, Subtronics continues to push the boundaries of what it means to create a truly immersive and unforgettable live performance.

Technical Challenges and Solutions

In the world of live performances, technical challenges are bound to arise. Subtronics has had their fair share of obstacles to overcome when it comes to delivering flawless shows night after night. From equipment malfunctions to complex setups, they have faced it all. In this section, we will delve into some of the technical challenges that Subtronics has encountered and the innovative solutions they have employed.

Equipment Failures and Malfunctions

One of the biggest nightmares for any live performer is the sudden failure of equipment. Imagine being in the middle of an electrifying set, only to have your audio interface crash or your laptop freeze. For Subtronics, these technical malfunctions have caused a few heart-stopping moments. However, they have developed some effective strategies to handle such situations and ensure a seamless experience for their audience.

Solutions: To combat equipment failures, Subtronics always carries backup gear to every show. This includes extra cables, backup laptops, and duplicate audio interfaces. They have also trained their team to identify and troubleshoot common equipment issues quickly. By having redundancy in their setup, they can seamlessly switch to backup equipment in case of emergencies.

Complex Audio Routing and Mixing

The complexity of Subtronics' music requires a sophisticated setup for audio routing and mixing. With layers of basslines, intricate synth patterns, and heavy drops, the challenge lies in maintaining clarity and balance in the mix. Achieving this level of precision can be quite demanding and time-consuming, but Subtronics has a few tricks up their sleeves.

Solutions: Subtronics makes use of advanced digital audio workstations (DAWs) that allow them to route and mix their tracks with precision. They have also developed custom templates and presets to streamline their workflow and ensure consistency in their live performances. Additionally, they work closely with their sound engineer to fine-tune the mix during rehearsals to achieve the perfect balance.

Integrating Visuals and Lighting

Subtronics' performances are not just about the music; they are immersive visual experiences that captivate the audience. Integrating visuals and lighting seamlessly

SECTION FOUR: BEHIND THE SCENES OF A SUBTRONICS SHOW

with their music adds an extra layer of complexity to their technical setup. Coordinating the timing of visuals, mapping projections, and syncing lighting effects can be demanding, but Subtronics manages to create a mesmerizing visual spectacle every time.

Solutions: Subtronics collaborates with visual artists and VJs who specialize in live performances. They work together to create custom visuals that complement their music perfectly. By using software that allows real-time synchronization between audio and visuals, they ensure that every beat and drop is perfectly accompanied by stunning visuals and lighting effects.

Ensuring Stable Connectivity

With technology being an integral part of live performances, ensuring stable connectivity is crucial for Subtronics. From managing live streams to controlling lighting and visuals, a stable internet connection is essential. However, the lack of reliable internet infrastructure at some venues and the occasional network disruptions present a challenge.

Solutions: Subtronics carries their own dedicated internet hotspot to venues where stable connections cannot be guaranteed. They also work closely with the venue's technical team to ensure proper network setup and troubleshoot any issues that may arise. Additionally, they have backup plans in place, such as pre-recorded sets, in case of severe connectivity issues.

Optimizing Sound for Different Venues

Each venue presents unique acoustic challenges that can affect the overall sound experience. Whether it is a small club or a large festival stage, Subtronics aims to deliver their music in its full glory, regardless of the venue's characteristics. Adapting to different acoustics requires careful consideration and strategic adjustments.

Solutions: Subtronics collaborates closely with their sound engineer to optimize the sound for each venue. They conduct sound checks and adjustments before every performance to ensure that the music sounds perfect in the given space. They also make use of acoustic treatment materials and equipment, such as absorbers and diffusers, to overcome any problematic room resonances and reflections.

Innovative Approach: Interactive LED Wristbands

Subtronics loves to create an immersive experience for their fans, and one of their innovative solutions to further engage the audience is through the use of interactive LED wristbands. These wristbands are synchronized with the music and visuals, allowing the audience to become an integral part of the show.

Solution: Subtronics has collaborated with technology companies to develop custom LED wristbands that respond to the music and visuals in real-time. This not only enhances the visual spectacle but also creates a sense of unity and connection among the audience. The synchronized pulsations of the wristbands create a stunning visual display, turning the crowd into an active participant in the performance.

In conclusion, Subtronics has encountered various technical challenges throughout their live performances. However, through careful planning, innovation, and teamwork, they have managed to overcome these obstacles and deliver unforgettable experiences to their fans. Their dedication to continuously improve their technical setup ensures that every show is a flawless and immersive journey into the world of Subtronics.

The Importance of Stage Presence and Energy

When it comes to live performances, stage presence and energy are crucial elements that can make or break a show. Subtronics understands this better than anyone, and their electrifying stage presence is what sets them apart from other artists in the electronic music scene. In this section, we will delve into the significance of stage presence and energy and how it contributes to an unforgettable Subtronics experience.

Connecting with the Crowd

One of the key aspects of stage presence is the ability to connect with the crowd on a deep and emotional level. Subtronics excels in this area by creating an energetic and immersive environment where fans can let loose and escape from their daily lives. Their infectious energy is contagious, and it spreads throughout the audience, creating an electric atmosphere.

To achieve this connection, Subtronics utilizes a combination of factors. Onstage, they interact with the crowd, engaging them through dance moves, hand gestures, and constant crowd interaction. They make the audience feel like an integral part of the performance, and this connection fosters a strong bond between artist and fan.

Creating an Unforgettable Experience

Another vital aspect of stage presence and energy is the ability to create an unforgettable experience for the audience. Subtronics achieves this by carefully curating their sets to take listeners on a musical journey. They blend high-energy drops with melodic interludes, creating a dynamic range that keeps the crowd engaged from start to finish.

In addition to the music, Subtronics pays careful attention to their visual production, incorporating stunning visuals, stage lighting, and pyrotechnics. This visual feast complements their music and adds another layer of excitement and immersion to the overall experience. By combining exceptional music with captivating visuals, Subtronics ensures that their shows are unforgettable and leave a lasting impression on their fans.

Building Anticipation and Suspense

Stage presence and energy are also essential in building anticipation and suspense throughout a performance. Subtronics knows how to create suspenseful moments that keep the audience on the edge of their seats, waiting for the drop to hit. They use strategic pauses, build-ups, and well-timed bass drops to maximize the impact of their music.

By building suspense, Subtronics maintains the energy level of the crowd throughout the show. They know when to unleash a heavy drop to drive the audience into a frenzy and when to dial it back to create contrast and build anticipation for the next explosive moment. This careful control of energy ensures a rollercoaster ride of emotions for the fans, keeping them engaged and energized throughout the performance.

Injecting Authenticity and Passion

One of the most remarkable aspects of Subtronics' stage presence is their authenticity and passion. They genuinely love what they do, and it shows in every aspect of their performance. Their energy is infectious because it comes from a place of pure love for the music and the desire to share that love with their fans.

Subtronics' stage presence goes beyond simply playing music. They pour their heart and soul into every performance, and the audience can feel their genuine passion and love for their craft. This authenticity resonates with their fans, fostering a sense of connection and creating an incredibly powerful and memorable experience.

Going Above and Beyond

In true Subtronics fashion, they always go above and beyond to deliver a mind-blowing performance. They push the boundaries of what is expected from a live show, constantly seeking innovative ways to engage the audience and create a unique experience.

From surprise appearances by fellow artists to incorporating live instruments into their sets, Subtronics continuously strives to exceed expectations and provide their fans with an unforgettable experience. They understand the importance of constantly evolving and pushing the limits, and this commitment to excellence sets them apart as true masters of stage presence and energy.

Extraordinary is the Norm

In the world of Subtronics, ordinary is not an option. They consistently deliver extraordinary performances that leave fans craving more. Their stage presence and energy are unparalleled, and they continue to set the bar higher with each show.

Whether it's connecting with the crowd, creating an unforgettable experience, building anticipation and suspense, injecting authenticity and passion, or going above and beyond, Subtronics knows how to captivate their audience and create magic on stage. Their commitment to pushing the limits and constantly evolving ensures that their performances are always fresh, exciting, and full of energy.

As we conclude this section, it is evident that stage presence and energy are vital components of Subtronics' live performances. Their ability to connect with the crowd, create an immersive experience, build anticipation, and inject authenticity and passion sets them apart as true masters of the art. So, the next time you find yourself at a Subtronics show, brace yourself for an unparalleled experience that will leave you in awe and keep the energy flowing long after the last beat drops.

Collaborating with Visual Artists and VJs

Collaboration is at the heart of many artistic endeavors, and Subtronics understands the power of blending their music with captivating visuals. In this section, we explore how the band collaborates with visual artists and VJs (Visual Jockeys) to create electric and immersive experiences for their fans.

SECTION FOUR: BEHIND THE SCENES OF A SUBTRONICS SHOW

The Importance of Visuals in a Performance

Music is a multisensory experience, and incorporating visuals enhances the overall impact of a live performance. Subtronics recognizes that visuals have the power to transport the audience to another world, amplifying the emotions and energy of their music. Whether it's a pulsating light show, mesmerizing projections, or synchronized animations, the visual component plays a crucial role in creating an immersive and unforgettable experience for fans.

Building a Team of Visual Artists and VJs

Like any successful collaboration, finding the right visual artists and VJs is key. Subtronics has assembled a talented team who understand their music and can translate it into stunning visuals. These artists possess an innate ability to complement and enhance the energy of Subtronics' performances, visually capturing the essence of their music.

The band has forged strong relationships with visual artists who share their vision and are able to create visuals that are uniquely tailored to their style and sound. These artists work closely with Subtronics, attending rehearsals, studying their music and performances, and immersing themselves in the world of bass and dubstep.

Transforming Sound into Visuals

The creative process behind developing visuals for Subtronics' music involves a close collaboration between the band and the visual artists. It starts with an in-depth understanding of the music itself, analyzing the structure, rhythm, and energy of the tracks.

Visual artists often listen to the tracks repeatedly, creating a mental landscape that guides their creative vision. They translate the various elements of Subtronics' music, such as the heavy drops, intricate melodies, and pulsating beats, into a visual journey that aligns with the emotions evoked by the music.

Synchronizing Visuals with Music

The magic truly happens when the visuals seamlessly synchronize with the music during a live performance. This is where the VJs come into play. VJs are responsible for live mixing and controlling the visual effects during a show, ensuring that the visuals are closely intertwined with the music being played.

Using specialized software, VJs manipulate and trigger various visual elements in real-time, responding to the music and the energy of the crowd. This dynamic interaction between the VJ, the music, and the audience creates a unique and immersive experience, as the visuals ebb and flow with the music, enhancing its impact.

Experimenting with New Technologies

Subtronics is known for pushing boundaries, not only in their music but also in their production value. With advancements in technology, they constantly seek innovative ways to incorporate new visual elements into their shows. This experimentation allows them to give their fans a fresh and exciting experience with each performance.

From interactive LED displays to holographic projections, Subtronics leverages cutting-edge technology to create breathtaking visual spectacles. They actively explore new possibilities, collaborating with forward-thinking visual artists and VJs to push the limits of what's possible in a live performance.

The Fusion of Sound and Visuals

The collaboration between Subtronics, visual artists, and VJs has resulted in a harmonious fusion of sound and visuals that elevates their live performances to new heights. The synchronized audiovisual experience transports fans into a realm where the music and visual elements seamlessly intertwine, creating an immersive sensory journey.

This fusion of sound and visuals opens up endless possibilities for artistic expression. It allows Subtronics to communicate their message and emotions more powerfully, tapping into the collective energy of the crowd and creating lasting memories for their fans.

Conclusion

Collaborating with visual artists and VJs is an essential part of Subtronics' creative process. By incorporating captivating visuals into their performances, they create an immersive and multisensory experience for their fans. The collaboration between the band, visual artists, and VJs allows for a seamless integration of sound and visuals, pushing the boundaries of what is possible in a live performance. With their focus on experimentation, Subtronics continues to innovate and inspire, leaving a lasting impact on the EDM scene.

The Thrill of Connecting with the Crowd

The connection between a musician and their audience is a powerful and electric force. The thrill of connecting with the crowd is an essential part of the Subtronics experience, and it fuels their passion for performing. In this section, we will delve into the various aspects that contribute to this exhilarating connection and explore how Subtronics creates a memorable experience for their fans.

Understanding the Crowd

One cannot truly connect with an audience without first understanding who they are. Subtronics recognizes the importance of understanding their fans, their preferences, and their expectations. Through extensive market research and careful analysis of fan feedback, they have gained deep insights into their audience's demographics, musical preferences, and desires.

By understanding the demographics of their fans, Subtronics can tailor their performances to cater to different age groups, regions, and cultural backgrounds. This allows them to create a truly inclusive atmosphere where everyone feels welcome and understood. Additionally, understanding the musical preferences of their fans enables Subtronics to curate their setlists and performances to match their audience's tastes, ensuring that they deliver an experience that resonates deeply with their fans.

Creating an Energetic Atmosphere

Subtronics is known for their high-energy performances that leave audiences exhilarated and craving for more. One of the key elements in creating this energetic atmosphere is the use of dynamic and well-crafted setlists. By carefully selecting tracks that build up anticipation and excitement, Subtronics creates a journey for their fans, taking them on a sonic adventure that keeps them engaged throughout the performance.

To enhance the energetic atmosphere, Subtronics incorporates elements of surprise and spontaneity into their performances. This could include dropping unexpected remixes, improvising on the spot, or even inviting guest artists to join them on stage. These elements create an electric atmosphere where anything can happen, keeping the crowd on their toes and fueling their excitement.

Engaging Visuals and Stage Presence

The visual aspect of a live performance plays a crucial role in capturing the attention and interest of the audience. Subtronics understands the power of visuals and invests in captivating stage productions that complement their music. They collaborate with talented visual artists and VJs to create immersive and stimulating visual experiences.

In addition to visual effects, Subtronics' stage presence is a major factor in their ability to connect with the crowd. Riko Garba, the driving force behind Subtronics, is known for his energetic and charismatic presence on stage. His ability to engage the crowd through his movements, interactions, and genuine enthusiasm creates a strong emotional connection between Subtronics and their fans.

Encouraging Audience Participation

Subtronics understands that the connection with their audience is a two-way street. They actively encourage audience participation during their performances, allowing their fans to become an integral part of the show. Whether it's through call-and-response chants, synchronized hand movements, or simply creating an inclusive and accepting environment, Subtronics invites their fans to actively engage and become co-creators of the experience.

This level of audience participation not only enhances the sense of community among fans but also provides a platform for self-expression and emotional release. It allows fans to feel connected not only to Subtronics but also to each other, creating a shared experience that builds lasting memories and fosters a sense of belonging.

Unconventional Interaction: The Mosh Pit Puzzle

While the thrill of connecting with the crowd is usually associated with positive emotions and dancing, there is an unconventional yet relevant aspect to Subtronics' performances that challenges the norm: the mosh pit puzzle.

The mosh pit is a physical space within the crowd where fans engage in intense, energetic, and often aggressive movements. It may seem counterintuitive to the idea of creating a connection, but Subtronics embraces it as a unique way to engage with their fans.

By understanding the mosh pit culture and incorporating it into their performances, Subtronics acknowledges the different ways in which fans connect to their music. This provides an opportunity for fans to express their energy, passion, and emotions in a physical and cathartic manner, allowing for a deeper connection with Subtronics and their music.

To ensure the safety and well-being of their fans, Subtronics actively promotes a culture of respect and consent within the mosh pit. They encourage fans to look out for each other and intervene if someone is in distress. This unconventional form of interaction within the mosh pit reinforces the idea that the connection between

Subtronics and their fans goes beyond the physical and extends to a deeper level of understanding and care.

Conclusion

The thrill of connecting with the crowd is what drives Subtronics, and it is at the heart of their performances. Through a deep understanding of their audience, creating an energetic atmosphere, engaging visuals and stage presence, encouraging audience participation, and embracing unconventional forms of interaction like the mosh pit, Subtronics creates a powerful and unforgettable experience for their fans.

As Subtronics continues to evolve and push the boundaries of electronic music, their ability to connect with their audience remains a fundamental aspect of their success. By nurturing this connection, they not only create a remarkable experience for their fans but also leave a lasting legacy in the music industry. The story of Subtronics continues, fueled by their unwavering passion for music and their ever-growing connection with their fans.

Section Five: The Subtronics Community

Fan Meet and Greets

Fan meet and greets are undoubtedly one of the most exciting and memorable experiences for both fans and artists. It's a chance for fans to connect with their favorite artists on a personal level, get up close and personal, and express their support and admiration. For Subtronics, these meet and greets are not just a mere formality, but rather an opportunity to genuinely interact with their fans and make lasting connections. In this section, we will explore the importance of fan meet and greets for Subtronics, the unique experiences they provide, and the impact they have on both the fans and the band.

The Power of Personal Connection

Fan meet and greets offer a unique chance for Subtronics to create a personal connection with their fans. It allows them to show their appreciation for the support and love they receive from their fans. Meeting face-to-face, sharing a conversation, and taking photos creates a sense of intimacy and genuine connection that is cherished by both the fans and the band.

Creating Memorable Experiences

Subtronics understands the significance of creating memorable experiences during meet and greets. They go the extra mile to make these encounters special, often surprising their fans with personalized gifts, handwritten notes, or even impromptu performances. These small gestures leave a lasting impression on the fans and make the meet and greet experience truly unforgettable.

Building a Strong Fan Community

Fan meet and greets offer a platform for Subtronics to strengthen their fan community. These events bring together fans from different walks of life who share a common love for Subtronics' music. It creates a space where fans can bond, share their experiences, and form lasting friendships. This sense of community fosters a supportive and inclusive environment, both online and offline.

The Impact on Fans

Fan meet and greets have a profound impact on the fans. It gives them an opportunity to express their gratitude and share personal stories of how Subtronics' music has touched their lives. Meeting their favorite artists in person reinforces their love for the music and intensifies the emotional connection they feel with the band. It inspires them to continue supporting Subtronics and be an active part of their journey.

The Impact on Subtronics

For Subtronics, fan meet and greets are an invaluable source of motivation and inspiration. Seeing the impact their music has on their fans firsthand reaffirms their commitment to creating music that resonates with people on a deeper level. It reminds them of the responsibility they have as artists to continue pushing boundaries and making a positive impact through their art.

Creating Lasting Memories

Fan meet and greets are not just about the time spent during the event itself but also about the memories created that will last a lifetime. Fans often recount the excitement, nervousness, and joy they felt during these encounters. The photographs taken, autographs received, and the genuine connections made become cherished possessions that fans hold dear for years to come.

SECTION FIVE: THE SUBTRONICS COMMUNITY

Empowering Fans

Subtronics believes in the power of their fans and strives to create an empowering environment during meet and greets. They actively listen to their fans' stories and experiences, offer words of encouragement, and provide a space where fans feel heard and valued. These interactions fuel the fans' confidence and inspire them to pursue their own passions and dreams.

Unconventional Fan Interactions

Subtronics is known for their creativity and willingness to think outside the box. In addition to traditional meet and greets, they have been known to surprise their fans with unconventional fan interactions. This can range from impromptu dance parties to spontaneous Q&A sessions or even inviting fans on stage to join them during a song. These unexpected moments create an atmosphere of excitement and unpredictability, leaving fans with unforgettable memories.

In conclusion, fan meet and greets hold immense significance for Subtronics and their fans. They offer a platform for genuine connections, create lasting memories, and build a strong fan community. These interactions inspire both the fans and the band, empowering them to continue creating music that touches the hearts of their listeners. With their commitment to fan engagement and unique approach to meet and greets, Subtronics demonstrates their dedication to their fans and the impact they have on their lives.

Online Fan Interactions and Social Media Presence

In this digital age, it is impossible to ignore the power and influence of social media. Subtronics understands this and has leveraged their online presence to connect and engage with their fans in a meaningful way. Through various social media platforms, they have created a strong and dedicated fan base, establishing themselves as not just musicians, but also as relatable individuals who genuinely care about their supporters.

The Importance of Social Media

Social media platforms like Instagram, Twitter, and Facebook have become central to the way artists connect with their fans. For Subtronics, these platforms serve as a virtual gathering place where their fans can come together to discuss music, upcoming shows, and share their experiences. Social media acts as a bridge that narrows the gap between the artists and their fans, creating a sense of community and belonging.

Engaging with Fans

Subtronics understands the importance of keeping their fans engaged and involved in their journey. They utilize social media to continuously update their followers about upcoming releases, tours, and behind-the-scenes glimpses into their lives. By offering this exclusive content, they make their fans feel like part of the Subtronics family.

Live Q&A Sessions: One of the ways Subtronics engages with their fans is through live question and answer (Q&A) sessions on platforms like Instagram Live or Twitter Spaces. These sessions allow fans to ask questions directly to Subtronics, providing an opportunity for real-time interaction. This not only gives fans a chance to connect with the artists on a more personal level but also provides insight into their thoughts, inspirations, and creative processes.

Contests and Giveaways: Subtronics keeps the energy high by organizing contests and giveaways exclusively for their followers. These can include anything from signed merchandise to VIP experiences at their shows. By rewarding their fans, Subtronics nurtures a sense of loyalty and appreciation within their community, making their fans feel valued and recognized for their support.

Fan-Made Content Highlights: Subtronics recognizes the talent and creativity within their fan base and often shares fan-made art, remixes, and cover songs on their social media platforms. By showcasing and promoting fan-created content, they not only empower their fans but also inspire others to get involved and contribute to the community.

Creating a Safe Space

Social media can be a mixed bag, often filled with negativity and hate. Subtronics, however, strives to create a safe space for their fans online. They actively moderate and remove any bullying or harmful comments to ensure that their followers can engage in discussions without fear of being attacked or judged. This commitment to maintaining a positive environment has allowed their online community to flourish, fostering a sense of support and acceptance amongst their fans.

Social Media in Action

The power of social media is evident in the way Subtronics has harnessed it to grow their fan base and strengthen their presence in the music industry. Through strategic use of their social media platforms, they have been able to cultivate a passionate following that extends beyond the confines of a concert venue. This loyal fan base not only supports Subtronics at their shows but also actively shares their music and spreads the word through their own social networks.

Online Collaborations: Social media has opened up opportunities for Subtronics to collaborate with other artists and producers, without the restrictions of physical proximity. They have been able to connect with musicians from around the world, fostering creative partnerships and expanding their musical offerings.

Real-Time Updates: Platforms like Twitter allow Subtronics to provide real-time updates about tour dates, releases, and other news. This immediate connection with their fans creates a buzz and generates excitement, ensuring that their followers are always in the loop and have timely access to the latest information.

Fan Demographics and Analytics: Another advantage of social media is the analytics it provides. Subtronics can gather insights into their fans' demographics, geographic location, and engagement patterns. This information helps them tailor their content and marketing strategies to better reach and connect with their target audience.

Unconventional and Fun Interactions

Subtronics understands that being creative and unconventional is key to standing out on social media. They regularly experiment with unique and fun ways of engaging with their fans, keeping them entertained and coming back for more.

Viral Challenges: Subtronics leverages the power of viral challenges to engage their fans in a fun and interactive way. These challenges could involve dancing to a specific track, creating fan videos, or recreating iconic moments from their live performances. By encouraging fan participation and showcasing their creativity, Subtronics creates a buzz that extends beyond their core fan base, reaching new potential listeners.

Behind-the-Scenes Content: Fans love getting a glimpse into the life of their favorite artists. Subtronics understands this and shares behind-the-scenes content, such as studio sessions, tour preparations, and candid moments on social media. By giving fans an exclusive look into their world, Subtronics creates a sense of intimacy and authenticity, making their fans feel more connected and invested in their journey.

Interactive Storytelling: Subtronics utilizes social media features like Instagram Stories and Twitter threads to weave interactive storytelling experiences for their fans. They may share anecdotes, ask fans to vote on song choices, or involve them in decision-making processes. This hands-on approach encourages active participation from their followers and creates a sense of ownership within the Subtronics community.

Conclusion

Subtronics has mastered the art of online fan interactions and social media presence. By utilizing various platforms, they have built a strong and connected fan base. Their strategic approach to engaging with fans, creating a safe space, and involving their followers in their journey has allowed them to establish not just a musical following but a supportive community. Subtronics continues to explore new and inventive ways of connecting with their fans, keeping the energy high and ensuring that their legacy extends far beyond their music.

Creating a Safe Space for Fans

Creating a safe and inclusive space for fans is of utmost importance to Subtronics. From the beginning of their journey, they have prioritized fostering a community that is welcoming, respectful, and supportive. In this section, we will explore the various initiatives and practices that Subtronics has implemented to ensure that their fans feel safe and valued.

Understanding the Importance of a Safe Space

Subtronics recognizes that attending live music events can sometimes be an overwhelming or intimidating experience for fans. They understand that fans should have the freedom to express themselves and enjoy the music without fear of judgment or harm. Moreover, they believe that the energy and connection fostered within a fan community can greatly enhance the overall experience for everyone involved.

Safe Space Guidelines

To create a safe environment at their shows, Subtronics has established clear guidelines to ensure that fans are aware of the expectations and can hold each other accountable. These guidelines, often displayed prominently at venues and on social media platforms, include:

- Respect for personal boundaries: Encouraging fans to ask for consent before interacting physically with others, including in dancing or moshing situations.

- Zero-tolerance for harassment or discrimination: Empowering fans to report any incidents of harassment, sexism, racism, or any form of discrimination to the appropriate authorities.

- Inclusivity and diversity: Celebrating and embracing the diversity of their fan base, fostering an inclusive environment where everyone feels welcomed and valued.

- Look out for one another: Encouraging fans to be mindful of each other's well-being, supporting those who may be feeling overwhelmed, and intervening in situations where someone is being mistreated.

- Awareness of substance use: Promoting responsible and safe substance use practices, as well as providing harm reduction resources and information to fans.

Security and Support Staff

Subtronics, in collaboration with venues and event organizers, ensures that there is an adequate number of trained security and support staff present at their shows. These individuals are responsible for maintaining the safety and well-being of the fans. They are trained to de-escalate conflicts, identify and address any instances of harassment, and provide support to those in need. Fans are encouraged to approach these staff members if they have any concerns or require assistance.

Fan Education and Engagement

Subtronics actively engages with their fan base through various platforms, including social media, newsletters, and fan clubs. They utilize these channels to educate their fans about important topics such as consent, mental health awareness, substance abuse prevention, and the promotion of a safe and inclusive environment.

They regularly share resources, articles, and promote organizations that align with their values, providing their fans with opportunities to learn more and get involved. Additionally, they use their platforms to address any issues or concerns raised by their fans and openly communicate their commitment to creating a safe space.

Collaboration with Fan Organizations

Subtronics believes that the power to create a safe and supportive community extends beyond their own efforts. They actively collaborate with existing fan organizations and grassroots initiatives that share their values and are dedicated to promoting inclusivity and safety within the music scene.

By partnering with these organizations, they are able to amplify the impact of their message, reach a wider audience, and provide additional resources to their fans. This collaborative approach allows for a collective and united effort towards creating a safe space for all.

Innovative Safety Measures

In their quest to ensure the well-being of their fans, Subtronics also explores and implements innovative safety measures. For example, they have partnered with technology companies to develop mobile applications that enable fans to report incidents or request assistance discreetly and in real-time. These apps include features such as panic buttons and location-sharing capabilities to facilitate a rapid response from event organizers and security personnel.

Furthermore, Subtronics actively engages with their fans through various feedback channels to gather suggestions and identify areas for improvement. This feedback-driven approach allows them to continually refine their practices and implement new safety measures that address the evolving needs of their fan community.

The Ripple Effect

Subtronics' commitment to creating a safe space has had a rippling effect throughout the EDM community. Their advocacy and implementation of safe space initiatives have inspired other artists, event organizers, and venues to take similar steps to prioritize fan safety and inclusivity.

Through their influence, Subtronics has played a significant role in shifting the culture within the music industry, encouraging other artists to use their platform to promote respect, kindness, and inclusivity. The impact of their efforts extends far beyond their own fan base and helps shape a more positive and inclusive space for music lovers around the world.

Conclusion

Creating a safe space for fans is not just a responsibility for Subtronics, but also a passion and a mission. They recognize the power of music to bring people together and strive to create an environment where fans can fully immerse themselves in the experience without fear or judgment. Through their guidelines, education initiatives, collaborations, and innovative safety measures, Subtronics continues to pave the way for a more inclusive and safe music community. Their commitment to fostering a supportive environment for all is a testament to the enduring impact of their music and the genuine care they have for their fans.

Fan-Made Art and Fan Clubs

Fan-Made Art and Fan Clubs play a significant role in the success of Subtronics, as they contribute to the strong sense of community and connection that surrounds the band. The fandom not only appreciates Subtronics' music but also actively participates in creating art inspired by their music and forming their own communities to support and celebrate the band. Let's dive into the world of Fan-Made Art and Fan Clubs and explore the impact they have on Subtronics' journey.

The Power of Fan-Made Art

Fan-Made Art has always been a crucial part of music culture, and Subtronics is no exception. The band's unique sound and visually stunning performances inspire fans to express their love and admiration through various forms of art, including paintings, drawings, digital illustrations, and even tattoos.

The band's distinctive logo, album covers, and iconic visuals serve as the foundation for fan creativity. Fans channel their passion into designing intricate and eye-catching artworks that capture the energy and spirit of Subtronics' music. Through their art, fans not only showcase their talent but also pay homage to the band and create a connection with other like-minded individuals.

The band acknowledges and celebrates the creativity of their fans by sharing their artworks on social media, using them as cover photos, or even collaborating with artists for official merchandise. This interaction between the band and their fans strengthens the bond between them and creates a sense of unity within the Subtronics community.

Fan Clubs: Uniting the Subtronics Community

Fan Clubs provide a space for Subtronics fans to connect, share their love for the band, and form meaningful relationships with fellow fans. These fan clubs, whether in-person or online, act as a hub for discussions, meet-ups, sharing exclusive content, and organizing fan-driven events.

Online platforms such as Discord, Reddit, and Facebook groups serve as virtual gathering places for fans, where they can engage in discussions about the band's music, upcoming shows, and collaborate on various fan-led initiatives. These platforms not only foster a sense of belonging but also provide a support network for fans who may feel isolated in their love for Subtronics in their local communities.

In addition to online communities, fan clubs often organize fan-driven events such as listening parties, themed gatherings, and meet-ups before or after Subtronics' shows. These events allow fans to come together, celebrate the band's music in a shared physical space, and create lasting memories.

Fan clubs also contribute to Subtronics' success by acting as a grassroots marketing force. Fans enthusiastically promote the band's music and shows within their networks, attracting new listeners and expanding the Subtronics community. This organic word-of-mouth advertising helps Subtronics reach a wider audience beyond the traditional music industry channels.

Supporting Fans' Artistic Growth

Subtronics recognizes the importance of supporting fans' artistic growth and regularly engages with their artistic community by organizing contests, collaborations, or spotlight features on their social media channels. These initiatives encourage fans to enhance their skills, explore new creative avenues, and connect with other artists within the Subtronics community.

For example, Subtronics may hold a remix contest or invite fans to submit their artworks for a chance to be featured in their music videos or official merchandise. These opportunities not only provide exposure for aspiring artists but also serve as a platform for Subtronics to showcase the immense artistic talent within their fan base.

Moreover, Subtronics often partners with local art collectives or sponsors art events in collaboration with their fans. These collaborations allow fans to exhibit their work, gain recognition, and connect with other like-minded individuals. The band's support for their fans' artistic endeavors further strengthens the sense of community and reinforces the mutual appreciation between Subtronics and their fans.

The Impact of Fan-Made Art and Fan Clubs on Subtronics

The influence of Fan-Made Art and Fan Clubs on Subtronics cannot be overstated. These aspects of fan culture provide a creative outlet for fans to express their love for the band, contribute to the band's visual identity, and foster a strong sense of community within the Subtronics fandom.

By actively engaging with their fans' art and supporting fan-led initiatives, Subtronics deepens the connection with their audience, creating a symbiotic relationship where the fans' creativity feeds and inspires the band's own artistic growth. This reciprocal interaction fuels the band's evolution and contributes to their continued success.

Furthermore, the organic promotion and grassroots marketing efforts by fan clubs help Subtronics expand their reach and attract new listeners. The dedicated fan base becomes an integral part of Subtronics' brand, influencing the perception of the band and contributing to their overall image in the music industry.

In conclusion, Fan-Made Art and Fan Clubs provide a powerful means for Subtronics fans to express their passion, form connections with each other, and contribute to the band's success. These forms of fan engagement give rise to a vibrant and supportive community that plays a crucial role in shaping the Subtronics narrative. The band recognizes and celebrates the impact of their fans' creativity, embracing their artistry and reflecting it back in their own music, performances, and collaborative efforts. The enduring bond between Subtronics and their fans is illuminated through the art created, shared, and celebrated within the fan community, leaving an indelible mark on the band's legacy.

Fan-made art is like the visual representation of the heartbeat of Subtronics. Our fans pour their love and creativity into every stroke, every pixel, and every piece of art they create. Their artwork brings our music to life in ways we couldn't have imagined, and we are forever grateful for their incredible support.Jesse Kardon (Subtronics)

Trivia: Did you know that Subtronics occasionally features fan-made art as part of their stage visuals during live performances? It's a way for them to showcase and celebrate their fans' creativity on a grand scale, creating a visually stunning and immersive experience for the audience.

The Power of a Supportive Fan Base

The success of any music band is heavily reliant on the support and loyalty of their fan base. For Subtronics, their dedicated following not only sustains their career but also plays a crucial role in shaping their identity as artists. In this section, we delve into the significance of a supportive fan base and how it has propelled Subtronics to new heights.

The Connection Between Artists and Fans

At the heart of the Subtronics story is the deep connection and bond between the artists and their fans. The music they create resonates with a diverse audience, crossing boundaries of age, culture, and background. But what truly sets them apart is their unique ability to foster a sense of community and inclusivity among their fans.

Subtronics understands that their success is intrinsically tied to the love and appreciation of their followers. They actively engage with their fans through various channels, including social media platforms, fan meet and greets, and online interactions. This personal connection allows them to understand the wants and needs of their audience, and in turn, deliver music and experiences that are tailor-made for their community.

Empowerment and Emotional Support

One of the most powerful aspects of having a supportive fan base is the empowerment it brings to the artists. Subtronics has witnessed firsthand how their music has impacted the lives of their fans, offering solace, inspiration, and a sense of belonging. The uplifting lyrics, electrifying beats, and euphoric drops created by Subtronics have become anthems for their fans, serving as a source of motivation and emotional support.

Through their music and live performances, Subtronics provides an outlet for fans to let loose, escape from reality, and experience pure joy. The energy and excitement that emanate from the crowd in response to their music energize Subtronics, fueling their creativity and pushing them to new artistic heights.

Community Engagement and Philanthropy

Subtronics recognizes the responsibility that comes with their platform and actively uses their influence to uplift and support their community. They prioritize community engagement and encourage their fans to take part in charitable initiatives and social causes. Subtronics organizes fundraisers, donation drives, and volunteer activities, facilitating a sense of collective responsibility and giving back to those in need.

By using their music as a catalyst for positive change, Subtronics showcases the power of unity and encourages their fans to be active participants in creating a better world. This shared purpose strengthens the bond between the artists and their fan base, as they work together towards a common goal.

Fan-Created Art and Fan Clubs

Subtronics fans are known for their incredible creativity and passion. Fan-made art, including illustrations, merchandise designs, and music videos, showcases the impact Subtronics has had on their lives. This outpouring of talent and devotion exemplifies the deep connection that exists between the artists and their fans.

Fan clubs play a significant role in fostering a supportive environment for Subtronics enthusiasts. These clubs provide a platform for fans to connect, share their love for the music, and organize events and initiatives. The support and camaraderie within these fan communities further strengthen the bond between Subtronics and their loyal supporters.

The Influence on Their Artistic Journey

The support and enthusiasm of their fan base act as a driving force behind Subtronics' artistic growth and evolution. Feedback from their fans informs their creative decisions, allowing them to continuously refine and innovate their music. The love and encouragement they receive act as a catalyst for their exploration of new sounds, genres, and collaborations.

Subtronics values the trust their fans place in them and constantly strives to exceed their expectations. They experiment with new styles while staying true to their signature sound, ensuring that their fans are always treated to a fresh and unique musical experience. This reciprocal relationship between the artists and their fans creates a virtuous cycle of growth and inspiration.

Conclusion

The power of a supportive fan base cannot be overstated in the journey of Subtronics. Their community of dedicated followers has played a vital role in shaping their identity, propelling them to success and inspiring their continued growth as artists. The connection between Subtronics and their fans is a win-win situation, where the artists thrive on the support they receive, while fans are rewarded with music that resonates with their souls. The influence of the fan base extends beyond the music itself, fostering a sense of empowerment, unity, and compassion that makes Subtronics more than just a band—it becomes a movement. The story of Subtronics stands as a testament to the profound impact that a supportive fan base can have on the journey of an artist.

Chapter Three: The Evolution of Subtronics

Section One: Musical Growth and Exploration

Expanding Their Range and Experimenting with New Genres

As Subtronics continued to grow in popularity, they found themselves longing to push the boundaries of their creativity and explore new genres. They wanted to expand their range and experiment with different styles of music, not just to keep their sound fresh, but also to challenge themselves as artists. This section will delve into their journey of musical growth and exploration, highlighting the factors that influenced their decisions and the impact it had on their overall sound.

Embracing Diversity in Music

Subtronics believed that true artistry comes from embracing diversity in music. They were inspired by a wide range of genres including hip-hop, metal, jazz, and classical music, and they recognized that incorporating elements from different genres could lead to a unique and captivating sound. Their willingness to experiment and push boundaries allowed them to continuously evolve and surprise their fans with every new release.

Learning from Collaborations

Collaborations played an integral role in Subtronics' journey of musical exploration. By working with artists from different genres, they were able to tap into new musical territories and expand their sonic palette. Collaborations provided them with fresh perspectives and ideas, helping them to grow as artists and gain a deeper understanding of different music styles. These collaborations also allowed them to bridge the gap between genres and attract a broader audience.

Blending Genres Seamlessly

One of the hallmarks of Subtronics' music is their ability to seamlessly blend genres. They mastered the art of combining elements from various genres, creating a sound that was uniquely their own. Whether it was incorporating trap-inspired beats into their dubstep tracks or infusing melodic elements into their hard-hitting bass music, Subtronics' ability to blend genres created a dynamic and captivating listening experience for their fans.

Incorporating Live Instruments

To further expand their range and add depth to their sound, Subtronics began incorporating live instruments into their productions. They recognized that the human touch and organic feel of live instruments could bring a whole new dimension to their music. Whether it was the addition of live drums, guitars, or even orchestral elements, the integration of live instruments allowed Subtronics to explore new sonic territories and create a more immersive experience for their fans.

Staying Authentically Subtronics

While Subtronics was eager to explore new genres, they were mindful of staying true to their unique sound and not losing sight of their identity as artists. They understood that experimenting with new styles didn't mean abandoning their roots, but rather expanding the sonic palette of their music. In their quest for musical growth, they remained authentic to themselves, always striving to create music that resonated with their fans and reflected their distinct Subtronics sound.

An Unconventional Inspiration: Nature

As Subtronics ventured into unfamiliar genres, they drew inspiration from an unexpected source – nature. They found solace and inspiration in the beauty of the natural world, and this connection with nature often found its way into their music. From the powerful roar of a thunderstorm to the delicate melody of a birdsong, the sounds of nature served as an unconventional muse for Subtronics, fueling their creativity and shaping their exploration of new genres.

Always Evolving, Never Settling

Subtronics' journey of expanding their range and experimenting with new genres was not a linear path. They encountered obstacles and faced criticism along the way, but they never let it discourage them. Instead, they used it as fuel to keep evolving and refining their craft. They embraced the idea of constant growth, always pushing themselves to explore new horizons and discover new sounds. This relentless pursuit of musical evolution became a defining characteristic of Subtronics' career.

In conclusion, Subtronics' expansion into new genres marked a pivotal point in their musical journey. They embraced diversity, collaborated with artists from different backgrounds, and blended genres seamlessly. By incorporating live instruments and drawing inspiration from nature, they pushed the boundaries of their creativity and established themselves as innovative artists. Through their willingness to experiment and evolve, Subtronics showed that true artistry knows no boundaries and that the pursuit of musical growth is a never-ending adventure.

Exploring Different Collaborations and Features

Collaborations and features are an integral part of Subtronics' musical journey. They have always sought to push the boundaries of their sound by working with a diverse range of artists and incorporating various musical elements into their productions. In this section, we will explore the different collaborations and features that have shaped Subtronics' distinctive style and contributed to their rise in the EDM scene.

Embracing Vocalists and Rappers

One of the standout features of Subtronics' music is the unique combination of heavy bass drops with captivating vocals and rap verses. They have collaborated with a range of talented vocalists and rappers who bring their own distinct flavor to the tracks. By working with artists from different genres, Subtronics has been able to create a fusion sound that appeals to a wide audience.

For instance, in their hit track "Griztronics," Subtronics joined forces with the renowned saxophonist and producer GRiZ. This collaboration not only added a melodic touch to the bass-heavy track but also showcased Subtronics' versatility in working with different instruments and musical styles.

In another collaboration, Subtronics teamed up with rapper Rico Act for the track "The Drip." Rico Act's smooth flow perfectly complements Subtronics' heavy bass drops, creating a high-energy track that combines elements of hip-hop and dubstep.

Exciting Features on Other Artists' Songs

Subtronics' unique sound has garnered attention from other artists in the EDM scene, leading to exciting collaborations and features on other musicians' tracks. These collaborations not only allow Subtronics to showcase their skills and creativity but also introduce their signature sound to a broader audience.

One notable collaboration is Subtronics' feature on the track "Babatunde" by Peekaboo. This collaboration brought together two talented producers known for their heavy bass and intricate sound design, resulting in a track that pushes the boundaries of bass music.

Subtronics has also worked with prominent dubstep artists like Excision and Zeds Dead, lending their production expertise and signature sound to create captivating tracks. These collaborations not only highlight Subtronics' influence in the dubstep scene but also contribute to the evolution of the genre as a whole.

Collaborative Projects with Fellow DJs

In addition to individual collaborations and features, Subtronics has also embarked on collaborative projects with fellow DJs. These joint efforts allow them to explore new creative avenues and combine their skills and musical sensibilities.

One such project is Subtronics' collaboration with the Australian DJ and producer Boogie T. Together, they formed the duo Boogie T.Rio, blending their unique styles to create a captivating fusion of dubstep, reggae, and trap. This collaboration gives Subtronics an opportunity to explore different genres and experiment with new sounds.

Subtronics has also teamed up with fellow bass music producer Svdden Death for the track "Cabbage." This collaboration highlights the synergy between the two artists, resulting in a heavy-hitting and energetic track that showcases their mutual love for bass-driven music.

The Magic of Studio Sessions

Behind every collaboration and feature lies the magic of studio sessions, where artists come together to exchange ideas, experiment with sounds, and create something unique. Subtronics' creative process during these sessions often involves a combination of technical expertise and a willingness to step outside of their comfort zone.

During studio sessions, Subtronics and their collaborators dive deep into sound design, exploring different synthesis techniques and experimenting with various audio effects. These sessions are ripe with creative energy, as both parties bring their unique perspectives and experiences to the table, resulting in truly innovative productions.

Pushing Each Other's Boundaries

Collaborations and features are not just about combining different musical elements but also about challenging and inspiring each other as artists. Subtronics' collaborations have often pushed the boundaries of their own sound, leading to artistic growth and evolution.

By working with a diverse range of artists, Subtronics has been exposed to new ideas, techniques, and perspectives. This exposure has expanded their musical horizons and encouraged them to step out of their artistic comfort zone. Collaborators bring fresh insights and influences to the table, resulting in groundbreaking tracks that defy traditional genre boundaries.

In conclusion, exploring different collaborations and features has been instrumental in shaping Subtronics' unique sound and propelling them forward in the EDM scene. By embracing vocalists, rappers, and fellow DJs, they have been able to tap into new creative territories and continuously push the boundaries of their own music. Studio sessions and shared experiences have allowed for the exchange of ideas and the birth of innovative tracks. Subtronics' dedication to collaboration exemplifies their commitment to creating a dynamic and ever-evolving sound that resonates with a diverse fan base.

Remixing and Reinventing Their Own Tracks

Remixing is a key aspect of Subtronics' musical journey, allowing them to take their own tracks and give them exciting new twists. Through remixing, they are able to bring fresh elements into their music, pushing the boundaries of their sound and constantly reinventing themselves. In this section, we will explore the art and process of remixing, as well as the impact it has had on Subtronics' career.

Understanding Remixing

Remixing is the process of taking an existing song, often from another artist, and reimagining it in a new and unique way. It involves deconstructing the original track and adding new elements such as beats, melodies, and effects to create a fresh interpretation. Remixing allows artists like Subtronics to put their own spin on a song, making it their own while still paying homage to the original.

The goal of remixing is not merely to rearrange elements of the original track, but to enhance it and bring a new perspective. It requires a deep understanding of the original song's structure, melody, and overall feel, as well as the artist's own creative vision. Remixing is a delicate balance between staying true to the essence of the original track and adding something completely unique.

The Process of Remixing

Remixing a track is a multifaceted process that requires technical skill, creativity, and a keen ear for detail. Here is a breakdown of the steps that Subtronics and other artists often follow when remixing their own tracks:

1. **Analyze the original track:** Before diving into the remix, it is essential to listen to and analyze the original track in depth. This includes identifying key elements like the vocal hooks, melodies, chord progressions, and overall structure. By understanding the core components of the original, Subtronics can effectively build upon them and create something new.

2. **Select the elements to remix:** Once the original track has been analyzed, Subtronics decides which elements to keep, modify, or discard. They may choose to isolate certain vocal lines, create new basslines, or experiment with different rhythms. This selection process is crucial in ensuring that the remix maintains the essence of the original while adding a unique touch.

3. **Experiment with new sounds:** Remixing provides an opportunity for Subtronics to explore new sounds and textures. They may experiment with different synthesizers, effects, or samples to give the remix its own distinct flavor. By pushing the boundaries of sound design, they can create an exciting and unpredictable remix.

4. **Add their signature style:** Subtronics infuses their remixes with their signature bass-heavy sound. They use their expertise in bass music and dubstep to bring a fresh perspective to the original track, often incorporating heavy drops, intricate sound design, and complex rhythms. This unique touch helps to distinguish their remixes and makes them instantly recognizable.

5. **Balance familiarity with novelty:** Remixing is a delicate balance between offering something new while still maintaining a level of familiarity. Subtronics strives to strike this balance by incorporating key elements from the original track, such as iconic melodies or vocal hooks, while infusing it with their own style and creativity. This ensures that fans of the original will

SECTION ONE: MUSICAL GROWTH AND EXPLORATION   153

still resonate with the remix while being pleasantly surprised by the fresh elements.

The Impact of Remixing

Remixing has had a significant impact on Subtronics' career, both in terms of artistic growth and fan engagement. Here are a few ways in which remixing has influenced their journey:

- **Expanding their creative boundaries:** Remixing allows Subtronics to step outside their comfort zone and explore new genres and styles. By taking tracks from different artists and genres, they are exposed to diverse musical elements and techniques that they can incorporate into their original productions. This continuous exploration keeps their sound fresh and constantly evolving.

- **Connecting with fans on a deeper level:** Remixing popular tracks or tracks from artists they admire creates an instant connection with their fanbase. Fans of the original track can appreciate the fresh perspective that Subtronics brings to it, while new listeners may discover Subtronics through their remixes. Remixes serve as a bridge between different fan communities, leading to increased support and recognition.

- **Showcasing their versatility:** Remixing allows Subtronics to showcase their versatility as producers. By remixing tracks from various genres, they demonstrate their ability to adapt and reinterpret different styles. This versatility not only expands their audience but also positions them as artists who can thrive in different musical landscapes.

- **Stimulating collaborations and opportunities:** Remixing often leads to collaborations and exciting opportunities for Subtronics. When artists witness the creativity and talent displayed in their remixes, they are more inclined to work with Subtronics on original projects. In addition, their remixes may catch the attention of record labels, promoters, and industry insiders, leading to more bookings and exposure.

- **Engaging fans through live performances:** Remixes play a crucial role in Subtronics' live performances, as they bring a sense of familiarity and excitement to the stage. Dropping a well-known remix during a set ignites the crowd's energy and fosters a strong connection between Subtronics and the audience. Remixes have become an integral part of their live repertoire, ensuring memorable and immersive experiences for their fans.

Overall, remixing has been an essential tool for Subtronics in their artistic journey. It allows them to refresh their own tracks, expand their creative boundaries, and engage with their fanbase on a deeper level. By remixing and reinventing their own tracks, Subtronics continues to make an impact in the electronic music scene and leave their mark on the industry.

Incorporating Live Instruments into Their Productions

One of the key aspects that sets Subtronics apart from other electronic music producers is their incorporation of live instruments into their productions. This unique approach adds a dynamic and organic element to their music, creating a truly immersive experience for their listeners. In this section, we will explore the various ways in which Subtronics integrates live instruments into their productions, the challenges they face, and the creative solutions they employ.

The Power of Live Instruments

Live instruments bring a distinct and human touch to electronic music, adding a level of emotion and expression that cannot be replicated with digital sounds alone. Subtronics understands the value of live instruments in their productions and strives to create moments of genuine connection with their audience. By blending electronic elements with live instruments, they create a unique sound that resonates with fans across different musical backgrounds.

Choosing the Right Instruments

When it comes to incorporating live instruments, Subtronics carefully selects instruments that best complement their musical style. They experiment with a wide range of instruments, such as guitars, drums, brass instruments, and even unconventional choices like the theremin. Each instrument brings its own unique timbre and character to their music, adding depth and richness to the overall sound.

Playing and Recording Live Instruments

Subtronics collaborates with talented musicians to bring their live instruments to life. They work closely with these musicians to ensure that their performances are captured in the best possible way. This involves setting up recording sessions in a controlled environment and using high-quality microphones to capture every nuance and detail of the instrument's sound.

Integrating Live Instruments with Digital Production

Once the live instrument recordings are captured, Subtronics seamlessly integrates them into their digital production workflow. This requires careful mixing and processing to ensure that the live instrument recordings blend harmoniously with the electronic elements. They use various techniques such as equalization, compression, and reverb to achieve the desired balance and sonic cohesion.

Creative Techniques and Innovations

Subtronics constantly explores innovative ways to push the boundaries of incorporating live instruments into their productions. They experiment with unconventional playing techniques, such as bowing a guitar or using extended techniques on brass instruments, to create unique and otherworldly sounds. They also combine live instrument recordings with sampling and synthesis to create hybrid sounds that are truly one-of-a-kind.

Challenges and Solutions

Incorporating live instruments into electronic music production presents its own set of challenges. One of the main challenges is achieving a seamless integration between the live instrument recordings and the digital elements. The different tonal characteristics, dynamics, and timing of live instruments can pose difficulties in creating a cohesive sound. To overcome these challenges, Subtronics meticulously aligns the timing of the live instrument recordings with the digital elements and applies careful processing to ensure a balanced and cohesive mix.

Another challenge is the practicality of incorporating live instruments into live performances. Electronic music performances often involve intricate setups and precise synchronization of various elements. To address this, Subtronics collaborates with experienced musicians who are adept at performing live with electronic music setups. They also invest in advanced technology and equipment that allows for seamless integration of live instruments into their live performances.

Case Study: The Electric Cello

One noteworthy example of Subtronics incorporating live instruments into their productions is the use of an electric cello. The rich and resonant sound of the cello adds an ethereal quality to their music, creating an emotional connection with the audience. By utilizing live looping techniques, Subtronics is able to layer different cello melodies and harmonies in real-time, creating lush and captivating soundscapes.

Conclusion

Incorporating live instruments into their productions is a key element that sets Subtronics apart in the electronic music scene. They embrace the power of live instruments to create a unique and immersive experience for their listeners. Through careful selection, recording, and integration of live instruments, they add a dynamic and organic element to their music, pushing the boundaries of electronic music production. Subtronics' innovative approach serves as an inspiration to aspiring producers and demonstrates the limitless creative possibilities that can be achieved by bridging the worlds of live instruments and electronic music.

The Influence of Other Genres on Their Sound

When it comes to the evolution of music, one cannot underestimate the impact of different genres on an artist's sound. For Subtronics, the boundaries of electronic music have always been an open playground for exploration. In this section, we will dive into the various genres that have influenced Subtronics' signature sound and how they have seamlessly incorporated elements from diverse musical styles.

Dubstep: The Foundation

At its core, Subtronics' sound is rooted in the genre of dubstep. With its heavy basslines, syncopated beats, and dark atmospheres, dubstep provided the foundation on which Subtronics built their unique sonic identity. The wobbles and growls characteristic of early dubstep tracks were instrumental in shaping Subtronics' sound palette.

Drawing inspiration from dubstep pioneers like Skream, Benga, and Excision, Subtronics incorporated the genre's distinct rhythmic patterns and intense sound design into their music. From the very beginning, they understood that fusing dubstep with their own creative twists would allow them to stand out in a crowded EDM landscape.

Trap: Blending Rhythms

While dubstep laid the groundwork for their sound, Subtronics also drew influence from the trap genre. Trap is known for its heavy beats, booming 808s, and trap snares that create a hypnotic rhythm. By incorporating trap elements into their tracks, Subtronics was able to infuse their music with a sense of energy and groove.

The combination of dubstep and trap rhythms created a powerful fusion that captivated audiences. It allowed Subtronics to dive into the world of hip-hop and experiment with different tempos and flows. This unique blend of dubstep and trap rhythms became a signature aspect of their sound, setting them apart from other artists in the EDM scene.

Drum and Bass: Driving Energy

In addition to dubstep and trap, Subtronics found inspiration in the high-octane genre of drum and bass. Known for its fast-paced beats, intricate drum patterns, and pulsating basslines, drum and bass injected a new level of energy into Subtronics' music.

By incorporating elements of drum and bass, Subtronics was able to create tracks that kept audiences on their toes, never knowing what sonic surprise was coming next. The frenetic pace of drum and bass allowed Subtronics to push the limits of their creativity, infusing their tracks with a relentless drive that became a hallmark of their sound.

Hip-Hop: Vocal Influences

Apart from the instrumental aspects, Subtronics also drew inspiration from the world of hip-hop in terms of vocal influences. Collaborating with hip-hop artists and incorporating rap verses into their tracks allowed Subtronics to expand their sonic palette and connect with a broader audience.

By featuring vocalists and rappers on their tracks, Subtronics brought a new dimension to their music. The fusion of electronic elements with hip-hop vocals added an organic and human touch to their sound, creating a unique listening experience for their fans.

Unique Blend: Breaking Boundaries

While Subtronics drew inspiration from dubstep, trap, drum and bass, and hip-hop, they were never confined by the limitations of these genres. Instead, they took elements from each and molded them into something entirely their own. This disregard for traditional genre boundaries allowed Subtronics to continuously push the envelope and explore new sonic territories.

Their fearless approach to incorporating diverse genres led to the creation of a sound that cannot be classified easily. Subtronics' music is a melting pot of influences, a sonic collage where dubstep, trap, drum and bass, and hip-hop coexist harmoniously.

The Unconventional Combination

Subtronics' ability to seamlessly blend and reimagine elements from different genres is a testament to their creative vision and technical prowess. Their sound resonates with fans across genres and has gained them a dedicated following worldwide.

By embracing new influences and refusing to be confined by genre conventions, Subtronics has paved the way for a new wave of electronic music that defies categorization. Their ability to create a unique blend of sounds is a testament to the power of musical exploration and the endless possibilities that lie within the realm of music.

In a world where genre boundaries are becoming increasingly blurred, Subtronics stands as a beacon of artistic freedom and innovation. Their music continues to evolve, drawing inspiration from an ever-expanding range of genres, and leaving an indelible mark on the music industry.

Beyond the Glow: Redefining Electronic Music

Subtronics' exploration and incorporation of various genres have not only shaped their own sound but have also influenced the larger electronic music scene. Their ability to seamlessly blend genres has inspired other artists and producers to experiment with their own unique combinations.

The impact of Subtronics' genre-blending approach can be seen in the rise of hybrid genres that incorporate elements from multiple styles. Artists are no longer constrained by the limitations of a single genre and are instead pushing the boundaries of what electronic music can be.

Subtronics' influence extends beyond their music. They have become a symbol of creative freedom and a reminder that genres are just labels that can be transcended. Their ability to create a sonic experience that resonates with fans from different backgrounds is a testament to the power of music to unite people.

In conclusion, the influence of other genres on Subtronics' sound cannot be understated. From dubstep to trap, drum and bass to hip-hop, they have seamlessly blended these genres to create a unique sonic identity. By breaking down genre boundaries and embracing diverse influences, Subtronics has redefined what electronic music can be, leaving an enduring impact on the industry and inspiring artists to push the limits of their own creativity.

Section Two: Pushing the Limits of Live Performances

Incorporating New Technologies and Gadgets

In their relentless pursuit of pushing the limits of live performances, Subtronics has always been at the forefront of embracing new technologies and gadgets. They are well known for their innovative use of cutting-edge equipment and devices to create mind-blowing audiovisual experiences for their fans. In this section, we will dive into some of the key technologies and gadgets that Subtronics has incorporated into their shows, exploring how these advancements have elevated their performances to new heights.

Motion Tracking Technology

One of the most visually striking elements of Subtronics' live shows is their use of motion tracking technology. By integrating motion sensors and cameras into their stage setup, they are able to capture the movements of the artists and the crowd in real-time. This data is then processed and used to generate interactive visuals and dynamic lighting effects that synchronize perfectly with the music.

The team behind Subtronics uses specialized software to analyze the motion data and map it onto various visual elements, such as LED screens, projections, and stage props. This creates a truly immersive experience for the audience, as the visuals react and evolve in response to the energy and movements of the performers and the crowd. The result is a seamless fusion of music, technology, and human expression that transports the audience into an electrifying digital realm.

Augmented Reality (AR) and Virtual Reality (VR)

Subtronics is known for pushing the boundaries of visual storytelling and creating immersive worlds within their performances. To achieve this, they have embraced augmented reality (AR) and virtual reality (VR) technologies as powerful tools for enhancing their live shows.

AR technology allows Subtronics to overlay computer-generated graphics onto the real world, blending the physical and digital realms. By wearing AR-enabled glasses or using smartphones, audience members can see virtual objects, characters, and effects seamlessly integrated into the environment. Subtronics leverages AR to create captivating visuals that interact with the real-world stage elements, adding an extra layer of depth and engagement to their performances.

In addition to AR, Subtronics also explores the use of virtual reality (VR) to transport their fans into fully immersive 3D environments. By donning VR headsets, audience members can experience being inside a virtual world where they can interact with Subtronics' music and visuals in unprecedented ways. This technology allows for a more intimate and personal connection with the music, amplifying the emotional impact of the live performance.

Interactive LED Panels

Subtronics' stage design is a sight to behold. At the heart of their visually stunning productions are interactive LED panels that serve as both decorative backdrops and interactive visual elements. These LED panels are programmed to display intricate patterns, animations, and colorful images that synchronize with the music.

What sets Subtronics apart is their use of touch-sensitive LED panels, allowing the performers to physically interact with the visuals. By touching or gesturing on the panels, they can trigger different effects and animations, creating a dynamic and immersive visual experience. This real-time interaction between the artists and the visuals adds an element of spontaneity and improvisation to their performances, making each show unique and unforgettable.

Live Sampling and Looping Equipment

Subtronics' music is characterized by intricate sound design and bass-heavy drops. To achieve their signature sound on stage, they rely on live sampling and looping equipment. These devices enable them to capture and manipulate audio in real-time, allowing for on-the-fly remixing and improvisation.

Live sampling involves recording snippets of sounds from various sources, such as the crowd's cheers, ambient noises, or even their own performance, and incorporating them into the music. This adds a layer of authenticity and immediacy to their live sets, making each show a truly unique sonic experience.

Looping equipment allows Subtronics to create repetitive musical patterns or sequences on the fly, which can be layered together to build complex and evolving soundscapes. This technique adds depth and richness to their music, creating a dynamic and hypnotic atmosphere that keeps the audience engaged from start to finish.

Unconventional Instrument Fusion

In addition to incorporating cutting-edge technologies and gadgets, Subtronics is also known for their experimentation with unconventional instrument fusion. They blend traditional instruments with electronic music production techniques to create a truly unique sonic palette.

For example, Subtronics has been known to incorporate live guitar or drums into their performances, layering these organic sounds with electronic elements. This fusion of analog and digital instruments brings a raw and visceral energy to their music, blurring the lines between genres and defying expectations.

Their ability to seamlessly merge different sounds and styles is a testament to their creativity and willingness to explore new sonic territories. By pushing the boundaries of musical fusion, Subtronics continues to redefine what is possible in the realm of electronic music.

In conclusion, Subtronics' incorporation of new technologies and gadgets has revolutionized their live performances, taking them to extraordinary levels of audiovisual spectacle. From motion tracking technology and AR/VR experiences to interactive LED panels and live sampling equipment, they have harnessed the power of innovation to create unparalleled concerts. By embracing these advancements, Subtronics continues to break new ground and set a high bar for future electronic music performances. The chapter concludes with a deeper exploration of the impact of Subtronics' evolution on the EDM scene and their enduring legacy.

Creating Immersive Visual Experiences

In the world of Subtronics, music is not just about sound. It is a multi-sensory experience that transports the audience to another dimension. With their captivating performances and mind-bending visual effects, Subtronics is known for creating immersive visual experiences that leave fans in awe.

To understand the magic behind these experiences, we must delve into the world of stage production, lighting design, and visual effects. It is a delicate balance between technology, artistry, and creativity that brings Subtronics' music to life on stage.

The Art of Stage Design

When it comes to creating immersive visual experiences, the stage is the canvas on which the magic unfolds. Subtronics and their team pay meticulous attention to every detail of the stage design, ensuring that it complements and enhances the music.

From the placement of LED panels to the arrangement of props and structures, each element is carefully curated to engage the audience visually. The design takes into account the overall theme and mood of the performance, aiming to create a cohesive and captivating visual narrative.

Lighting as a Powerful Tool

One of the key components of Subtronics' immersive visual experiences is lighting design. Lighting serves as a powerful tool to set the atmosphere, evoke emotions, and guide the audience's attention.

With an array of lighting fixtures, including moving lights, lasers, and strobes, Subtronics transforms the stage into a vibrant and dynamic visual spectacle. The seamless integration of lighting cues with the music adds an extra layer of excitement and intensity to the performance.

The careful coordination between the lighting designer and the music producer is crucial to achieve synchronization between visual effects and drops. It requires precise timing and a deep understanding of the music's structure and dynamics.

Visual Effects for the Senses

Immersive visual experiences wouldn't be complete without the mesmerizing visual effects that Subtronics incorporates into their performances. These effects aim to stimulate the senses and transport the audience into a new realm.

From mesmerizing projections to intricate laser shows, the visuals intertwine with the music, creating a mesmerizing symphony of sight and sound. The synchronization of the visuals with the beats and drops of the music enhances the overall impact and creates an immersive atmosphere that captivates the audience.

Subtronics also experiments with unconventional visual effects to surprise and intrigue their fans. Smoke machines, confetti cannons, and pyrotechnics are expertly utilized to create moments of heightened excitement and awe.

The Role of Technology

Technology plays a vital role in bringing Subtronics' immersive visual experiences to life. State-of-the-art equipment and software enable their team to push the boundaries of creativity and deliver cutting-edge performances.

Advanced lighting control systems, such as DMX (Digital Multiplex), provide precise control over every light fixture on the stage. This allows for intricate lighting choreography and synchronized effects that enhance the overall visual impact.

Visual effects are often powered by powerful computers and specialized software, which enable the real-time manipulation and projection of complex graphics and animations. This allows Subtronics to create mesmerizing visual backdrops that seamlessly integrate with the music.

Fusing Art and Technology

Creating immersive visual experiences requires a delicate balance between art and technology. Subtronics and their team are not just music producers or technical experts; they are artists who use technology as a medium to express their creativity.

The visual elements are carefully crafted to complement and enhance the music, creating a cohesive narrative that allows the audience to dive deeper into the world of Subtronics. The combination of music, lights, and visual effects creates a multisensory experience that transcends the boundaries of traditional live performances.

Unconventional Example: Augmented Reality Spectacle

As technology continues to evolve, so do the possibilities for immersive visual experiences. One unconventional example that Subtronics could explore in the future is an augmented reality (AR) spectacle.

Imagine a live performance where the audience wears AR glasses that overlay virtual elements onto the real world. As Subtronics unleashes their music, visual effects and animations erupt around the audience, creating an otherworldly experience.

The AR glasses could also allow for interactive elements, where the audience can manipulate virtual objects or contribute to the visual narrative in real-time. This would blur the line between performer and spectator, further immersing the audience in the Subtronics universe.

Of course, the implementation of such technology would come with its challenges, including hardware requirements, synchronization, and ensuring a seamless user experience. However, the potential for creating an unparalleled immersive visual experience with AR is both exciting and intriguing.

Exercises

1. Research and analyze the stage design of a different electronic music artist. How does their stage design contribute to the overall visual experience? Compare and contrast their approach with Subtronics.

2. Experiment with lighting design using household items. Transform a room into a visually captivating environment using different light sources and techniques. Consider the mood and atmosphere you want to create and how lighting can enhance it.

3. Watch live performance videos of Subtronics and other electronic music artists. Pay close attention to their visual effects and how they synchronize with

the music. Identify specific moments that stand out to you and explain why they are impactful.

4. Imagine you are part of Subtronics' visual production team. How would you incorporate unconventional visual effects, such as holograms or virtual reality, into their live performances? Describe the specific moments or songs where these effects would have the greatest impact and why.

5. Reflect on your most memorable concert experience. What were the visual elements that stood out to you? How did they enhance your overall enjoyment of the performance? Discuss with friends or fellow music enthusiasts and compare your experiences.

Surprise B2B Sets and Guest Appearances

One of the hallmarks of Subtronics' live performances is their penchant for surprise back-to-back (B2B) sets and the inclusion of guest appearances. These unexpected collaborations with other artists add an element of excitement and unpredictability to their shows, leaving audiences buzzing with anticipation.

The Thrill of B2B Sets

Subtronics is known for their affinity for B2B sets, where two artists take turns playing tracks, often improvising and reacting to each other's music in real-time. These sets create a unique atmosphere where the energy of two individuals combines to create an electric live experience.

The art of a successful B2B set lies in the seamless transition between artists, maintaining a cohesive flow while still allowing each artist's distinct sound to shine through. It requires a deep understanding and familiarity with each other's music, as well as an ability to read and respond to the crowd's energy in the moment.

To achieve this, Subtronics frequently collaborates with artists who share their passion for pushing boundaries and are equally skilled at captivating crowds. These B2B sets not only create an unforgettable experience for the audience but also foster a sense of camaraderie and community among artists in the EDM scene.

The Element of Surprise

Surprise plays a crucial role in Subtronics' live performances. In a world where setlists tend to be meticulously planned in advance, Subtronics takes pride in keeping their fans on their toes by incorporating unexpected tracks or genre switches into their sets. This unpredictability keeps the energy high and ensures that no two shows are ever the same.

Similarly, surprise guest appearances are a common occurrence during Subtronics' performances. Inviting fellow artists to join them on stage adds an element of mystique and excitement, leaving fans eagerly guessing who might make an appearance. These surprise collaborations often result in impromptu B2B sets, creating an electrifying atmosphere that is hard to replicate.

Remembering the Past, Inspiring the Future

Subtronics pays homage to the rich history of electronic music through their surprise B2B sets and guest appearances. By collaborating with artists from different generations and subgenres, they bridge the gap between the past and the present, ensuring that the roots of electronic music are never forgotten.

These surprise collaborations also serve to inspire the next generation of artists. Seeing Subtronics and their peers seamlessly blend their unique styles on stage highlights the limitless potential of creativity and collaboration in the EDM scene. It encourages aspiring artists to push boundaries, experiment with new sounds, and forge their own path in the industry.

Unconventional yet Relevant

To take their surprise B2B sets to the next level, Subtronics often employs unconventional approaches. For example, they might incorporate live instruments into their performances, such as guitars or drums, to add an extra layer of depth and complexity to their sound. This fusion of electronic and live music blurs the line between genres and creates a truly immersive experience for the audience.

Additionally, Subtronics is known for their unique stage production and visuals. They work closely with visual artists and VJs to create stunning visual displays that complement their music. These visuals enhance the surprise element of their sets, captivating the audience's senses and taking them on a mesmerizing journey.

Exercises and Challenges

1. Think about an artist or DJ you admire. Imagine doing a surprise B2B set with them. What songs or elements of their style would you incorporate into your performance? How would you ensure a seamless transition between your sets?

2. Research the history of B2B sets in the EDM scene. Choose a notable B2B performance and analyze how the artists complemented each other's styles. What made their collaboration memorable?

3. Experiment with surprise elements in your own DJ sets. Add unexpected tracks or genre switches to see how it affects the energy of the crowd. Take note of the audience's response and use it as a learning experience for future performances.

4. Collaborate with a fellow artist or musician on a mini B2B set. Share your music with each other and find common ground where your styles intersect. Create a setlist together and practice transitioning between your tracks to ensure a cohesive performance.

5. Watch live performances by Subtronics or other artists known for surprise B2B sets. Pay attention to how they engage with the crowd and deliver unexpected moments. Take inspiration from their stage presence and incorporate those techniques into your own performances.

Remember, surprise B2B sets and guest appearances are about creating a unique and unforgettable experience for both the artists and the audience. Embrace the element of surprise and let your creativity shine to leave a lasting impact on your fans.

Concept Shows and Special Effects

Concept shows and special effects are an essential part of Subtronics' live performances. They go beyond just playing music and aim to create a unique and immersive experience for the audience. In this section, we will delve into the world of concept shows and explore how Subtronics uses special effects to captivate their fans.

The Art of Concept Shows

Concept shows are a way for Subtronics to tell a story or convey a specific theme through their music and visuals. These shows often have a cohesive narrative or a central idea that guides the entire performance. By creating a storyline or a concept, Subtronics aims to immerse their audience in a different world and evoke emotions that go beyond just the music.

To design a concept show, Subtronics collaborates with visual artists, stage designers, and lighting technicians to bring their vision to life. They carefully select visuals, props, and costumes that align with the theme and help enhance the overall experience. The goal is to create a multisensory journey for the audience, where every element, from the music to the visuals, works together seamlessly.

One example of a concept show by Subtronics is "The Space Odyssey." This performance takes the audience on a cosmic journey, with each track representing a different stage in the story. The visuals depict distant galaxies, alien landscapes, and surreal imagery that transport the audience to another dimension. The use of interstellar props, like spaceships and futuristic clothing, further enhances the immersive experience.

Special Effects: The Wow Factor

Special effects play a crucial role in concept shows and help create the "wow" factor that leaves the audience in awe. Subtronics utilizes a variety of special effects techniques to elevate their performances and make them visually stunning. Let's explore some of these techniques:

- **Pyrotechnics:** Fire effects, such as fireballs, flame projectors, and fireworks, add a dramatic and intense element to the show. They create a sense of excitement and enhance the energy of the performance.

- **Lasers and Lighting:** Subtronics employs intricate laser setups, synchronized with the music, to create mesmerizing visual patterns and beams of light. The lighting design, including moving lights, strobes, and LEDs, helps set the mood and adds depth to the overall visual aesthetic.

- **Projection Mapping:** Projection mapping allows Subtronics to transform any surface into a dynamic display. By mapping visuals onto different objects, such as stage structures or props, they can create illusions, distortions, and 3D effects, bringing their concept to life in a captivating way.

- **CO2 Cannons and Confetti Blasts:** These effects are often used to create impactful moments and enhance specific drops or build-ups in the music. CO2 cannons release blasts of cold cryogenic fog, while confetti blasts fill the air with a shower of colorful paper, adding a festive and celebratory element to the performance.

- **Holograms and Augmented Reality:** Subtronics explores the cutting-edge realm of holograms and augmented reality to push the boundaries of their concept shows. By incorporating holographic projections or AR elements, they blur the line between reality and fantasy, creating mind-bending visual experiences that leave the audience spellbound.

Creating Unforgettable Moments

The goal of concept shows and special effects is to create unforgettable moments that stay with the audience long after the performance. Subtronics pays attention to the pacing, flow, and surprises within their shows to ensure an engaging and dynamic experience for their fans. Here are some techniques they use to achieve this:

- **Climactic Build-ups and Drops:** Subtronics understands the power of a well-crafted build-up and drop. They build anticipation with intense visuals and perfectly timed lighting effects, creating a sense of excitement and release that energizes the crowd.

- **Unexpected Transitions and Mashups:** To keep the audience on their toes, Subtronics incorporates unexpected transitions between tracks and surprises the crowd with unique mashups. These unexpected moments add an element of surprise and keep the audience engaged throughout the show.

- **Interactive Elements:** Subtronics loves to involve the audience in their performances. They often include interactive elements, such as throwing inflatable props or releasing large-sized beach balls into the crowd. These interactions create a sense of unity and shared experience among the audience members.

- **Visual Storytelling:** Through carefully curated visuals and animated graphics, Subtronics tells a story that complements their music. Whether it's a journey through a mystical forest or an exploration of futuristic worlds, the visual storytelling enhances the emotional impact of the performance.

- **Surprise Guest Appearances:** Subtronics occasionally brings surprise guest artists to their concept shows, adding an element of surprise and excitement for the audience. These collaborations create unique moments and allow for unexpected on-stage chemistry between artists.

Pushing the Boundaries: Exploring New Technologies

Subtronics is always at the forefront of pushing boundaries and embracing new technologies to enhance their concept shows. They constantly seek out innovative tools and techniques that can take their performances to the next level. Some of the emerging technologies they have explored include:

- **Virtual Reality (VR):** Subtronics has experimented with virtual reality, allowing the audience to fully immerse themselves in their concept shows. By using VR headsets, fans can experience the performance from different perspectives, interact with virtual objects, and even have a front-row view of the stage.

- **Augmented Reality (AR):** By incorporating AR elements into their shows, Subtronics adds an extra layer of interactivity and magic. They have utilized AR filters or apps that allow the audience to engage with virtual avatars, objects, or environments, blurring the line between the physical and digital realms.

- **Wearable Technology:** Subtronics has explored the integration of wearable technology into their concept shows. They have experimented with LED costumes, interactive accessories, and biometric sensors that react to the music or the audience's movements, creating a truly immersive and interactive experience.

It is through their dedication to pushing the boundaries and embracing new technologies that Subtronics continues to amaze and captivate their fans. Their concept shows and special effects not only showcase their musical talent but also demonstrate their commitment to creating unforgettable experiences for their audience.

Conclusion

Concept shows and special effects are the pinnacle of Subtronics' live performances. By creating immersive environments and utilizing stunning visual effects, they transport their audience into different worlds and leave a lasting impact. Subtronics' dedication to pushing boundaries and embracing new technologies ensures that their concept shows continue to evolve and amaze, solidifying their status as one of the most innovative and exciting acts in the EDM scene.

As we conclude our exploration of concept shows and special effects, we can't help but be in awe of Subtronics' ability to create a sensory experience that goes beyond just the music. They have mastered the art of storytelling and incorporated visual elements that captivate and engage their audience. Their relentless pursuit of pushing the boundaries of technology ensures that their shows will continue to dazzle and inspire for years to come.

Never-Ending Quest to Dazzle Their Fans

In their never-ending quest to dazzle their fans, Subtronics has always pushed the boundaries of live performances, constantly seeking new ways to create memorable experiences. Through incorporating cutting-edge technologies, imaginative stage productions, surprise sets, and mind-blowing special effects, they strive to captivate and amaze their audience on a whole new level.

Incorporating New Technologies and Gadgets

Subtronics understands that technology plays a crucial role in enhancing live performances. They are known for embracing the latest advancements and incorporating them seamlessly into their shows. From custom-designed MIDI controllers and innovative mixing techniques to interactive visuals and lighting, Subtronics consistently raises the bar.

One example of their innovative use of technology is the incorporation of gesture-based controllers. These controllers allow the duo to manipulate and control various elements of their performance using hand movements. By doing so, they create a mesmerizing and interactive experience for their fans, where every gesture translates into jaw-dropping visual effects and mind-bending soundscapes.

Creating Immersive Visual Experiences

Visuals are an integral part of Subtronics' live performances, as they add depth and immerse the audience in their sonic world. They collaborate closely with visual artists and VJs to create mind-bending visual displays that synchronize with their music. Through intricate mapping techniques, they transform the stage into a vibrant and dynamic canvas, transporting their fans into a visually captivating realm.

They also make use of live 3D projection mapping, a technique that allows visuals to be precisely mapped onto physical objects. By mapping their visuals onto custom-built structures and props on stage, they create a multi-dimensional and immersive experience that fully complements their music. This innovative approach results in an otherworldly spectacle that fans remember long after the show ends.

Surprise B2B Sets and Guest Appearances

Subtronics loves to surprise their fans with unexpected collaborations and guest appearances during their performances. They believe that these moments not only add an element of excitement but also give their audience a unique and unforgettable experience.

Subtronics frequently invites fellow artists to join them on stage for spontaneous B2B (back-to-back) sets. These sets create an electric atmosphere as the artists feed off each other's energy, pushing the limits and creating unprecedented moments of musical brilliance. The element of unpredictability keeps the audience on the edge of their seats, never knowing who might step on stage next.

In addition to B2B sets, Subtronics occasionally brings surprise guest performers to join them for specific tracks or segments of their shows. These surprise appearances not only elevate the overall performance but also provide a platform for emerging talent to showcase their skills to a wider audience. It's a testament to Subtronics' commitment to fostering a strong sense of community within the EDM scene.

Concept Shows and Special Effects

Subtronics' commitment to dazzling their fans is further exemplified in their concept shows and the use of special effects. They strive to curate immersive experiences that transport their audience to different worlds, blurring the line between reality and imagination.

One of their most remarkable concept shows is the "Neon Dreams" tour. With neon-themed visuals, ethereal lighting effects, and euphoric soundscapes, Subtronics creates an otherworldly atmosphere that feels like a dream come true. This concept show takes the audience on a journey through a neon-lit wonderland, where the boundaries of time and space cease to exist.

Special effects such as pyrotechnics, confetti cannons, and CO_2 blasts are also employed to enhance the overall impact of their performances. These effects add an extra layer of excitement and spectacle, leaving their fans in awe and craving for more.

Never-Ending Quest to Dazzle Their Fans: A Personal Touch

What sets Subtronics apart in their quest to dazzle their fans is their unwavering commitment to creating a personal connection. Despite their rise to stardom, they have always prioritized their fans, recognizing their importance in their journey.

They often interact with their audience during performances, taking the time to engage with the crowd, exchanging smiles and energy. This personal touch makes their shows feel intimate, even in front of thousands of fans. Subtronics values the relationships they have built with their supporters and strives to make each show a memorable experience for every individual in attendance.

In conclusion, Subtronics' never-ending quest to dazzle their fans involves pushing the boundaries of live performances through innovative technologies, immersive visuals, surprise appearances, and concept shows. It's not just about delivering mind-blowing music but also about creating memorable experiences that leave a lasting impact. With each show, they continue to explore new ways to captivate and amaze, ensuring that their fans always leave with a sense of wonder and excitement. Their commitment to connecting with their audience on a personal level adds an even more profound dimension to their performances, making every fan feel like an integral part of their journey. Subtronics' relentless pursuit of astonishment is what fuels their success and solidifies their place as mesmerizing performers in the EDM scene.

Section Three: The Impact on the EDM Scene

Pioneering the Next Generation of Bass Music

Subtronics, with their unique style and innovative sound, has been at the forefront of shaping the next generation of bass music. Through their groundbreaking productions and electrifying performances, they have not only pushed the boundaries of the genre but also inspired a new wave of artists and producers.

Exploring New Sonic Landscapes

One of the key ways in which Subtronics has pioneered the next generation of bass music is through their exploration of new sonic landscapes. In their productions, they blend elements from various genres such as dubstep, trap, and drum and bass, creating a hybrid sound that is uniquely their own. This fusion of genres not only keeps their music fresh and exciting but also attracts a wider audience.

To achieve this, Subtronics experiments with different sound design techniques and incorporates unconventional elements into their tracks. They constantly push the boundaries of what is considered traditional within the bass music realm, exploring new textures, rhythms, and tonalities. This fearless creativity has allowed them to carve out a distinct sonic identity and inspire other artists to think outside the box.

Embracing Collaborations and Cross-Pollination

Another way Subtronics has contributed to the evolution of bass music is through their collaborations with fellow artists from various genres. By teaming up with vocalists, rappers, and other producers, they introduce their bass-focused sound to new audiences and further expand the boundaries of the genre.

These collaborations not only result in exciting and dynamic tracks but also foster a cross-pollination of ideas and styles. Subtronics' willingness to work with artists from different backgrounds encourages a collaborative mindset within the bass music community, leading to the emergence of fresh sounds and innovative approaches.

Blurring the Lines Between Live and Electronic Music

Subtronics understands the importance of delivering an engaging live performance that goes beyond simply playing DJ sets. They have been instrumental in blurring the lines between live and electronic music, incorporating live elements into their shows.

During their performances, Subtronics combines DJing with live instrumentation, bringing a vibrant energy to their sets. By incorporating instruments such as drums, guitars, and synthesizers, they create a dynamic and immersive experience for their audience. This unique approach not only sets them apart but also inspires other electronic artists to explore the possibilities of incorporating live elements into their own performances.

Influencing the Bass Music Community

Through their success and groundbreaking sound, Subtronics has had a significant influence on the bass music community. Their rise to prominence has motivated aspiring producers to experiment with their own styles, leading to a diversification of bass music as a whole.

Moreover, Subtronics' commitment to accessibility and inclusivity has helped foster a strong and supportive community around their music. They actively engage with their fans through social media, fan meetups, and charitable initiatives. By creating a safe space for fans to connect and share their love for their music, Subtronics has fostered a community that supports and uplifts its members.

Championing Innovation

Above all, Subtronics champions innovation within the bass music scene. They constantly challenge themselves and their peers to push the boundaries of what is possible, driving the evolution of the genre forward.

Whether it's through their groundbreaking productions, electrifying performances, or collaborations with artists from different genres, they consistently strive to bring something fresh and exciting to the table. Subtronics' unwavering commitment to pushing the boundaries of bass music influences the entire industry and inspires future generations of artists to think beyond the conventions of the genre.

Example: The Creativity of Sound Design

To illustrate the innovative approach of Subtronics, let's consider the topic of sound design. One of the hallmarks of their music is the intricate soundscapes they create, which often feature a wide range of unique and unconventional sounds.

In their track "Griztronics," a collaboration with GRiZ, Subtronics showcases their creativity in sound design. The song incorporates a variety of distinct and intricate bass sounds, each with its own character and texture. These sounds are created through a combination of synthesis techniques, modulation effects, and meticulous attention to detail.

For example, they might start with a raw, heavily distorted bass sound and then layer it with subtle modulations and effects to add movement and depth. They might also experiment with different wavetables, filters, and envelopes to shape the sound further. Through this process of trial and error, they craft unique and recognizable bass drops that captivate listeners.

By pushing the boundaries of sound design, Subtronics sets a new standard for the bass music genre. Their innovative approach inspires other producers to experiment with their own sound design techniques, ultimately driving the evolution of bass music as a whole.

Summary

Subtronics' contributions to the next generation of bass music are far-reaching and significant. Through their fearless exploration of new sonic landscapes, cross-genre collaborations, incorporation of live elements into their performances, and dedication to championing innovation, they have shaped the future of the genre. Their unique sound and creative approach have inspired countless artists and producers to push the boundaries of what is possible within bass music. As they continue to evolve and explore new horizons, Subtronics leaves an enduring glow on the bass music scene.

Influencing Other Artists and Producers

Subtronics, with their unique and groundbreaking sound, has left an indelible mark on the electronic music scene. Their innovative approach to music production and fearless experimentation has influenced a new wave of artists and producers, inspiring them to push the boundaries of their own creativity. In this section, we will explore the ways in which Subtronics has influenced other artists and producers and examine the lasting impact of their musical contributions.

Challenging Conventional Genres

Subtronics' fearless approach to music production has challenged the conventional boundaries of genres, inspiring other artists and producers to explore new sonic territories. Their fusion of bass music and dubstep, coupled with elements of other genres such as trap and hip-hop, has paved the way for a fresh sound that resonates with a diverse range of listeners. As a result, artists from various backgrounds have been inspired to think outside the box and experiment with genre-blending in their own productions.

Example:
One such artist is XYZ, who was initially rooted in a traditional dubstep sound. After being introduced to Subtronics' music, XYZ was inspired to push beyond the confines of the genre and incorporate elements of bass music and trap into their own productions. The result was a unique and refreshing sound that gained XYZ recognition and critical acclaim. In turn, XYZ's experimental approach has influenced a new generation of producers, creating a ripple effect in the electronic music community.

Innovative Sound Design Techniques

Subtronics' attention to detail and impeccable sound design have become a source of inspiration for aspiring producers. Their ability to create unique and recognizable drops, often characterized by heavy basslines and intricate synth work, has set a new standard for production excellence. As a result, other producers have been motivated to delve into the art of sound design and experiment with unconventional techniques.

Example:
Producer ABC, who was struggling to find their own signature sound, turned to Subtronics' music for inspiration. By studying Subtronics' tracks and dissecting their sound design techniques, ABC was able to develop a fresh approach to their own productions. The incorporation of unconventional sound design elements, inspired by Subtronics, set ABC's music apart from the crowd and garnered attention from both fans and industry professionals.

Creative Collaboration and Cross-Pollination

Subtronics' willingness to collaborate and cross-pollinate with other artists has contributed to their influence in the music industry. By working with vocalists, rappers, and fellow DJs, they have not only expanded their own creativity but also exposed their collaborators to a wider audience. These collaborations have sparked new ideas and inspired other artists to collaborate across genres, resulting in the emergence of exciting and innovative music.

Example:

In a recent collaboration, Subtronics teamed up with singer/songwriter LMN to create a track that seamlessly blended electronic elements with soulful vocals. The success of this collaboration opened doors for LMN, introducing her to a fanbase she may not have reached otherwise. Furthermore, the unique combination of Subtronics' production style and LMN's distinctive vocals inspired other artists to explore similar cross-genre collaborations, bridging the gap between different musical communities.

Pushing the Boundaries of Performance

In addition to their impactful music production, Subtronics' high-energy performances and stage presence have left a lasting impression on both fans and fellow artists. Their ability to captivate audiences with intense and immersive live shows has raised the bar for live performance in the electronic music scene. As a result, other artists and producers have been compelled to elevate their own live performances to match the level of energy and engagement that Subtronics consistently delivers.

Example:

Producer DEF, who previously relied heavily on pre-recorded sets, was inspired by Subtronics' dynamic live performances. Witnessing the crowd's response to Subtronics' energy and stage presence prompted DEF to rethink their own approach to live shows. In an effort to provide a more authentic and engaging experience, DEF incorporated live instruments and interactive elements into their performances. This transformation not only revitalized DEF's career but also had a ripple effect, influencing other artists to explore new possibilities in their own live shows.

Fostering a Supportive Community

Subtronics' dedication to their fans and their efforts to create a supportive and inclusive community have had a profound impact on the electronic music scene. Their genuine interactions with fans, both in-person and online, have cultivated a sense of belonging and unity among their fan base. This has inspired other artists and producers to prioritize building a community around their music, fostering a supportive environment for fans to connect with each other and the artists they admire.

Example:

Artist GHI, who initially struggled to connect with their audience, drew inspiration from Subtronics' community-building efforts. Realizing the importance of fan engagement, GHI started actively communicating with their fans through social media platforms, hosting meet and greets, and encouraging fan-made art. This genuine connection and focus on creating a supportive community not only strengthened GHI's fan base but also inspired other artists to adopt a similar approach.

Reflection on the Influence

Subtronics' influence on other artists and producers extends far beyond their music. Their fearless experimentation, innovative sound design, and dedication to their fans have set a new standard for excellence in the electronic music community. By challenging conventional genres, pushing the boundaries of performance, and fostering a supportive community, Subtronics continues to shape the future of electronic music. As the industry evolves, the impact of their contributions will endure, leaving a lasting imprint on the music industry for years to come.

Shaping the Sound of Music Festivals

In the realm of electronic dance music (EDM), Subtronics has played a significant role in shaping the sound of music festivals around the world. Their unique blend of heavy bass music, dubstep, and experimental sound design has created a seismic impact on the festival circuit. Through their exhilarating performances, innovative stage production, and collaborations with other artists, Subtronics has left an indelible mark on the EDM scene.

Setting the Tone for High-Energy Performances

When it comes to music festivals, energy is everything. Subtronics understands this concept and has mastered the art of delivering high-octane performances that leave crowds buzzing with excitement. Their ability to create a sonic ecosystem where bass drops reign supreme is unparalleled. By merging elements of dubstep, trap, and other bass-heavy genres, Subtronics crafts a thrilling auditory experience that resonates with festival-goers.

From the moment they step on stage, Subtronics commands attention with heart-pumping beats and infectious basslines. Their intense and dynamic sets keep audiences engaged, leaving them craving more. By carefully selecting tracks and building tension with strategic drops, Subtronics creates an electrifying atmosphere that takes festival-goers on a wild musical journey.

Innovative Visuals and Stage Production

Subtronics not only captivates audiences with their music but also with their visually captivating stage production. They understand that a visually stimulating experience is just as important as the music itself. By incorporating innovative lighting setups, mesmerizing visuals, and stunning stage designs, Subtronics creates a truly immersive experience for festivalgoers.

Their attention to detail in stage production helps to transport the audience into a different world. From synchronized light shows that accentuate the drops to custom-designed visuals that complement the music, Subtronics ensures that every aspect of the performance is a feast for the senses. The integration of cutting-edge technology and artistic vision creates a visually stunning spectacle that amplifies the impact of their music.

Unforgettable Sets at Major Festivals

Through their unrivaled talent and reputation for delivering mind-blowing performances, Subtronics has earned a spot on some of the most prestigious stages at major music festivals around the world. Their sets have become a must-see attraction for festival-goers, drawing massive crowds eager to witness their electrifying performances.

Whether it's commanding the main stage at Electric Daisy Carnival (EDC), headlining at Ultra Music Festival, or igniting the energy at Tomorrowland, Subtronics consistently sets the bar high. Their ability to curate unforgettable experiences filled with non-stop energy and bass-heavy drops has established them as festival favorites.

Collaborations with Big-Name Artists

Subtronics' influence extends beyond their solo performances. They have also made waves in the EDM scene through their collaborations with big-name artists. These partnerships have not only pushed the boundaries of their sound but have also shaped the overall sound of music festivals.

By working with artists from different genres and backgrounds, Subtronics injects fresh perspectives into their music. These collaborations bridge the gap between various styles of electronic music and create a fusion of sounds that influences the industry as a whole. With each collaboration, Subtronics adds a new layer to their sonic repertoire, further expanding their reach and impact on music festivals.

Establishing a Legacy in the Music Festival Scene

The impact of Subtronics on the music festival scene goes beyond their performances and collaborations. They have played a pivotal role in inspiring a new generation of artists and producers to explore bass-heavy genres and experiment with innovative sound design.

Through their trailblazing career, Subtronics has demonstrated that embracing unconventional sounds and pushing the limits of electronic music can lead to success and recognition in the industry. Their unwavering commitment to their unique style and dedication to delivering unforgettable live performances has cemented their place in the history of music festivals.

As Subtronics continues to evolve and explore new sonic territories, their influence on the sound of music festivals persists. Their legacy serves as a reminder of the power of experimentation and the importance of captivating performances in the EDM world.

Conclusion

Shaping the sound of music festivals has been a significant achievement for Subtronics. Through their high-energy performances, innovative stage production, collaborations with other artists, and their overall commitment to pushing the boundaries of electronic music, Subtronics has left an unforgettable mark on the EDM scene. Their impact on music festivals will continue to reverberate for years to come, inspiring future generations of artists and shaping the evolution of the genre. As their story continues, we can only imagine the new heights they will reach and the incredible experiences they will create for fans around the world.

The Role of Subtronics in the Rise of Dubstep

Dubstep, a genre of electronic music characterized by its heavy basslines, intricate rhythms, and unique sound design, has exploded in popularity in recent years. And at the forefront of this movement is none other than Subtronics - a dynamic duo that has undeniably played a significant role in the rise of dubstep. In this section, we will explore how Subtronics has made their mark on the genre, shaping its sound and influencing the next generation of dubstep artists.

Understanding the Origins of Dubstep

To appreciate Subtronics' impact on the genre, it's essential to understand the origins of dubstep. Born in the late 1990s in the underground clubs of South London, dubstep emerged as a fusion of genres such as 2-step garage, drum and bass, and dub reggae. It was characterized by its half-time beats, syncopated rhythms, and a focus on sub-bass frequencies.

Dubstep's early pioneers, such as Skream, Benga, and Digital Mystikz, laid the foundation for the genre, experimenting with new sounds and pushing the boundaries of electronic music. These artists paved the way for the dubstep movement to gain momentum, reaching audiences far beyond the clubs of London.

The Rise of Subtronics

Subtronics, consisting of Jesse Kardon and Chris Kirk, burst onto the dubstep scene in the early 2010s. Their unique sound, characterized by heavy basslines, intricate sound design, and relentless energy, captivated listeners and set them apart from other artists in the genre.

Expanding on the Dubstep Sound

One of the key contributions of Subtronics to the rise of dubstep is their ability to expand on the existing sound of the genre. They were not content with replicating what had already been done; instead, they pushed the boundaries and added their own distinctive elements to the music.

Subtronics' productions seamlessly blend influences from various genres, incorporating elements of trap, hip-hop, and even metal into their dubstep tracks. This fusion of styles created a unique sonic experience that resonated with listeners craving something new and exciting.

Innovative Sound Design

Another aspect that sets Subtronics apart is their impressive sound design. Their tracks are carefully crafted, with attention to every detail, resulting in a sound that is rich, powerful, and utterly captivating.

Subtronics explore unconventional soundscapes, experimenting with different textures, layers, and effects to create mind-bending drops and memorable melodies. Their attention to detail and willingness to take risks with their sound design have propelled them to the forefront of the dubstep scene.

Creating a Community of Dubstep Fans

Subtronics has not only made an impact through their music but also by creating a vibrant community of dubstep fans. Through their energetic performances, engaging social media presence, and collaborative projects with other artists, Subtronics has brought together a dedicated fan base.

By connecting with their fans on a personal level, Subtronics has fostered a sense of belonging and community within the dubstep scene. This has not only boosted their popularity but has also contributed to the overall growth and success of the genre.

Shaping the Future of Dubstep

Subtronics' influence extends beyond their own music. They have played a significant role in shaping the future of dubstep by inspiring and mentoring budding artists.

Mentoring New Talent

Subtronics actively seeks out and collaborates with up-and-coming artists, providing them with a platform to showcase their talents. Through these collaborations, Subtronics helps to elevate the next generation of dubstep producers and ensure the genre's continued evolution.

They share their knowledge and expertise, offering guidance and support to emerging artists. By fostering this collaborative spirit, Subtronics builds upon the sense of community within the dubstep scene and encourages artistic growth.

Influencing the Sound of Dubstep

Subtronics' innovative approach to music production has influenced the sound of dubstep as a whole. Many emerging dubstep artists take inspiration from Subtronics' distinct sound design, experimenting with similar techniques to create their own unique styles.

The duo's willingness to push boundaries and experiment with different sounds and genres has inspired a wave of creativity within the dubstep community. As a result, the genre continues to evolve and push the limits of what is possible.

Performing at Major Festivals

Subtronics' captivating live performances at major festivals have also contributed to the rise of dubstep. Their high-energy sets, combined with their undeniable stage presence, have introduced countless listeners to the genre.

By showcasing dubstep on large stages and captivating audiences with their dynamic performances, Subtronics has helped bring the genre to the mainstream. This exposure has increased the visibility and popularity of dubstep, attracting new fans and ensuring its longevity.

The Enduring Impact of Subtronics

As the dubstep genre continues to evolve, one thing remains clear: Subtronics has left an indelible mark on the genre. Through their unique sound, innovative productions, and dedication to fostering a sense of community, they have helped to elevate dubstep to new heights.

Their contributions to the rise of dubstep go beyond their own success. Subtronics has influenced the sound of the genre, paved the way for emerging artists, and ensured the continued growth and evolution of dubstep.

Looking towards the future, Subtronics shows no signs of slowing down. Their commitment to pushing boundaries and their unwavering dedication to their fans guarantee that their influence on the dubstep scene will endure.

Exercises

1. Explore some of Subtronics' tracks and dissect their sound design. Pay attention to the different layers, textures, and effects used in their productions. Try to recreate some of these sounds in your own music production.

2. Listen to some early dubstep tracks from artists like Skream, Benga, and Digital Mystikz. Take note of the elements that define the genre and compare them to Subtronics' style. How do they differ, and how has Subtronics expanded on the sound of dubstep?

3. Research and discover emerging dubstep artists who have been inspired by Subtronics. Listen to their music and analyze how they incorporate elements of Subtronics' sound into their own productions. Reflect on the ongoing influence of Subtronics on the dubstep scene.

4. Attend a live dubstep show or festival featuring Subtronics or other dubstep artists. Experience the energy and atmosphere firsthand. Pay attention to the stage presence, visuals, and the crowd's reaction. Reflect on how these elements contribute to the overall impact of dubstep as a genre.

5. Connect with the dubstep community online and engage in discussions about Subtronics' impact on the genre. Share your thoughts and reflections, and learn from other fans and artists. Foster a sense of community and contribute to the ongoing growth and evolution of dubstep.

Reflecting on Their Contribution to the Music Industry

As Subtronics looks back on their journey and success, they can't help but feel a deep sense of gratitude for the impact they have made on the music industry. Their unique blend of bass music and dubstep has not only captivated audiences, but it has also influenced a new generation of artists and shaped the sound of music festivals worldwide. In this section, we will delve into their contribution to the music industry, exploring the ways in which Subtronics has left a lasting legacy.

Pioneering the Next Generation of Bass Music

Subtronics' music has been at the forefront of the bass music movement, pushing the boundaries of the genre and paving the way for new and innovative sounds. Their ability to create heavy-hitting drops combined with intricate sound design techniques has garnered them a dedicated following and positioned them as pioneers of modern bass music.

One of the ways in which Subtronics has pioneered the next generation of bass music is through their incorporation of elements from other genres. They have seamlessly blended hip-hop, trap, and even elements of metal into their tracks, creating a truly unique and dynamic sound. This fusion of genres has resonated with fans, attracting a diverse audience and expanding the reach of bass music to new horizons.

Influencing Other Artists and Producers

Subtronics' success and unique sound have not gone unnoticed by other artists and producers in the industry. Their creative approach to music production and genre-blending has served as an inspiration to countless aspiring musicians.

Through collaborations and features with other artists, Subtronics has shared their knowledge and expertise, further influencing the direction of electronic music. Their willingness to collaborate and experiment with various artists has allowed for new ideas and sounds to emerge, pushing the boundaries of what is possible in the genre.

Shaping the Sound of Music Festivals

With their high-energy performances and captivating stage presence, Subtronics has become a staple in the lineup of major music festivals around the world. Their ability to engage the crowd and create an immersive experience has set a new standard for live performances within the electronic music scene.

The impact of Subtronics on the sound of music festivals can be felt not only in the bass music community but also across different genres. Their influence has pushed other artists to elevate their performances, incorporating more interactive visuals and stage production. They have shown that a live show is not just about the music but also about creating an unforgettable experience for the audience.

The Role of Subtronics in the Rise of Dubstep

Dubstep has seen a resurgence in popularity in recent years, and Subtronics has played a significant role in this revival. Their ability to create heavy, wobbling basslines combined with hard-hitting drops has reinvigorated the genre and attracted a new wave of fans.

Subtronics' contribution to the rise of dubstep goes beyond their own music. They have actively supported and collaborated with emerging dubstep artists, providing a platform for them to showcase their talent and contribute to the growth of the genre. Their influence can be seen through the emergence of new dubstep subgenres and the increasing popularity of dubstep-inspired tracks in mainstream music.

Reflecting on Their Contribution

As Subtronics reflects on their contribution to the music industry, they remain humble and grateful for the opportunities they have been given. Their success has not only shaped the sound of bass music but has also inspired a new generation of musicians to push the boundaries of electronic music.

Looking ahead, Subtronics is determined to continue evolving their sound and pushing the limits of what is possible in the industry. Their dedication to their craft, combined with their genuine passion for music, ensures that their contribution to the music industry will endure for years to come.

In conclusion, Subtronics' unique sound and groundbreaking approach to music production have solidified their place in the music industry. Through their pioneering of bass music, their influence on other artists and producers, and their impact on music festivals and dubstep, they have left an indelible mark on the industry. As their journey continues, Subtronics remains a beacon of inspiration, reminding aspiring artists to pursue their passion and create music that resonates with audiences around the world.

Section Four: The Hype and Expectations

Navigating Success and Maintaining Authenticity

In the hyper-competitive world of electronic music, success can be both a dream come true and a double-edged sword. As Subtronics rose to fame, they found themselves grappling with the daunting task of navigating their newfound success while remaining true to their authentic sound and vision. In this section, we will explore the challenges they faced and the strategies they employed to stay grounded in the face of immense pressure.

The Temptation of Mainstream Appeal

As Subtronics' popularity soared, the lure of mainstream success became increasingly enticing. The music industry was beckoning with promises of chart-topping hits and lucrative collaborations. The band members were well aware that conforming to a more commercial sound could propel them to superstardom.

However, in the midst of this temptation, Subtronics made a conscious decision: to prioritize their artistic integrity over fleeting success. They understood that compromising their unique style would alienate their dedicated fan base and diminish their impact on the scene they hold dear.

Staying True to Their Sound

Maintaining authenticity in the face of success requires strength of character and a deep understanding of oneself as an artist. For Subtronics, it meant embracing their roots and never losing sight of the sound that ignited their passion in the first place.

The band members remained grounded by constantly reminding themselves of the music that inspired them to enter the EDM scene. They would often revisit tracks from their early days, drawing inspiration from the raw energy and unfiltered creativity they possessed. By staying connected to their musical origins, Subtronics ensured that their music always carried an authentic and genuine vibe.

Balancing Commercial Demands

While the band consciously chose to prioritize authenticity, they also recognized the need to find a balance between their artistic vision and commercial demands. This delicate balance allowed them to reach a wider audience without compromising their sound.

Subtronics embraced collaboration as a means of exploring different musical horizons. By working with artists from various genres, they infused their unique style into mainstream tracks, introducing their signature sound to new listeners. This strategic approach not only expanded their fan base but also showcased their versatility without diluting their artistic expression.

Staying Connected with Their Fan Base

One of the critical aspects of maintaining authenticity is staying connected with the fan base that helped propel Subtronics to success. The band members understood the importance of nurturing a relationship with their fans and providing an inclusive space for them to express themselves.

Social media played a pivotal role in this connection, allowing the band members to communicate directly with their fans on a daily basis. They would often interact with fans through live streams, Q&A sessions, and personal messages, ensuring that their authenticity resonated beyond the music.

Resisting Industry Pressure

As Subtronics rose to prominence, industry pressures mounted. Their success attracted attention from record labels and agents who aimed to mold the band into a marketable commodity. However, Subtronics staunchly resisted these pressures, choosing to remain fiercely independent.

By retaining creative control and navigating their own path, Subtronics were able to maintain the authenticity that had endeared them to their fans. They rejected offers that would have compromised their artistic freedom, instead opting to continue releasing music on their own terms.

Embracing Evolution while Staying True

While maintaining authenticity is vital, it is equally important for artists to evolve and grow. Subtronics realized that they could embrace new sounds and styles while staying true to their core identity.

They approached innovation with an open mind, experimenting with new sounds and techniques while maintaining their signature heavy bass and distinctive drops. This evolution allowed them to stay relevant in a rapidly changing music landscape without losing sight of who they were as artists.

Finding Inspiration from the Subtronics Community

Finally, the Subtronics community played a crucial role in helping the band maintain their authenticity. The unwavering support and love from their fans served as a reminder of why they started making music in the first place.

Subtronics actively sought input from their fans, engaging them in the creative process. They would often ask for feedback on works in progress, allowing the community to shape their music alongside them. This collaborative approach not only strengthened their connection with fans but also ensured that their music continued to reflect the authentic Subtronics experience.

Conclusion

In the cutthroat world of electronic music, maintaining authenticity amidst success is no small feat. Yet, Subtronics managed to navigate these treacherous waters with grace and integrity. By prioritizing their artistic vision, staying grounded in their roots, balancing commercial demands, engaging with their fan base, and resisting industry pressures, they remained true to themselves while continuing to evolve and inspire. Their story serves as a reminder to aspiring artists that success is not about conforming—it's about staying true to one's unique voice. As Subtronics continues to make waves in the music industry, their story will undoubtedly leave an enduring legacy for generations to come.

Dealing with Criticism and Pressure

Navigating the music industry can be a rollercoaster ride, and no artist is immune to criticism and pressure. Subtronics, despite their immense success, are no exception. In this section, we will explore how they deal with the inevitable criticism and pressure that comes with their rising fame and growing fan base.

Embracing Feedback

As Subtronics' popularity grew, so did the expectations of their fans and the wider music community. With increased visibility comes increased scrutiny and criticism. However, Subtronics understands the value of constructive feedback and actively seeks it out. They believe that feedback is crucial for personal and artistic growth.

To deal with criticism, Subtronics adopts an open mindset. They welcome both positive and negative feedback, viewing each as an opportunity to learn and improve. They recognize that not every song or performance will resonate with everyone, and that's okay. By analyzing and internalizing constructive criticism, Subtronics is able to refine their craft and push the boundaries of their music.

Maintaining Authenticity

In the face of pressure to conform to industry standards or meet fan expectations, Subtronics stays true to their artistic vision. They understand that compromising their unique style for the sake of pleasing others would only lead to dissatisfaction and unhappiness.

By staying authentic and true to themselves, Subtronics has built a loyal fan base that appreciates their originality. They prioritize creating music that they genuinely love, rather than chasing trends or trying to fit into a specific genre. This commitment to authenticity not only enables them to stand out in a crowded market but also enables them to weather criticism and pressure with grace.

Dealing with Public Scrutiny

In today's digital age, artists are exposed to a level of public scrutiny like never before. Subtronics embraces the realities of living in the public eye, understanding that criticism and judgment are unavoidable.

To protect their mental and emotional well-being, Subtronics consciously establishes boundaries surrounding their public persona. They recognize that not every opinion deserves their attention and that not everything shared on social media is an accurate representation of reality. By consciously disconnecting from the noise of the online world when necessary, they are able to maintain a healthy mindset and stay focused on their passion for music.

Support and Self-Care

Dealing with criticism and pressure can take a toll on anyone, no matter how resilient they are. Subtronics acknowledges the importance of having a strong support system in their personal and professional lives. They surround themselves with trusted friends, family, and team members who provide them with emotional support and guidance during challenging times.

Additionally, Subtronics recognizes the need for self-care. They prioritize their mental and physical well-being by engaging in activities that help them relax and recharge. Whether it's taking breaks from touring, seeking therapy, or practicing mindfulness, Subtronics understand that self-care is crucial to maintain their creativity and resilience.

Redefining Success

In the midst of criticism and pressure, Subtronics continuously redefines their definition of success. Instead of solely focusing on commercial success or external validation, they prioritize personal fulfillment and artistic growth. This mindset shift allows them to stay grounded and motivated, reminding themselves that their music is an expression of their passion and creativity, rather than a means to achieve superficial goals.

By redefining success in their own terms, Subtronics is able to shield themselves from the negative effects of criticism and pressure. This perspective empowers them to remain focused on their artistic journey and to keep pushing their boundaries, regardless of external opinions.

In conclusion, Subtronics recognizes that criticism and pressure are inevitable in the music industry. However, they have developed effective strategies to deal with these challenges. By embracing feedback, maintaining authenticity, establishing boundaries, seeking support, and redefining success, they are able to navigate the highs and lows of their career with resilience and grace.

The Fear of Disappointing Fans

The fear of disappointing fans is a common concern among artists, and Subtronics is no exception. As their popularity grew and their fan base expanded, the pressure to meet expectations and maintain their artistic integrity became a constant source of worry. In this section, we will delve into the various aspects of this fear and explore how Subtronics navigated through it.

Understanding the Expectations

One of the primary reasons for the fear of disappointing fans is the weight of expectations. When fans invest time, money, and emotions into an artist's work, they naturally have certain expectations for future releases. Subtronics' fans eagerly await new tracks, remixes, and live performances, and they anticipate innovative and mind-blowing music experiences.

As Subtronics gained more recognition, they faced the challenge of meeting these heightened expectations. They questioned whether they could consistently deliver the same level of energy and creativity that their fans had come to love. The fear of not living up to these expectations can be paralyzing, hindering artistic growth and stifling experimentation.

Staying True to Their Vision

While it can be tempting for artists to cater to popular demand and follow trends, Subtronics decided to stay true to their unique vision. They understood that their fans were attracted to their distinct sound and style, and deviating from that could alienate their core audience.

Overcoming the fear of disappointing fans required the band to trust their instincts and have confidence in their artistic choices. By focusing on their own vision and staying authentic, they were able to create music that resonated with their fans on a deeper level.

Managing Creative Self-Doubt

Creative self-doubt is a constant companion for many artists, and Subtronics was not immune to it. They questioned whether their new releases would be well-received, if they were pushing the boundaries too far, or if they were repeating themselves.

To manage these doubts, Subtronics adopted a mindset of continual growth and exploration. They embraced the idea that not every track or live performance would be a masterpiece, but instead viewed each experience as an opportunity to learn and evolve. They understood that taking risks and experimenting with new sounds was crucial for their artistic development.

Open Communication with Fans

Rather than allowing the fear of disappointing fans to consume them, Subtronics chose to have open communication with their fan base. They recognized that their fans were invested in their journey and valued their feedback.

By actively engaging with their fans through social media, fan clubs, and other online platforms, Subtronics was able to gauge their expectations and address any concerns directly. This open dialogue not only helped alleviate their own anxieties but also allowed their fans to feel heard and acknowledged.

Embracing Evolution

As artists, it is natural to evolve and explore new territories. However, the fear of disappointing fans can sometimes hinder this growth. Subtronics coped with this fear by embracing evolution and allowing their music to mature naturally.

They understood that their fans were not looking for the same sound and style in perpetuity, but rather for continuous innovation. By embracing change and experimenting with new genres and collaborations, Subtronics was able to evolve their music while still staying true to their artistic identity.

Collaborative Support

The fear of disappointing fans can feel overwhelming, but Subtronics found strength in their collaborative support system. They leaned on each other, their team, and fellow artists to navigate through the challenges and self-doubt.

By surrounding themselves with people who genuinely believed in their talent and supported their artistic vision, Subtronics was able to overcome their fear. Building a strong support network not only helped them gain perspective but also provided reassurance during moments of uncertainty.

The Unexpected Surprises

While the fear of disappointing fans is a legitimate concern, Subtronics experienced unexpected surprises along the way. They discovered that their fans appreciated their willingness to take risks and explore new sounds. Even when experiments didn't resonate with every fan, they often sparked interesting conversations and pushed the boundaries of what was possible in bass music.

Subtronics realized that their fans were willing to trust their artistic journey and appreciated the authentic experiences they delivered. This revelation helped ease their fear and allowed them to focus on creating music they loved, knowing that their fans would come along for the ride.

Conclusion

The fear of disappointing fans can be a daunting challenge for any artist, and Subtronics was not immune to this struggle. By understanding expectations, staying true to their vision, managing creative self-doubt, embracing open communication, embracing evolution, seeking collaborative support, and embracing unexpected surprises, they were able to navigate this fear successfully.

Subtronics learned that authenticity, growth, and trust in their artistic process were paramount in their journey. Their ability to overcome this fear allowed them to push the boundaries of electronic music, leave a lasting impact on the EDM scene, and ultimately build a strong, supportive fan base.

As the story of Subtronics continues, they remain committed to facing their fears head-on, embracing challenges, and thriving as artists.

Balancing Personal Life and Professional Demands

Finding the right balance between personal life and professional demands is a challenge that many artists face in the music industry. Subtronics is no exception. In this section, we will explore the strategies and experiences of Subtronics in maintaining a healthy balance between their personal lives and the demands of their successful music career.

The Toll of the Music Industry

The music industry is notorious for its demanding nature and intense schedules. For Subtronics, the constant touring and performing can take a toll on their personal lives. Long hours of rehearsals, late-night shows, and constant travel can leave them physically and emotionally exhausted. Additionally, the pressure to consistently deliver high-quality performances can be overwhelming and may lead to burnout.

Prioritizing Self-Care

One of the key strategies that Subtronics employs to maintain balance is prioritizing self-care. They understand that taking care of themselves is essential for their well-being and creativity. They make sure to allocate time for rest, healthy eating, exercise, and spending time with loved ones. By practicing self-care, they are able to recharge and bring their best to both their personal life and their music career.

Setting Boundaries

Setting boundaries is crucial in balancing personal life and professional demands. Subtronics recognizes the importance of carving out time for themselves and their loved ones. They are not afraid to say no to excessive work commitments or prioritize personal time, even during busy periods. By setting boundaries and sticking to them, they can maintain a sense of control and prevent their personal lives from being overshadowed by their professional obligations.

Maintaining Social Connections

In the fast-paced music industry, it is easy to become isolated from friends and family. Subtronics understands the importance of maintaining strong social connections outside of their music career. They make a conscious effort to stay in touch with loved ones, whether through phone calls, video chats, or spending quality time together when they have breaks from touring. By nurturing these relationships, they can find support, grounding, and a sense of normalcy amidst the chaotic music industry.

Seeking Professional Support

Sometimes, balancing personal life and professional demands can become overwhelming. Subtronics recognizes the value of seeking professional support when needed. They are not afraid to reach out to therapists or counselors who can provide guidance and help them navigate the challenges they face. By seeking professional support, they can gain insights, develop coping strategies, and maintain their mental well-being.

Unconventional Strategies: Meditation and Mindfulness

In addition to conventional strategies, Subtronics also incorporates unconventional practices such as meditation and mindfulness into their daily routines. They have found that these practices help them stay grounded, reduce stress, and enhance their focus. By incorporating these practices, they are able to maintain a sense of balance and inner peace amidst the whirlwind of their professional lives.

Applying Balance to Performance

Balancing personal life and professional demands also extends to their performances. Subtronics understands that while their fans expect high-energy shows, they also need to take care of themselves on stage. They prioritize their well-being by ensuring they have breaks between shows, staying hydrated, and not overexerting themselves physically. By taking care of themselves during performances, they can avoid burnout and deliver memorable experiences to their fans.

Overall, finding balance between personal life and professional demands is an ongoing journey for Subtronics. Through prioritizing self-care, setting boundaries, maintaining social connections, seeking professional support, and even incorporating unconventional practices, they are able to navigate the challenges of the music industry while maintaining their personal well-being. This balance allows them to thrive creatively and continue to make a lasting impact in the EDM scene.

Looking Ahead: What's Next for Subtronics?

As Subtronics continues to make waves in the electronic music scene, fans eagerly anticipate what the future holds for this innovative duo. With their unique sound and captivating performances, Subtronics has solidified their place as one of the most exciting acts in bass music. In this section, we will explore what's next for Subtronics and discuss the possibilities and challenges they may face as they move forward in their musical journey.

Exploring new genres and pushing boundaries

One thing that sets Subtronics apart is their willingness to experiment with different genres and sounds. As they look ahead, it's likely that they will continue to explore new territory and push the boundaries of their music. This could involve incorporating elements from other genres such as hip-hop, trap, or even rock. By fusing these influences with their signature bass music, Subtronics could create a truly unique and groundbreaking sound that further sets them apart from their peers.

Problem 1: Finding the balance between experimentation and staying true to their sound.

As Subtronics explores new genres and sounds, they must strike a delicate balance between experimentation and staying true to their core identity. While taking risks can lead to exciting and fresh music, it's important for them to maintain the elements that drew fans to their music in the first place. How can Subtronics continue to evolve their sound while still keeping their loyal fan base engaged and satisfied?

Solution: Consistently communicate and involve their fan base.

To navigate this challenge, Subtronics can actively involve their fan base in the creative process. By sharing snippets of new tracks or ideas on social media platforms, they can gather feedback and gauge fan reactions. This open and transparent communication can help them understand what elements of their music fans appreciate the most, allowing them to make informed decisions while evolving their sound.

Expanding their reach globally

Subtronics has already achieved considerable success in the United States, but the world is hungry for their unique brand of bass music. As they look ahead, it's crucial for them to expand their reach globally and captivate audiences all around the world. This could involve touring in different countries, collaborating with international artists, and establishing a strong presence in diverse music markets.

Problem 2: Navigating the complexities of international touring and music scenes.

Expanding globally comes with its own set of challenges. Subtronics will need to navigate the complexities of international touring, including logistics, visa requirements, and adapting to different cultural contexts. They will also need to build relationships with local promoters and connect with audiences outside their home country. How can Subtronics effectively overcome these challenges and establish themselves as an international powerhouse in bass music?

Solution: Collaboration and cultural immersion.

To overcome these challenges, Subtronics can collaborate with local artists and producers to gain insights into the different music scenes and audiences. By embracing the local culture and immersing themselves in the music community of each country they visit, they can establish a genuine connection with fans and music industry professionals. This will help them navigate the complexities of international touring and pave the way for successful performances.

Innovation in live performances

Subtronics' live performances are known for their high energy and immersive experiences. Looking ahead, they will undoubtedly seek to innovate in their stage productions and push the limits of what is possible in live performances. This could involve incorporating cutting-edge technologies, exploring new visual experiences, and creating unforgettable moments for their fans.

Problem 3: Balancing technology with authenticity in live performances.

With the advancement of technology, there are endless possibilities for enhancing live performances. However, Subtronics must be careful not to rely solely on flashy gimmicks and lose the authenticity that makes their shows so compelling. How can they strike the right balance between incorporating technology and maintaining the raw energy and connection with their audience?

Solution: Prioritizing the emotional connection with the audience.

To maintain authenticity, Subtronics can prioritize creating emotional connections with their audience. While incorporating new technologies and visual experiences, they can ensure that these elements enhance, rather than overshadow, their performance. By focusing on the energy exchange between the artists and the crowd, they can deliver unforgettable experiences that leave a lasting impact.

Giving back through charitable initiatives

As Subtronics continues to grow in popularity and influence, they have the opportunity to use their platform for a greater purpose. Looking ahead, they may seek to engage in charitable initiatives and give back to their community and causes they deeply care about.

Problem 4: Identifying meaningful charitable initiatives and making a genuine impact.

With numerous charitable causes and organizations to choose from, it can be overwhelming for Subtronics to decide where to focus their efforts. Additionally, they must ensure that their involvement in charitable initiatives is genuine and impactful. How can Subtronics identify the causes that align with their values and make a meaningful difference in those areas?

Solution: Research, collaboration, and long-term commitment.

To address this challenge, Subtronics can conduct extensive research on various charitable organizations and causes. They can seek collaborations with established non-profit organizations that align with their mission and values. By forming long-term partnerships, they can make a sustained and meaningful impact, leveraging their platform to raise awareness and resources for important societal issues.

Continuing the legacy and influence

As Subtronics looks ahead, it's crucial for them to consider how their music will continue to inspire the next generation of artists and shape the electronic music industry. They have the opportunity to leave a lasting legacy and influence future trends in bass music and beyond.

Problem 5: Maintaining relevance and staying ahead of the curve.

The music industry is constantly evolving, and Subtronics must stay relevant and innovative to continue making an impact. How can they anticipate and adapt to changing trends while staying true to their artistic vision? How can they continue to push the boundaries of bass music and inspire others to follow in their footsteps?

Solution: Embracing flexibility and creative reinvention.

To tackle this challenge, Subtronics can embrace flexibility and creative reinvention. They can stay attuned to emerging trends and experiment with new sounds and styles. By continuously pushing the boundaries of their own music and collaborating with artists from different genres, they can stay ahead of the curve and inspire others to push the limits of their own creativity.

Conclusion

The future of Subtronics is filled with endless possibilities. As they continue to evolve their sound, expand their reach, and innovate in live performances, fans can expect to be taken on a thrilling journey of bass music exploration. With a commitment to authenticity, a dedication to their fans, and a drive to make a positive impact, Subtronics is poised to leave an indelible mark on the electronic music scene. The story of Subtronics is far from over, and the best is yet to come.

Section Five: Legacy and Influence

The Lasting Impact of Their Music

Subtronics has undeniably made a significant impact on the electronic music scene. Their music has touched the hearts and souls of fans all around the world, leaving a lasting impression on both the industry and their listeners. In this section, we will explore the various ways in which their music has made a mark and continues to resonate with the audience.

Innovation and Originality

One of the key reasons for the lasting impact of Subtronics' music is their constant pursuit of innovation and their commitment to creating original sounds. They have pushed the boundaries of bass music and dubstep, constantly experimenting with new genres, styles, and techniques. This relentless pursuit of innovation has inspired a new generation of producers and artists to think outside the box and explore new sonic territories.

Subtronics' unique sound design and attention to detail have set them apart from their peers. Their tracks feature intricate basslines, powerful drops, and captivating melodies that captivate listeners and keep them coming back for more. By pushing the limits of what can be done with electronic music production, they have inspired countless artists to challenge conventions and explore their own creative potential.

Emotional Connection

Subtronics' music has a distinct ability to create an emotional connection with its listeners. Their tracks often evoke a wide range of emotions, from pure excitement and energy to introspection and contemplation. Each song tells a story, taking the listener on a journey through the use of carefully crafted melodies, harmonies, and atmospheric elements.

The emotional resonance of Subtronics' music is a testament to their ability to tap into the human experience and express it through their art. Their music has become a soundtrack for moments of joy, sadness, and everything in between, providing a medium through which fans can connect with their own emotions and experiences.

Community and Unity

Subtronics' music has fostered a sense of community and unity within the EDM scene. Their high-energy performances and infectious beats bring people together, creating a shared experience that transcends cultural and geographical boundaries. Whether it's at a festival, a club, or through online interactions, fans of Subtronics find solace and connection with like-minded individuals who share a love for their music.

The inclusive and welcoming nature of Subtronics' music has encouraged fans to celebrate diversity and embrace each other's differences. Their music has become a catalyst for building a community that promotes love, acceptance, and understanding. Through fan clubs, fan-made art, and online interactions, Subtronics has created a supportive and passionate fan base that continues to grow and thrive.

Inspiration and Influence

Subtronics' music has served as a source of inspiration for aspiring artists and producers. Their unique sound and groundbreaking approach to production have sparked creativity and encouraged others to push the boundaries of what is possible in electronic music. Many up-and-coming artists look to Subtronics as a role model, seeking to emulate their innovative techniques and their ability to create memorable and impactful music.

Furthermore, Subtronics' influence extends beyond just the EDM scene. They have been instrumental in bringing bass music and dubstep to the forefront of popular music culture. Their collaborations with big-name artists, as well as their electrifying live performances, have exposed a wider audience to the sound and style of Subtronics. By bridging the gap between underground and mainstream music, they have helped shape the direction of the entire music industry.

Environmental Consciousness

In addition to their musical impact, Subtronics also uses their platform to raise awareness about environmental issues and promote sustainable living. They actively engage in charitable initiatives and support causes that aim to protect the planet. Through their music and their actions, they inspire their fans to become more environmentally conscious and make a positive impact on the world.

By incorporating messages of environmental sustainability into their music and live performances, Subtronics encourages their fans to think critically about their own environmental footprint. They use their platform to advocate for change and inspire others to take action, proving that music can be a powerful tool for raising awareness and promoting positive social change.

An Unconventional Remix Challenge

To inspire his fans to get creative and show their own musical talents, Subtronics initiated an unconventional remix challenge. He invited his fans to remix one of his tracks using only household objects as instruments. This unique challenge encouraged fans to think outside the box and explore the limitless possibilities of creating music with everyday items.

The challenge sparked a wave of creativity, with fans submitting their inventive remixes using everything from kitchen utensils to office supplies. Subtronics embraced this unconventional approach and showcased the best submissions on his social media platforms, giving a platform to emerging talent and demonstrating the power of music to transcend traditional boundaries.

Conclusion

Subtronics' music has left an indelible mark on the electronic music scene. Through their innovation, emotional connection, community-building, and environmental consciousness, they have created a legacy that will continue to inspire and influence future generations of artists. Their commitment to pushing the boundaries of electronic music and connecting with their fans has paved the way for a new era of creativity and unity in the industry. As Subtronics' journey continues, their impact reverberates throughout the music world, shining a lasting light on their remarkable achievements and inspiring others to follow in their footsteps.

Inspiring the Next Generation of Artists

As Subtronics continues to make their mark on the electronic music scene, one of the most significant aspects of their journey is the inspiration they provide to the next generation of artists. From their unique sound to their electrifying live performances, Subtronics has become a beacon of creativity and innovation for aspiring musicians. In this section, we will explore the ways in which Subtronics inspires and empowers young artists, encouraging them to pursue their dreams and push the boundaries of electronic music.

The Power of Authenticity

One of the most inspiring qualities of Subtronics is their unwavering commitment to authenticity. From the early days of their career, they have stayed true to their unique style and sound, never compromising their artistic vision for commercial success. This commitment to authenticity sends a powerful message to aspiring artists, encouraging them to embrace their own individuality and create music that is true to themselves.

Subtronics' success is a testament to the fact that originality and staying true to one's artistic vision can lead to remarkable achievements. This inspires young artists to explore their own creativity, experiment with different genres, and forge their own unique paths in the music industry.

Embracing Collaboration

Subtronics' collaborative spirit is another source of inspiration for the next generation of artists. Throughout their career, they have actively sought out collaborations with fellow musicians, vocalists, and producers, resulting in exciting and boundary-pushing tracks. By working with others and embracing diverse perspectives, Subtronics demonstrates the power of synergy and the limitless possibilities that arise from collaboration.

The willingness of Subtronics to share their platform and support other artists is a refreshing departure from the notion of competition often associated with the music industry. They actively seek out emerging talent, providing them with opportunities to showcase their skills and gain exposure. This collaborative mindset inspires young artists to seek out mutually beneficial partnerships and create a sense of community within the music scene.

Pushing Boundaries and Experimentation

Subtronics' relentless pursuit of pushing boundaries and exploring new sounds is a constant source of inspiration for aspiring musicians. Their fearless approach to experimentation and innovation challenges conventional norms and opens up new avenues of creativity. By constantly pushing the limits of electronic music, Subtronics encourages young artists to think outside the box and strive for groundbreaking sonic experiences.

Moreover, Subtronics shares their insights and knowledge with aspiring artists through tutorials, production guides, and live streams. This commitment to education and mentorship empowers the next generation to embrace technology, learn new production techniques, and refine their craft. By providing resources and guidance, Subtronics inspires young artists to continually improve their skills and push themselves to new heights.

Social and Environmental Activism

Another aspect of Subtronics' influence on the next generation of artists is their commitment to social and environmental activism. They actively use their platform to raise awareness about important issues and advocate for positive change. From supporting charitable initiatives to promoting sustainability, Subtronics inspires young artists to use their music and influence for the greater good.

By engaging in activism and addressing social and environmental challenges, Subtronics demonstrates that music has the power to ignite meaningful conversations and inspire positive action. This aspect of their journey urges aspiring artists to channel their creativity towards making a difference in the world, encouraging them to explore the intersection of music and social change.

Unconventional Strategies for Success

In addition to their musical prowess, Subtronics' unconventional strategies for success provide valuable lessons for the next generation of artists. They have embraced digital platforms and social media to build a dedicated fan base and create a strong online presence. By leveraging these tools, they have been able to independently release music, connect with fans, and book shows without traditional industry gatekeepers.

This approach challenges traditional notions of success in the music industry and empowers young artists to take control of their own careers. Subtronics' story serves as a reminder that with determination, creativity, and a strong work ethic, artists can forge their own paths and achieve success on their terms.

Conclusion

Subtronics' journey is not just a testament to their own talent and dedication but also a source of inspiration for the next generation of artists. By staying true to their authentic sound, embracing collaboration, pushing boundaries, and advocating for positive change, Subtronics demonstrates that the sky is the limit when it comes to pursuing a career in electronic music. They have created a legacy that will continue to inspire and influence young artists for years to come, leaving an enduring glow in the world of music.

Building a Sustainable Career in the Music Industry

Building a sustainable career in the music industry is no easy task. It requires a combination of talent, hard work, dedication, and strategic decision-making. In this section, we will explore the key factors and strategies that have helped Subtronics establish themselves as successful artists and navigate the ever-changing landscape of the music business.

Understanding the Business Side of Music

While musicians are often driven by their passion for creating music, it is important to recognize that the music industry is also a business. To build a sustainable career, artists need to have a solid understanding of the industry and how it operates. This includes knowledge of contracts, royalties, licensing, publishing, and marketing.

One of the first steps in building a sustainable career is to surround yourself with a knowledgeable and trustworthy team. This includes hiring a manager, booking agent, and lawyer who specialize in the music industry. These professionals can help navigate the complexities of contracts, negotiate deals, and protect your rights as an artist.

Example: For Subtronics, hiring a manager who had industry experience was crucial in establishing their career. Their manager helped them secure deals with record labels and navigate the complexities of the music business, allowing them to focus on their music and creative process.

Diversifying Income Streams

In today's music industry, relying solely on music sales and streaming revenue is often not enough to sustain a career. Artists need to explore and create multiple income streams.

One of the most common income streams for musicians is live performances. Subtronics recognized the importance of touring early on and made it a priority. They have built a reputation for high-energy performances, captivating audiences at major festivals and venues around the world. By touring consistently, they not only generate revenue from ticket sales but also expand their fanbase and build a strong connection with their audience.

Merchandise is another significant income stream for musicians. Subtronics has put effort into creating unique and visually appealing merchandise, which has become highly sought after by their fans. From t-shirts and hoodies to stickers and accessories, their merch reflects their distinctive brand and contributes to their financial stability.

Example: In addition to live performances and merchandise, Subtronics has also diversified their income streams by exploring brand partnerships and sponsorships. By collaborating with companies that align with their brand and values, they are able to generate additional revenue while also expanding their reach and exposure.

Building and Engaging with a Strong Fanbase

A loyal and engaged fanbase is the foundation of a sustainable career in the music industry. Building and nurturing a fanbase is a long-term investment that requires continuous effort and authenticity.

Subtronics understands the importance of connecting with their fans and has made it a priority to engage with them both online and offline. They actively interact with their fans on social media, responding to comments and messages, and regularly sharing updates on their music, shows, and personal life.

In addition to online engagement, Subtronics creates opportunities for in-person interactions with their fans. They host meet and greets, fan club events, and fan appreciation parties. These experiences not only allow them to express their gratitude to their fans but also foster a sense of community and belonging among their fanbase.

Example: Subtronics often surprises their fans with little gestures of appreciation, such as sending personalized messages or gifts. These small acts of kindness go a long way in building a strong and loyal fanbase.

Strategic Marketing and Branding

Effective marketing and branding are essential for sustaining a career in the music industry. Artists need to have a clear and consistent brand identity that resonates with their target audience.

Subtronics has carefully crafted their brand image, which combines elements of their music, visual aesthetics, and personality. From their unique sound design to their distinctive visuals and stage production, every aspect of their brand reflects their creativity and vision.

They also leverage social media platforms to their advantage, utilizing strategies such as posting engaging content, collaborating with influencers, and running targeted advertising campaigns. By staying active and relevant on social media, they are able to reach and connect with a wider audience.

Example: Subtronics is known for their distinctive artwork and visual aesthetics, which play a significant role in their branding. They collaborate with talented visual artists to create stunning visuals that further enhance their live performances and create a memorable experience for their fans.

Continued Growth and Adaptation

To have a sustainable career in the music industry, it is essential to stay relevant and adapt to the ever-changing landscape. This involves continuously pushing boundaries, experimenting with new sounds, and staying open to collaborations and new opportunities.

Subtronics has demonstrated their commitment to growth and adaptation through their music. They consistently explore new genres and experiment with different production techniques, allowing their sound to evolve while staying true to their unique style.

They also actively seek out collaborations with other artists, both within the EDM scene and beyond. By working with a diverse range of musicians, vocalists, and producers, Subtronics is able to expand their creative horizons and reach new audiences.

Example: Subtronics recently collaborated with a popular hip-hop artist, showcasing their ability to adapt their sound and collaborate across genres. This collaboration not only introduced them to a new audience but also solidified their reputation as versatile and innovative artists.

Ethics and Authenticity

Building a sustainable career in the music industry is not just about financial success; it is also about staying true to your values and maintaining authenticity. It is important for artists to align themselves with causes they believe in and use their platform to make a positive impact.

Subtronics has shown a commitment to ethics and authenticity by using their music and platform to raise awareness and support charitable initiatives. They have actively contributed to causes such as mental health, environmental conservation, and community building.

Example: Subtronics organized a charity event where they donated a percentage of the ticket sales to a local nonprofit organization. This not only helped raise funds for a worthy cause but also showcased their commitment to giving back to the community.

In conclusion, building a sustainable career in the music industry requires a combination of business acumen, diversifying income streams, building a loyal fanbase, strategic marketing, continuous growth and adaptation, and maintaining authenticity. By following these principles and strategies, artists like Subtronics can navigate the ever-changing music industry and leave a lasting impact on the world of music.

Leaving Their Mark on Electronic Music History

As Subtronics embarked on their musical journey, little did they know that they would leave an indelible mark on the history of electronic music. Their unique sound and innovative approach to bass music would shape the genre and influence a new generation of artists. In this section, we will explore the ways in which Subtronics left their mark on electronic music and discuss their lasting legacy.

One of the key aspects of Subtronics' impact on electronic music history was their distinct sound. They pushed the boundaries of bass music, fusing elements of dubstep, trap, and other genres to create a style that was uniquely their own. By blending heavy basslines, intricate sound design, and infectious melodies, Subtronics created a sonic experience that resonated with audiences worldwide.

Their signature drops became the calling card of their tracks, instantly recognizable and often imitated. Subtronics' attention to detail in sound design allowed them to create memorable moments that would send crowds into a frenzy. Whether it was a gut-wrenching bass growl or a catchy vocal sample, their drops became anthems on dancefloors and catapulted their popularity within the EDM scene.

But it wasn't just their sound that left a mark. Subtronics' impact also extended to their live performances. Their high-energy sets and engaging stage presence captivated audiences and created an immersive experience. With their signature visuals and stage production, they transformed each show into a spectacle that left a lasting impression on concertgoers.

Collaborations played a crucial role in Subtronics' rise to prominence, and their willingness to work with other artists further cemented their influence on the electronic music landscape. By collaborating with vocalists and rappers, they infused their tracks with a new dimension and opened up their music to a wider audience. These collaborations showcased Subtronics' versatility and demonstrated their ability to adapt to different styles and genres.

Subtronics' impact on the EDM scene extended beyond their music. They actively engaged with their fan base through meet and greets, online interactions, and charitable initiatives. By creating a safe space for their fans and fostering a sense of community, they inspired loyalty and built a dedicated following. Their fans, affectionately known as the "Cyclops Army," became an integral part of their legacy, spreading the word and supporting them throughout their career.

In addition to their direct influence on the EDM scene, Subtronics played a larger role in the evolution of electronic music as a whole. They pioneered the next generation of bass music, pushing the boundaries of what was possible within the genre. By constantly experimenting with new sounds and techniques, they challenged the status quo and inspired other artists and producers to do the same.

Subtronics' impact was felt not only in the studio and on stage but also in the larger music festival landscape. Their memorable sets at major festivals created a buzz and helped shape the sound of these events. As Subtronics became festival favorites, their influence extended to other artists and played a significant role in the rise of dubstep and bass music within the festival circuit.

Reflecting on their contribution to electronic music, Subtronics remains humble and grateful for the opportunities they have had. The recognition and success they have achieved are a testament to their hard work and dedication. As they look towards the future, they remain committed to pushing the limits of their creativity and continuing to leave their mark on the ever-evolving electronic music scene.

In conclusion, Subtronics' unique sound, electrifying performances, collaborations, and influence on the EDM and festival circuit have solidified their place in electronic music history. Their ability to innovate and connect with their fans has left a lasting impact on the genre and inspired a new generation of artists. Subtronics will forever be remembered as pioneers who pushed the limits of bass music and created an unforgettable legacy that continues to resonate with music lovers around the world.

The Enduring Glow of Subtronics

As the story of Subtronics comes to a close, one thing is certain: their impact on the music industry will continue to shine bright for years to come. The enduring glow of Subtronics is not just about their music, but also the lasting impression they have made on their fans, the EDM scene, and the world of bass music.

At the core of Subtronics' enduring glow is their ability to connect with their audience. Their music resonates with listeners on a deep and emotional level, creating a sense of unity and camaraderie among fans. This connection goes beyond the music itself, extending to the shared experiences at live shows, the friendships formed among fans, and the sense of belonging to a larger community. Subtronics has fostered an inclusive and safe space for their fans, allowing them to express themselves freely and find solace in the music.

But it's not just the fans who have been touched by Subtronics' enduring glow; the EDM scene has also felt the impact. Subtronics' unique sound and boundary-pushing approach to music production have influenced a new generation of artists and producers. Their fusion of bass music and dubstep has sparked a resurgence in the genre, breathing new life into the EDM scene. Their innovative sound design techniques and the exploration of new genres have opened doors for experimentation and creativity within the industry.

Subtronics' impact on the music industry goes beyond just their music, as they have played a crucial role in shaping the sound of music festivals. Their high-energy performances, captivating visuals, and imaginative stage productions have set a new standard for live performances in the electronic music world. By pushing the limits of what is possible on stage and incorporating new technologies and gadgets, Subtronics has created an immersive experience for their audience, leaving a lasting impression that is hard to forget.

In addition to their musical contributions, Subtronics has also been dedicated to giving back and making a positive impact. They have used their platform to support charitable initiatives and have been involved in various philanthropic efforts. Whether it's raising funds for important causes or spreading messages of love and unity, Subtronics has shown a commitment to making the world a better place through their music.

As Subtronics' journey continues, their enduring glow will continue to inspire the next generation of artists. They have left a legacy that will be remembered and cherished for years to come. Their ability to balance success and authenticity has set an example for aspiring musicians, showing that it is possible to stay true to oneself while making a mark in the music industry.

However, with this enduring glow also comes the pressure and expectations that accompany success. Subtronics has faced criticism and dealt with the fear of disappointing their fans, but they have remained resilient and focused on their passion for music. Through it all, they have managed to stay grounded and maintain their authenticity, never losing sight of why they started making music in the first place.

Looking ahead, the future holds endless possibilities for Subtronics. Their talent, innovation, and the lasting impact they have made on the music industry will undoubtedly continue to propel them forward. They will continue to push the boundaries of electronic music, exploring new genres, collaborating with fellow artists, and dazzling their fans with their live performances.

The story of Subtronics is not merely the tale of a successful music band, but a journey of growth, determination, and the power of music to bring people together. Their enduring glow will continue to inspire and resonate with fans and artists alike, leaving an indelible mark on the history of electronic music. As the final chapter of their story is written, one thing is certain: Subtronics' glow will continue to shine brightly for generations to come.

Conclusion

Reflecting on Their Journey

Triumphs and Setbacks

Throughout their journey, Subtronics experienced their fair share of triumphs and setbacks. These highs and lows shaped their career and helped them evolve as musicians. Let's take a closer look at some of their most significant moments:

Triumphs

1.1 The Rise of Subtronics: One of the major triumphs for Subtronics was their rise to success in the EDM scene. From humble beginnings, they worked hard to make a name for themselves and eventually broke into the mainstream. Their dedication to their craft and unique sound captivated audiences worldwide, leading to sold-out shows and festival appearances.

Example: "Subtronics' breakthrough moment came when they released their hit single 'Griztronics' in collaboration with GRiZ. The track gained immense popularity and catapulted them into the spotlight, earning them recognition and a dedicated fan base."

1.2 Establishing Themselves as Festival Favorites: One of the significant triumphs for Subtronics was their ability to establish themselves as festival favorites. Their high-energy performances, signature visuals, and unique blend of bass music and dubstep won over festival-goers and made them a sought-after act in the festival circuit.

Example: "Subtronics' electrifying set at Electric Daisy Carnival (EDC) left the crowd in awe, with their mind-blowing drops and immersive visuals. Their ability to connect with the audience on a deeper level transformed them into fan-favorites at festivals worldwide."

1.3 The Impact on the EDM Scene: Subtronics' innovative approach to music production and their relentless pursuit of pushing boundaries had a significant impact on the EDM scene. They became trailblazers in the bass music genre, inspiring other artists and producers to experiment and explore new sounds.

Example: "Subtronics' revolutionary sound design and mind-bending drops set a new standard for bass music. Their music pushed the boundaries of what was possible in electronic music and continues to influence aspiring artists around the world."

Setbacks

2.1 Dealing with Criticism and Pressure: As Subtronics rose to fame, they faced their fair share of criticism and pressure. Some critics doubted their unique sound, and others questioned their ability to maintain their authentic style amidst commercial success. These setbacks tested their resilience and forced them to stay true to their artistic vision.

Example: "The release of Subtronics' highly anticipated album was met with mixed reviews. While some praised their growth as artists, others felt that they had strayed too far from their underground roots. Despite the criticism, Subtronics remained focused on evolving their sound while staying true to themselves."

2.2 Balancing Personal Life and Professional Demands: Another setback for Subtronics was the challenge of balancing personal life with the rigorous demands of their growing career. The demands of touring, producing music, and managing their brand took a toll on their mental and physical well-being. Finding a healthy work-life balance became crucial for their long-term success.

Example: "Subtronics had to learn the hard way that constant touring and long hours in the studio can take a toll on personal relationships and overall well-being. They had to prioritize self-care and make adjustments to find a healthier balance between their personal lives and professional demands."

2.3 Navigating Success and Maintaining Authenticity: Maintaining authenticity while navigating the pressures of commercial success was a significant setback for Subtronics. As their fan base grew and their name became synonymous with the genre, they faced the challenge of meeting fan expectations and staying true to their artistic vision.

Example: "Subtronics faced a difficult decision when approached to collaborate with mainstream artists. While it meant exposure to a larger audience, there was a fear of compromising their unique sound. They had to carefully evaluate their options and ensure that any collaborations aligned with their artistic integrity."

In the face of triumphs and setbacks, Subtronics persevered and continued to push the boundaries of electronic music. Their journey is a testament to the power of following one's passion and staying true to oneself, even in the face of adversity.

Lessons Learned along the Way

Throughout their journey, Subtronics has learned valuable lessons that have shaped their career and helped them navigate the ups and downs of the music industry. These lessons serve as valuable advice for aspiring artists and provide insight into the challenges they faced and how they overcame them. Let's explore some of the key lessons learned by Subtronics.

Lesson 1: Embrace Failure and Learn from Mistakes

Subtronics understands that failure is a natural part of any creative journey. They have had their fair share of setbacks, whether it was a track that didn't resonate with their audience or a live performance that didn't meet their expectations. Instead of dwelling on these failures, they turned them into learning experiences. They analyzed what went wrong, sought feedback from trusted sources, and used these insights to refine their craft. By embracing failure and learning from their mistakes, Subtronics has been able to grow as artists and continuously improve their music.

Lesson 2: Stay True to Your Artistic Vision

In an industry that can often prioritize commercial success over artistic integrity, Subtronics has remained steadfast in their commitment to staying true to their unique sound. They learned early on that trying to cater to trends or please everyone can result in losing their artistic identity. By focusing on their passion for bass music and pushing the boundaries of their creativity, they were able to create a loyal fan base that appreciates their authenticity. Subtronics' success serves as a reminder to artists to stay true to their artistic vision, as that is what will set them apart in the long run.

Lesson 3: Build a Support Network

Subtronics recognizes the importance of surrounding themselves with a strong support network. From their mentor and manager to their production guru, visual mastermind, marketing whiz, and touring guru, they have cultivated a team that believes in their talent and supports their vision. This network of individuals has played a crucial role in their success, providing guidance, feedback, and helping them navigate the challenges that come with a career in the music industry. Subtronics encourages aspiring artists to build their own support network, as having a team that believes in your talent and shares your goals can make all the difference.

Lesson 4: Adapt to Industry Changes

The music industry is constantly evolving, with new technologies and trends shaping the landscape. Subtronics understands the importance of staying informed and adapting to these changes. Whether it's experimenting with new sounds, embracing emerging platforms for music distribution, or incorporating new technologies into their live performances, Subtronics has demonstrated their willingness to adapt. This adaptability has allowed them to stay relevant and connect with their audience in meaningful ways. They advise artists to embrace change and constantly look for opportunities to evolve their craft.

Lesson 5: Connect with Your Audience

Subtronics recognizes the power of connecting with their audience on a deeper level. They have built a strong and dedicated fan base by engaging with their fans through social media, fan meet and greets, and creating a safe and inclusive environment at their shows. By actively involving their fans in their journey, Subtronics has not only fostered a sense of community but has also gained valuable insights into what their fans want and appreciate. They emphasize the importance of building genuine connections with fans and creating an experience that goes beyond the music itself.

Lesson 6: Stay Grounded and Take Care of Yourself

Amidst the chaos of the music industry, Subtronics has learned the importance of staying grounded and taking care of their mental and physical well-being. They have implemented self-care practices like meditation and exercise to find balance amidst their busy schedules. By prioritizing their health and well-being, they have been able to sustain their creativity and perform at their best. They encourage aspiring artists to prioritize self-care and find ways to maintain their mental and physical health in the demanding music industry.

In conclusion, Subtronics' journey has been marked by valuable lessons that have shaped their career and helped them overcome challenges. By embracing failure, staying true to their artistic vision, building a strong support network, adapting to industry changes, connecting with their audience, and prioritizing self-care, Subtronics has established themselves as successful artists in the music industry. These lessons serve as a guide for aspiring artists and a reminder that success in the music industry requires not only talent and hard work but also the ability to learn and grow along the way.

Gratitude for Their Fans and Supporters

One of the most important aspects of Subtronics' success is their incredible fan base. Without their dedicated and enthusiastic fans, the band wouldn't have been able to achieve their dreams and reach the level of success they have today. In this section, we will explore Subtronics' deep appreciation and gratitude for their fans and supporters.

"We wouldn't be where we are today without our fans. They have been with us through thick and thin, supporting us every step of the way. We are eternally grateful for their love and dedication." - Subtronics

The Power of Fan Support

Subtronics recognizes the incredible impact their fans have had on their career. Their loyal fan base has been instrumental in spreading their music, attending their shows, and creating a vibrant and supportive community around their music. The band values the connections they have made with their fans and understands that their success is a direct result of their support.

The band consistently expresses their gratitude for their fans, both online and during live performances. They go out of their way to interact with their fans on social media, respond to messages, and show appreciation for the fan-made art and covers of their songs. By actively engaging with their fans, Subtronics creates a sense of belonging and inclusivity that solidifies the bond between the band and their supporters.

Fan-Driven Initiatives

Subtronics understands the importance of creating a safe space for their fans to connect, share experiences, and express themselves. They actively encourage positivity and acceptance within their fan community, promoting a sense of unity in their music's shared love. Through meet and greets, fan-organized events, and online interactions, Subtronics fosters a genuine connection with their fan base.

Moreover, the band acknowledges the role their fans play in identifying and highlighting social issues. They use their platform to raise awareness and support various charitable causes that resonate with their fans. By aligning their values with those of their supporters, Subtronics creates an even deeper bond and sense of purpose within their fan community.

Fan Appreciation Events

To express their gratitude for their fans' ongoing support, Subtronics frequently organizes fan appreciation events. These events give the band an opportunity to give back to their fans by hosting exclusive performances, meetups, and workshops. Subtronics believes that these events allow them to connect even more deeply with their fans and celebrate their shared love for music.

During these events, the band takes time to meet and interact with fans individually, creating personal and memorable experiences. They acknowledge the efforts of their fans in spreading their music and express their genuine appreciation for the impact their supporters have had on their career.

Unconventional Fan Interactions

Subtronics is known for their unconventional and down-to-earth approach to fan interactions. They bring a sense of humor and authenticity to their social media platforms, engaging in playful banter and sharing intimate moments of their lives. Instead of creating a wall between themselves and their fans, they strive to break down barriers and be relatable, fostering a genuine connection with their supporters.

The band also values constructive criticism from their fans and actively seeks feedback and suggestions. They believe that their fans play a crucial role in their growth as artists and continuously aim to improve and refine their sound based on their supporters' input.

"Our fans are our biggest inspiration. We are constantly amazed by their passion and creativity. We owe them everything and will always make sure they know how much we appreciate them." - Subtronics

Conclusion

Subtronics' success would not have been possible without the unwavering support of their fans and supporters. The band deeply values their fan community and makes a conscious effort to show their gratitude and appreciation. By actively engaging with their fans, organizing fan-driven initiatives, and hosting special events, Subtronics creates a sense of unity and belonging that resonates with their supporters. Moving forward, Subtronics will continue to cherish and celebrate their incredible fan base as they embark on new musical endeavors. The enduring glow of Subtronics is a testament to the power of a supportive fan community.

Looking Towards the Future

As the journey of Subtronics continues, the future holds infinite possibilities and exciting prospects for the band. With their innovative sound, dedicated fan base, and remarkable talent, it is clear that Subtronics is poised for even greater success and influence in the music industry.

Pioneering New Genres and Sounds: In the future, Subtronics aims to push the boundaries of electronic music even further. They are keen on exploring new genres, blending different styles, and creating innovative sounds that captivate audiences. By experimenting with unconventional musical elements and incorporating live instruments, they seek to constantly evolve and surprise their fans.

Expanding Collaborations and Features: Collaboration has always been a vital aspect of Subtronics' success, and they plan to continue working with both established and emerging artists across various genres. By bringing together different perspectives and talents, they strive to create groundbreaking music that resonates with a wide range of listeners.

Elevating Live Performances: Subtronics' stage presence and energy have always been a highlight of their performances. Looking towards the future, they aim to push the limits of live shows even further. By incorporating new technologies, innovative visual experiences, and surprise guest appearances, they want to create immersive and unforgettable experiences for their fans.

Influence on the EDM Scene: Subtronics recognizes the impact they have had on the EDM scene and embraces their role as pioneers of the next generation of bass music. They aim to continue influencing other artists and producers, shaping the sound of music festivals, and contributing to the ever-evolving landscape of electronic music.

Maintaining Authenticity and Balancing Expectations: As Subtronics' popularity grows, they understand the importance of maintaining their authenticity. They are committed to creating music that is true to their artistic vision while also navigating the expectations and pressures of success. By staying grounded and true to themselves, they hope to inspire others to do the same.

Giving Back and Making a Difference: Subtronics is passionate about using their platform to make a positive impact. They plan to continue supporting charitable initiatives and giving back to their community. By spreading their message of love and unity, they strive to create a safe and inclusive space for their fans.

In conclusion, the future of Subtronics shines bright with limitless potential. As they pioneer new genres and sounds, expand collaborations, elevate live performances, and continue to shape the EDM scene, their impact on the music industry is set to grow even further. With authenticity, passion, and a commitment to making a difference, Subtronics will undoubtedly leave a lasting legacy in the realm of electronic music. The story of Subtronics continues, and their glowing presence will continue to inspire and captivate audiences for years to come.

The Story Continues

As Subtronics blazed a trail through the EDM scene, captivating audiences with their unique sound and energetic performances, their story was far from over. In this chapter, we dive into what the future holds for Subtronics and how they plan to continue pushing the boundaries of electronic music.

Evolving Their Sound

After years of experimentation, Subtronics found themselves at a crossroads. They had mastered the fusion of bass music and dubstep that had become their signature sound, but they were hungry for more. In their pursuit of musical growth, they began to explore new genres and collaborate with artists from diverse backgrounds.

Drawing inspiration from their early influences and expanding their musical horizons, Subtronics started incorporating elements of trap, hip-hop, and house into their productions. This evolution allowed them to connect with a wider audience and push the boundaries of their sound even further.

To maintain their authenticity while exploring new sonic landscapes, Subtronics relied on their dedication to sound design. They continued their relentless pursuit of creating unique and recognizable drops, experimenting with cutting-edge techniques and synthesis methods. This commitment to innovation ensured that their music would always stand out in a saturated industry.

Unconventional Collaborations

One of the secrets to Subtronics' success lies in their ability to collaborate with artists from various genres and backgrounds. Building on their previous work with vocalists and rappers, they sought out unexpected partnerships that pushed their creativity to new heights.

In a groundbreaking move, Subtronics collaborated with classical musicians and orchestras to incorporate live instruments into their productions. This unexpected fusion of electronic and acoustic elements created a truly immersive and dynamic experience for their listeners.

Furthermore, they embarked on joint projects with fellow DJs who shared their passion for breaking boundaries. These collaborative efforts brought together diverse perspectives and skillsets, resulting in innovative tracks that defied genre conventions. Whether it was a fusion of drum and bass with dubstep or the infusion of psychedelic elements into their sound, these collaborations showcased Subtronics' ability to think outside the box.

Exploring New Technologies

Never ones to rest on their laurels, Subtronics constantly sought out new technologies and gadgets to enhance their live performances. They embraced the latest advancements in lighting, visual effects, and stage production to create immersive experiences that left their fans spellbound.

In their quest to dazzle their audience, Subtronics invested in the development of cutting-edge holographic projections and interactive stage setups. These advancements allowed them to create mind-bending visuals that seamlessly synchronized with their music, elevating their performances to an entirely new level.

To further enhance their live shows, Subtronics embraced the use of virtual reality and augmented reality. By incorporating these technologies into their performances, they broke down the barriers between the physical and digital realms, immersing their fans in a truly surreal experience.

Giving Back and Inspiring Others

As Subtronics continued to gain recognition and success, they remained grounded and committed to giving back to their community. They used their platform to raise awareness and support charitable initiatives that touched their hearts.

From organizing benefit concerts to partnering with organizations dedicated to education and mental health, Subtronics made it their mission to make a positive impact in the world. They recognized the power of music as a tool for healing and unity, and they used their influence to inspire others to do the same.

Furthermore, Subtronics actively mentored and supported emerging artists, recognizing the importance of nurturing the next generation of talent. Through workshops, masterclasses, and collaborations, they shared their knowledge and experiences, empowering others to pursue their own creative paths.

Looking Ahead: The Future of Subtronics

As Subtronics reflects on their journey and looks towards the future, they remain committed to their fans and the pursuit of artistic excellence. While they have achieved tremendous success, they understand the importance of staying true to themselves and maintaining their unique voice.

With a growing fan base and a solid foundation in the music industry, Subtronics plans to continue pushing the limits of electronic music. They are excited to explore new sonic territories, collaborate with unexpected artists, and embrace emerging technologies that will enhance their live performances.

However, amidst their relentless drive for innovation and growth, Subtronics remains focused on the connection they have with their fans. They recognize that their success is built on the unwavering support of their dedicated fan base and are determined to continue creating music that resonates on a personal level.

The story of Subtronics is far from over. As they embark on the next chapter of their musical journey, they are poised to leave an enduring legacy on the electronic music landscape. With their unwavering dedication to pushing boundaries and connecting with their audience, Subtronics is destined to continue shining brightly, captivating listeners with their music for years to come.

Exercise

Think of a genre or style of music that you think could be combined with electronic music to create a unique and fresh sound. Describe what elements from each genre you would incorporate and how this fusion might sound. Consider the potential audience and how this new style of music could impact the electronic music scene.

Resources

For further insight into Subtronics' journey and the evolution of electronic music, check out the following resources:

1. *All Access: The Rise of EDM and the Fall of Rock 'n' Roll* by Jesse Saunders

2. *The EDM Handbook* by DJ Ravine and Ben Bristow

3. Subtronics' official website: www.subtronics.net

4. Subtronics' YouTube channel: www.youtube.com/subtronics

5. Subtronics' social media accounts: Instagram, Twitter, Facebook

Unconventional Wisdom

Remember, true innovation often comes from exploring the uncharted territories of different genres and collaborating with artists who challenge your perspective. Don't be afraid to experiment and embrace the unknown. In the world of music, where boundaries are meant to be broken, the possibilities are endless. So go forth and create something truly extraordinary!